T0167445

100 THINGS
BREWERS FANS
SHOULD KNOW & DO
BEFORE THEY DIE

100 THINGS
BREWERS FANS
SHOULD KNOW & DO
BEFORE THEY DIE

Tom Haudricourt

TRIUMPH
BOOKS

The Library of Congress has catalogued the previous edition as follows:

Haudricourt, Tom, 1954–
    100 things Brewers fans should know & do before they die / Tom Haudricourt.
        p. cm.
    ISBN 978-1-60078-788-1
    1. Milwaukee Brewers (Baseball team)—History. 2. Milwaukee Brewers (Baseball team)—Miscellanea.   I. Title. II. Title: One hundred things Brewers fans need to know and do before they die.
    GV875.M53H34 2013
    796.357'640977595—dc23
                                        2012041001

This book is available in quantity at special discounts for your group or organization. For further information, contact:
    Triumph Books LLC
    814 North Franklin Street
    Chicago, Illinois 60610
    (312) 337-0747
    www.triumphbooks.com

Printed in U.S.A.
ISBN: 978-1-62937-546-5
Design by Patricia Frey
Photos courtesy of AP Images unless otherwise indicated

For my wife, Trish, who has made the best of building a life with a husband whose work schedule allows little flexibility. Believe me when I say that I value her love, understanding, and support.

We never had children but happily and enthusiastically became dog people, which only other dog people truly understand. Brundy and Basil always will remain in our hearts, and now we have Digger and Dexter to carry on their weiner dog legacy.

Contents

Foreword

I grew up as a Braves fan, following Hank Aaron, Eddie Mathews, Johnny Logan, and those guys. I was really a National League fan back then. When the Brewers moved to Milwaukee in 1970, I was a junior in high school at Campbellsport High. I didn't really follow the Brewers at first because nobody knew much about them.

Then one day the Brewers sent a scout to watch me and work me out in Eden, Wisconsin. That's when I really started thinking about them. I went to UW-Oshkosh for two years. Then the Brewers drafted me in the 12th round of the 1974 draft. That was a big deal in Eden, getting drafted by the Brewers. All of my friends and family were excited about it because it was the state's team. I got called up in '76 and again in '77 and finally came up for good in 1978. The Brewers were getting good, and everybody in the state was getting pumped up about them. When I made it to the big leagues, everybody back home was so proud. I didn't know I had so many friends.

When we started winning, it was awesome. You couldn't go anywhere without people coming up to you. You'd go through the parking lot at County Stadium, and fans would offer you a brat or a beer. That was a lot of fun. There was a lot of electricity at the ballpark. We had a great bunch of guys on those teams. The clubhouse was a lot of fun. We were a close group, and everybody messed with each other. That was special. You don't see that much today.

We had a lot of characters back then, but when it was time to play the game, everybody was serious. We knew how to have fun but also play hard. Getting to play with Robin Yount and Paulie Molitor for all those years was great. You don't see things like that anymore. I got to play 15 years with two Hall of Famers. You can't beat that.

The Brewers had some down years after that, so it was great to see them start winning again and end a 26-year playoff drought in 2008. I knew the fans would support a winning team. They always have in Milwaukee. This organization has been great to me. I still enjoy coming around and being part of it. I felt so great for the players, the organization, the city, and the state.

It's incredible to draw more than 2 million fans a year in this market. That shows how great our fans are. You knew if the team won, the fans would come out. This is an awesome baseball town. All they talk about is the Brewers, everywhere you go. I'm glad I'm still a part of it.

—Jim Gantner

Introduction

When originally presented with the challenge of finding 100 things for Brewers fans to know and do before they die, my immediate reaction was: will I be able to come up with that many? The Brewers, after all, do not have 100 years, or even half that, of history to provide nuggets readers might enjoy.

But as I delved into the project, I eventually found myself deleting items in favor of others I enjoyed more and hoped readers would, as well. Attaching sidebars also became a natural process, because often a particular theme or story could not be told completely without an addendum.

Next came the task of arranging the segments in supposed order of importance. This is where it became tricky, because the Racing Sausages certainly are not more important in team history than, say, Robin Yount's 3,000th career hit. But in terms of what the team is best known for these days, those costumed, oversized wieners are more famous than many of the players, past and present.

Accordingly, I tried to mix some of the seminal moments in Brewers history with other things fans consider important, such as tailgating. What resulted was a combination of historical events and Brewers pop culture, which I hope readers find both diverse and entertaining.

I also quickly came to terms with the notion that funny and bizarre items would be and should be a part of the book. For one thing, I like funny and bizarre items. So beyond detailing the Suds Series in 1982 and the Brewers' long-awaited return to the postseason 26 years later, homage is paid to the likes of Chris "One and Done" Saenz, Gus "the Wonder Dog," garbage collector turned reliever Joe Winkelsas, the Chuckie Carr mutiny, the worst interview ever by Jeff Juden, those dreaded "Sweep Suits" of 2001, and the night a Brewers fan actually fought with an opposing player under the stands.

As I waded into the 100 things, what immediately struck me was how many of these events and items I covered as a Brewers beat writer, first for the *Milwaukee Sentinel* and later for the merged *Milwaukee Journal Sentinel*. I first began covering the team during the 1985 season and have continued to do so since, with the exception of a brief period in 2002–03 when I covered the New York Yankees for *The Record* of Bergen, New Jersey.

Invariably, when searching through the archives of the *Sentinel* and *Journal Sentinel* to recapture details of segments in the book, I would see my byline atop the stories. Many times, my immediate reaction would be: where did all the years go?

In essence, I have covered the Brewers for two-thirds of their existence. I missed the glory year of 1982 and had to wait a long time to see champagne sprayed in the Brewers clubhouse, but the things I witnessed were almost enough to fill this book (adding events prior to my arrival on the scene completed the task).

The opening of Miller Park and the team's revival in recent years proved without doubt that Milwaukee is a good, perhaps great, baseball town. The team now draws 2 to 3 million fans or thereabouts every year, an extraordinary level considering the market size. Put a good and/or interesting team on the field, and they will come.

Now, four years after the original 100 things, I have added new chapters with an updated ranking. Some interesting episodes have caught our attention, such as Hank the Ballpark Pup, as well as the player known as "God" in Korea. To show you how baseball has changed in the modern era of analytical evaluation (not to mention how old I am), the Brewers have a general manager who was born during my first year on the beat in 1985. Let's just say it took some time to process that bit of information.

It is with that knowledge and great hope that I present these augmented 100 things that Brewers fans should know and do before they die, with wishes that you have plenty of time to absorb them all before that final inevitability.

1 Bud Wouldn't Take No for an Answer

Simply put, without Bud Selig, there would be no Milwaukee Brewers.

A Milwaukee native, Selig took it personally when the Braves moved to Atlanta after the 1965 season. Selig was a devout baseball fan growing up in the city, and no one was happier when the Braves relocated from Boston in 1953, and no one was more devastated when they left town in a huff.

Before the moving vans were packed, Selig formed Teams, Inc., later renamed Brewers, Inc., a group that unsuccessfully sued to keep the Braves in town. He was haunted by a conversation he had with an elderly female baseball fan at the Braves' final game at County Stadium on September 22, 1965. "You're all we've got now," the woman told Selig. "Don't let us down."

Selig knocked on every baseball door he could find, attended every Major League Baseball meeting—in essence, making a supreme pest of himself. He was determined to get big league ball back to Milwaukee, begging the game's leaders for an expansion team and coming oh-so-close to buying the Chicago White Sox. Looking back at that frustrating time, Selig calls it "probably the toughest five years of my life. But it taught me to be tenacious and have patience."

That determination and unwillingness to take no for an answer was rewarded in 1970, when Selig's group was allowed to purchase the Seattle Pilots out of bankruptcy. The transaction was concluded just days before the start of the season, and hurried preparations were made to transform the club from the Pilots to the Brewers, a nod to the city's rich tradition of beer making.

Always a fan, even as the team's principal owner, Selig lived and died with the Brewers. In the early years, it was mostly the latter as the club battled to become relevant in the American League. The Brewers finally broke through in 1982 to win their only pennant, though that glorious season ended in disappointment when the St. Louis Cardinals rallied to win Games 6 and 7 of the World Series, otherwise known as the "Suds Series."

Selig was not merely content to operate a major league club, however. Born to lead, he found the time to be active in any number of ownership committees, learning the ins and outs of the game. He slowly emerged as a go-to guy to get things done on the management end. So it was no shock when owners ousted commissioner Fay Vincent on Labor Day weekend in 1992 and named Selig to that post on an interim basis days later.

September 9, 1992 remains emblazoned in Selig's memory as a special day on two fronts. In a meeting in Texas, he officially was voted in as interim commissioner. He then rushed back to Milwaukee and County Stadium to watch Robin Yount collect the 3,000th hit of his career.

But it soon became evident to Selig that he would not be able to continue running his beloved Brewers while also trying to navigate the sport through difficult economic issues. He turned over the reins of the club to his daughter, Wendy Selig-Prieb, a shift that became official on July 9, 1998, when he was named commissioner on a full-time basis.

Before transitioning to that new role, Selig's determination and perseverance paid off once again. He led the charge to build Miller Park, convincing civic leaders and state legislators through long and painful debate that the stadium was absolutely necessary to keep the Brewers in Milwaukee. It was that knack for persuasion, that ability to build consensus, and his refusal to take no for an answer that made Selig a natural to lead the Brewers and later the sport. There were painful times, such as ongoing labor strife that led to

A Fan Through and Through

Before he became owner of the Brewers and later commissioner of baseball, Bud Selig was a true baseball fan. And, as with most fans, he was in a good mood when his team was winning and miserable when it was losing.

That fan-like behavior continued when Selig was running the Brewers. By his own admission, he cheered wildly when the club was winning and did a slow burn when they lost, especially if they lost in an ugly fashion.

Selig's private box in County Stadium was adjacent to the press box, with a small landing in between. His door was made of metal, and when things weren't going well for the Brewers, you often heard it slam with a loud bang that shook the press box. Selig often joked that his wife, Sue, wouldn't sit with him when the team was losing because she was too embarrassed by his behavior.

There also was a seating area in front of the press box, and during games Selig often would pace back and forth, forth and back, alternately clapping and wringing his hands, depending on the Brewers fortunes. When one of his players would do something wrong, Selig often would turn around and look at me, shrugging his shoulders and rolling his eyes. While Selig's actions were somewhat comical, I always admired his passion. He wanted to win so badly.

One night when the Brewers were faring particularly poorly, Selig came into the press box and spied team media relations director Tom Skibosh and assistant Mario Ziino sitting in the corner, laughing about something unrelated to the game. Selig walked up behind them and roared, "If you want to have fun, go someplace else!"

The entire press box fell silent as Selig stomped out, slamming that door, as well as the door to his box, almost simultaneously. Being the smart-alecky cut-up that I am, I walked over to Skibosh and Ziino and said, "You know, he's right. If we want to have fun, we should go someplace else!" That broke the tension, and everyone started laughing. After leaving the Brewers a few years later, Skibosh wrote about his years with the club in a book titled, *If You Wanna Have Fun, Go Someplace Else!*

To this day, Bud and I talk about his temper tantrums when the Brewers played badly, and we always end up chuckling about it.

the strike in 1994 and cancellation of the World Series. But, as always, Selig persevered.

As a nod to his love for his hometown, he convinced baseball leaders to allow him to establish a new commissioner's office in a downtown high-rise in Milwaukee. True to his roots as a baseball fan, and later, owner of the Brewers, he simply refused to relocate. A creature of habit if there ever was one, Selig continues to regularly eat lunch at Gilles, a landmark frozen custard stand not far from Miller Park, always ordering the same modest meal—hot dog smothered in ketchup and Diet Coke. After 22 years on the job, he retired as commissioner of baseball in January 2015 but was given a new title, commissioner emeritus, and continues to conduct baseball business out of a new office in downtown Milwaukee.

It was only fitting that the Brewers dedicated a bronze statue to Selig outside of Miller Park on August 24, 2010. It honored his status as founding father of the franchise, driving force behind that retractable roof facility, and innovative commissioner of baseball—leading the way with significant changes such as interleague play, the wild-card playoff format, revenue sharing, and comprehensive drug testing.

The team was sold after the 2004 season to a group led by Los Angeles money manager and investor Mark Attanasio, officially ending the long tenure of Selig family ownership. But there was no denying the impact in the club's history of Allan H. Selig, a persistent man simply known as "Bud."

On July 30, 2017, on Selig's 83rd birthday no less, he reached the pinnacle of the sport by being inducted into the Baseball Hall of Fame in Cooperstown, New York. He admitted to being "overwhelmed" by that great honor but still does not consider that his greatest achievement in the game. When asked that question, he always gives the same answer: bringing baseball back to Milwaukee in 1970. "That will always be my biggest accomplishment because the odds were stacked against us tremendously," he said.

2 Mr. Baseball

When the Brewers announced in March 2012 that a statue of Bob Uecker would be unveiled later in the year at Miller Park, it was not surprising that "Mr. Baseball" made light of the honor.

Asked what took so long for the club to dedicate a statue to him, Uecker replied with a straight face, "It was kind of a finance thing. I didn't have enough for the down payment." Uecker's schtick carried on for several minutes, during which he described the pose on the statue as "kind of a Schwarzenegger-type thing... beefcake, speedo, pretty buffed."

You didn't really expect Uecker to play it straight, did you? It's not the style of one of the funniest men to ever wear a baseball uniform or sit behind a microphone in a radio booth. "Ueck," as he is known to friends and fans alike, can find a funny element in nearly every topic, including the serious heart surgery that forced him to miss much of the 2010 season.

In many ways, Uecker has been the face of the franchise. He has been the club's radio voice since 1971, the year after the team came to Milwaukee. A native of the city, Uecker was the perfect fit not only because of his baseball knowledge, but also because the sometimes slow tempo of the game provides the perfect platform for his unique style of self-deprecating, deadpan humor. Anything but a Hall of Famer as a player—he batted .200 in 297 games as a backup catcher—he evolved into one in the radio booth with his must-listen brand of storytelling and observation.

Along the way, Uecker became a national celebrity. It was during one of his many appearances on *The Tonight Show* that Johnny Carson dubbed him "Mr. Baseball," a moniker that stuck like glue. It was a comedic nod to Uecker's underachieving playing career, but it made perfect sense in so many other ways.

Uecker quickly became a friend and associate of former Brewers owner Bud Selig, who loves to tell the story about trying to make a scout out of the former catcher. Selig swears that Uecker's first scouting report landed on the desk of general manager Frank Lane

It Just Came Naturally

Some broadcasters work hard on their home run calls, finding just the right mix of words and intonation to make it their signature statement on the long ball. For Bob Uecker, it took no work whatsoever.

Uecker's renowned call, "Get up, get up, get out of here! Gone!" is as familiar to Brewers fans as a bratwurst and a beer at the ballpark. But it was not the product of an extensive search by the Hall of Fame radio voice to put his stamp on a home run. "That goes back to when I was a player," Uecker said. "When a guy would hit one deep, we'd all jump up out of the dugout and yell, 'Get up! Get up!' That's what we'd do. Everybody was jumping off the bench and saying that. I did it from Day One [on the air], because that's what we said when we played. I never really thought about it when I first started saying it [on the air]. I didn't think I needed my own home run call. I just did it from the start and kept doing it. It was just a habit.

"If people think it's one of the best calls, that's nice. It makes you feel good, but I don't really think much about stuff like that. When I see a ball go deep, I just say it. I don't really think about it beforehand."

Uecker said he was taken aback when the Brewers told him they wanted to put his home run call in neon lights next to Bernie Brewers' slide in Miller Park. "I never really thought it was that big of a deal until [former club vice president] Laurel Prieb came to me one day and said, 'Would you mind if we put your home run call up there?' I said, 'If you want to, sure.' It didn't matter to me. I didn't want them to make a big deal about it.

"I guess it has become my call, but I didn't really set out to do it that way. I know some guys work on what they want to say. I just said it. I don't really work hard at anything. I just show up and go along with things."

covered with remnants of mashed potatoes and gravy. "I knew then that he wasn't going to make it as a scout, so we decided to try him as a broadcaster," Selig recalled.

The wisest move in franchise history, many would call it.

Uecker finally was recognized by the Baseball Hall of Fame in Cooperstown, New York, in 2003, when he received the Ford C. Frick Award for excellence in broadcasting. People still talk about the hilarious acceptance speech he gave on that late-July day.

Uecker often says—perhaps only half-kidding—that he plans to keep broadcasting games until he drops in the booth. "They can take me right from there to my 'dirt bath,'" he says.

How widespread is Uecker's popularity? Not only is he in the Baseball Hall of Fame, he has likewise been honored by the Radio Hall of Fame, the National Association of Broadcasters Broadcasting Hall of Fame, the National Association of Sportscasters and Sportswriters Hall of Fame, the WWE Hall of Fame (Uecker hosted Wrestlemania III and IV), the Wisconsin Performing Artists Hall of Fame, and the Meat-Packing Industry Hall of Fame.

That's what you call cutting a wide swath through the sports and entertainment industries.

Uecker still regularly hears folks recite famous lines from his once-popular Lite Beer commercials ("I must be in the front row!") as well as from his hysterical portrayal of announcer Harry Doyle in the *Major League* movies ("Just a bit outside!"). He even had a memorable television career on the hit show *Mr. Belvedere*, which put 117 episodes into syndication and introduced him to an entirely new audience that had little or no interest in baseball.

Along the way, Uecker has never forgotten his Milwaukee roots. He still lives in the city much of the year and contributes to many philanthropic endeavors in the community. He can't go anywhere in the city without fans flocking to him. Players, club officials, and even owners have come and gone, but the one constant has been the voice greeting all residents of Brewer nation who follow the club via radio.

When you are that iconic to a franchise, one statue just isn't enough. In 2014 the Brewers announced a second tribute to Uecker would be placed in the last row of the upper deck behind home plate—below the pivot to Miller Park's retractable roof. That bronze figure depicts Uecker sitting—and certainly not in the front row—next to an empty seat, allowing fans to pose for photos with "Mr. Baseball." The price of admission to a Uecker seat is $1, the best bargain in baseball.

As for the enjoyment of spending nearly 50 years in the Brewers radio booth, Uecker said, "I hope the fans have enjoyed listening as much as I've enjoyed doing the games. I don't ever go to the park where I don't have a good day. I don't like losing. But I don't think I ever go to the park where I have a bad day. I don't think once.

"That's discounting playing. I had a lot of bad days there."

Try the veal, folks. "Mr. Baseball" will be here all week.

Forever "The Kid"

Robin Yount is hardly a kid anymore. In fact, he turned 62 in September 2017. Nevertheless, for those who played with him and watched him perform, Yount forever will be known as "The Kid." That's what happens when you break into the big leagues at the tender age of 18.

It was the spring of 1974, and the Brewers' brain trust was pondering who was going to play shortstop. The previous season, Tim Johnson batted .213 and committed 25 errors at the position, and club executives were, well, underwhelmed, to be honest.

Yount, the third pick overall in the '73 draft, had played only 64 games in the minors. But manager Del Crandall and his staff were willing to overlook that inexperience, primarily because they didn't have anybody better to play short, one of the most important positions in the field.

The Brewers took Yount north with them to begin the season, and a Hall of Fame career was born. But it was anything but smooth sailing at the start. Yount batted .250 with three home runs and 26 RBIs that first season. He was no threat to win AL Rookie of the Year honors.

The following season, Yount got a case of the yips in the field, committing a whopping 44 errors in 145 games at short. The jury was out as to whether "The Kid" was going to make it. "I was learning at the big league level," Yount said. "Those first few years were pretty tough. I'm sure a lot of people were wondering what the Brewers were doing, putting a raw kid like me at short. It took me a number of years before I really felt like a major league player."

All young players need a mentor to help smooth out the rough edges, and Yount found one in hitting coach Harvey Kuenn, who would later manage the Brewers to the 1982 World Series. Though Yount struggled in those early years, Kuenn could see that it wasn't breaking him mentally. Kuenn saw an innate toughness and determination, along with true baseball instincts, that he knew would win the day when all was said and done. "Harvey was really like a father figure to me," Yount said. "I don't know what I would have done without him."

Year by year, Yount became a better player. He broke through in a big way in '82, leading the Brewers to their only World Series appearance with a .331 batting average, 29 home runs, and 114 RBIs. Yount was voted the American League Most Valuable Player and also won a Gold Glove, an unthinkable feat for a player who once committed 44 errors in a season.

Allergic to Leather

When Robin Yount committed 44 errors during his second season in the major leagues, some wondered if he'd ever cut it at shortstop. By 1982, however, he had improved to the point that he was awarded the Gold Glove at his position.

The Brewers went 31 years before another player would be recognized for defensive prowess until center fielder Carlos Gomez earned recognition in 2013. That's a long time to go without a Gold Glove, but the national nightmare finally came to an end.

Here's a look at the short (and old) list of Brewers who have won Gold Gloves:

1B George Scott (5): 1972, 1973, 1974, 1975, 1976.
1B Cecil Cooper (2): 1979, 1980.
OF Sixto Lezcano: 1979.
SS Robin Yount: 1982.
CF: Carlos Gomez: 2013

Along the way, Yount became like a son to team owner Bud Selig, who beamed over his play, as any proud father would. Selig also learned that Yount could be extremely stubborn, especially when it came to playing with injuries—to the point where the owner had to come down to the clubhouse on one occasion and tell his banged-up star player that he wouldn't be in the lineup.

That was the kind of example Yount set for other players. He figured if he was in the lineup, whether 100 percent or not, he might find a way to help the Brewers win a game. No one was more miserable sitting on the bench.

Stubbornness and determination, however, could do nothing to change the shoulder injury that Yount suffered in 1984. Surgery was required to repair the damage, and when he no longer had the zip on his throws necessary to play shortstop, he reluctantly made the switch to center field. "I still couldn't throw," he said. "I never really liked playing the outfield as much as I did playing shortstop. But if I had to play out there, I was going to give it all I had."

And Yount did exactly that. On April 15, 1987, he made a diving catch in the gap in right-center off a drive by Eddie Murray to put the lid on Juan Nieves' no-hitter in Baltimore, still the only no-no in club history. Two years later, Yount claimed his second AL MVP award at age 33, becoming only the third player to claim that honor at different positions.

Yount wasn't done providing thrills for the fans of Milwaukee. On September 9, 1992, in the final game of a homestand at County Stadium, Yount assured his berth in Cooperstown, New York, by collecting his 3,000[th] hit, an opposite-field single off Cleveland Indians pitcher Jose Mesa. He was the third youngest player to reach that magic plateau, trailing only Ty Cobb and Hank Aaron.

Yount wore his Brewers uniform for 20 years before he took it off and called it a career. By the time he retired, there was no question he would be the first player in the organization's history to go to the Hall of Fame. Yount became a franchise icon, a player so identified with the team that he, in essence, became a lifetime Brewer.

To this day, whenever Yount visits Miller Park and runs into a former teammate such as Jim Gantner or Gorman Thomas, he still answers to "The Kid." He'll be forever known as such, even though he can't quite remember who first called him that when he showed up in Sun City, Arizona, in the spring of '74. "I'm sure they all called me that," he said. "When you're a teenager, that's what the older guys call you. I certainly wasn't going to complain." After the magnificent 20 years that Yount spent in a Brewers uniform, neither was anybody else.

4 Pick the Winning Wiener

In most ballparks around the country, fans look forward to the seventh-inning stretch when they can stand up, shake off the cobwebs, and sing "Take Me Out to the Ballgame." That tradition is observed in Milwaukee, as well, but most fans at Miller Park get more excited for what happens in the middle of the sixth inning.

Ladies and gentlemen, we bring you the Racing Sausages.

Some ideas are so silly that they are dismissed almost immediately. Luckily for fans of the Brewers, both near and far, that was not the case with this notion. Dress up some young folks in oversized, ethnic wiener costumes and have them race around the outer boundaries of the playing field to a finish line?

Sure, why not? And excuse us while we place a friendly wager on the outcome.

Officially known as the Klement's Racing Sausages—rest assured that the sponsor never envisioned the immense popularity of this daily event—five really big wiener costumes are worn by the participants:

- **The Bratwurst:** A longtime favorite ballpark treat in Milwaukee wears green lederhosen for the proper Austrian/Bavarian "flavor."
- **The Polish Sausage:** This contestant wears sunglasses and a blue and red rugby shirt. (Don't ask why.)
- **The Italian Sausage:** Sporting a chef's outfit, presumably from an Italian restaurant.
- **The Hot Dog:** This traditional ballpark food is decked out in a baseball uniform, of course.
- **The Chorizo:** The late-comer to the party wears a huge sombrero—not exactly the ideal aerodynamic accessory.

The signature Milwaukee Brewers event, the sausage race, occurs before the bottom of the sixth inning of every home game.

Club employees, including members of the grounds crew, usually run the race, but certain celebrities have been known to don the top-heavy costumes and make the trek—from the left-field corner, around home plate, and onward to the right-field corner—at paces that vary from game to game.

The Racing Sausages became popular beyond the wildest dreams of club officials and make frequent appearances at local events, including charitable causes. They also sponsor and participate in an annual 5K run/walk that benefits the Brewers Community Foundation.

The sausage race began at County Stadium in the early 1990s as a scoreboard animation. Then came the idea to make over-sized costumes of the wieners and have an actual on-field race on Sundays only, mostly for the enjoyment of children at the ballpark. The first live sausage race took place on May 29, 1994, the day the Brewers retired Robin Yount's No. 19 jersey.

Thus a tradition was born. By the turn of the century, the costumed racers went from a Sunday-only event to a gameday ritual. At the start, there were only three Racing Sausages: the Bratwurst, the Polish, and the Italian. Soon came the obvious fourth entrant, the Hot Dog, and much later, in a nod to the growing Latin involvement in the game, the Chorizo.

In the dark days of the franchise in the late '90s and early 2000s when the team staggered to one losing season after another, former Brewers beat writer Drew Olson coined the phrase, "Some people have the pennant race. We have the sausage race."

They became known on a national scale due to an unfortunate incident on July 9, 2003 during a game between the Brewers and Pittsburgh Pirates. As the sausages raced past the visiting dugout, Pirates first baseman Randall Simon, not realizing how top-heavy the costumes were, reached out with his bat and tapped the Italian Sausage. Mandy Block, who was wearing that costume, went tumbling to the ground, knocking over the Hot Dog like a bowling pin.

Assaulting a racing sausage is a capital offense in Milwaukee, and Major League Baseball arrested, fined, and suspended Simon for three games. The next day, he held an apologetic press conference and presented autographed bats to the two young ladies who hit the deck. Shortly afterward, T-shirts surfaced bearing the slogan, "Don't Whack Our Wieners!" Only in America, right?

On occasion, players have sneaked into the race, including Japanese pitcher Hideo Nomo, who developed a fondness for the event, which prompted his inclusion one day in 1999. With the massive calves of a big league pitcher sticking out below the costume, Nomo was easy to spot as he raced to victory.

You can never have too much of a good thing, so the Brewers decided to turn the Sunday races into a tag-team event, with youngsters, wearing miniature sausage outfits, finishing the race. Kids do the darnedest things, so you never know what will transpire after the original Racing Sausages tag off to the "cocktail wienies."

It is said that imitation is the sincerest form of flattery, and sure enough, other teams decided to capitalize on the growing popularity of the Racing Sausages by staging their own locally-themed costume races. The Pirates introduced the Racing Pierogies. The Washington Nationals stumbled upon a big sensation with the Racing Presidents of George Washington, Thomas Jefferson, Abraham Lincoln, and Theodore Roosevelt. The four figures atop Mount Rushmore try to outrun each other. (Alas, the Nationals never let Teddy win until the last regular season game of the 2012 season, his 534th race.)

Other clubs chimed in with, shall we say, lamer versions of the race. The Kansas City Royals have racing condiments; the Atlanta Braves feature racing hand tools; the Houston Astros went with racing hot sauce packets. As with most things in life, however, nothing beats the original. What former club vice president Laurel Prieb admitted began as "a lark" is now a Brewers institution. In the middle of the sixth inning of games at Miller Park, you won't see many fans head to the restrooms—they'll miss the sausage race if they do.

Heaven forbid.

5 The Suds Series

When the Brewers took on the St. Louis Cardinals in the 1982 World Series, it instantly was labeled the "Suds Series" because of the beer-making background of both cities. The Cards were owned by the Anheuser Busch family, makers of Budweiser. Several breweries— led by Miller and Schlitz—were still going in Milwaukee.

Fresh off their thrilling come-from-behind American League Championship Series, where they won the final three games in Milwaukee to dispatch the California Angels, the Brewers roared into St. Louis and stomped the Cardinals 10–0 in Game 1. Leadoff hitter Paul Molitor collected a record five hits in his very first World Series game, and veteran left-hander Mike Caldwell tossed a three-hitter. "I'd probably have to consider this one of my best performances this year," Caldwell said, "and probably my career, since this is the World Series."

The embarrassing loss snapped the Cardinals to attention, however, and they came back to win Game 2 in a 5–4 thriller. Ever since, Brewers owner Bud Selig has insisted that his club would have won the title had closer Rollie Fingers not been sidelined with an arm injury, and he often points to Game 2 to back that claim.

Rookie Pete Ladd, who filled in admirably for Fingers in the final stages of the season, took over for Bob McClure in the eighth inning with two on, one out, and the game tied at four. Ladd walked Lonnie Smith on a close 3–2 pitch—that he thought was a strike—lost his composure and walked pinch-hitter Steve Braun on four pitches to force in what would be the winning run. Manager Harvey Kuenn, not one to make excuses, refused to blame the loss on umpire Bill Haller's ball four call to Smith, however. "You can't blame one call for losing the game," said Kuenn, well aware his club held an early 3–0 lead in the game with veteran Don Sutton on the mound.

The Series shifted to Milwaukee for Game 3 with the Brewers' raucous fans filling County Stadium to the brim to experience their first Fall Classic. Those fans soon fell quiet as the Cardinals rolled to an easy 6–2 victory behind two home runs from Willie McGee, an unlikely power threat whose lanky frame and facial features led to the nickname "E.T." McGee hit only four homers during the regular season but twice got to Brewers ace Pete Vuckovich, who would be named the American League Cy Young Award winner a few weeks later. McGee also hurt the Brewers with his glove. With a man on and no outs in the ninth, Gorman Thomas crushed a pitch to deep left-center, which had home run written all over it, off of Cards closer Bruce Sutter. But McGee raced back, leaped, and reached over the fence to make a sensational catch, and the Brewers were done.

Undaunted by that loss, the Brewers bounced back to take Games 4 and 5 by scores of 7–5 and 6–4, respectively. St. Louis seemed in control of Game 4 with a 5–1 lead entering the seventh, but Milwaukee rallied for six runs. Thomas, who was having a tough Series and made the first out of the inning, capped the outburst with a two-run single. "I started the inning with a pop-up to the catcher. Hey, you could say I started the winning rally," Thomas joked afterward.

The Brewers rallied to take Game 5, again displaying the fighting spirit that got them this far. Without the good stuff he flashed in Game 1, Caldwell had to battle from start to finish, giving up 14 hits in 8⅓ innings but refusing to allow St. Louis a big rally.

McClure got closing duty this time and finished off the Cardinals, putting the Brewers within one victory of the crown.

Alas, that one victory never came. The Series shifted back to St. Louis where the Cardinals took a resounding 13–1 triumph in Game 6 to even it at three games apiece. Sutton, the late-season acquisition who pitched the Brewers to the AL East crown on the final day of the regular season and came up big again in the ALCS against California, had nothing left and was knocked out early. "I ran out of gas," Sutton said. "As much as it pains a professional to say it, I had pitched a lot of innings in September and October, and I flat ran out of gas. I regret that to this day."

Adding further insult to the lop-sided loss, commissioner Bowie Kuhn refused to shorten a World Series game when heavy rain soaked Busch Stadium in the sixth inning with the Cardinals ahead 8–0. The teams waited for more than two hours for the Brewers to absorb the inevitable defeat.

It was do-or-die for both teams in Game 7, but after winning the division on the last day of the season and taking the last three games of the ALCS against the Angels, the Brewers felt this was their year. The Cardinals had other ideas, however, even when they fell behind 3–1 in the sixth inning.

A three-run rally in the bottom of the sixth put St. Louis on top to stay, and Game 3 winner Joaquin Andujar made it stand up. The ever-reliable Sutter pitched the final two frames, retiring all six hitters he faced, striking out a flailing Thomas for the championship-clinching out.

With Fingers sidelined, the Cardinals knew they had the upper hand with Sutter in their bullpen. To this day, Brewers fans think the Series never would have made it back to St. Louis had Fingers been available for the late innings of the Game 2 defeat. "I don't know if I would have made a difference," said a disconsolate Fingers. "But I will say this: I would have liked to have been there to try."

6 It's Miller (Park) Time

As the 1990s rolled around, it had become apparent that County Stadium was on its last legs. A building boom in Major League Baseball had begun across the country, and it became evident to team owner Bud Selig that the Brewers would need a modern facility to remain competitive as a small-market franchise.

Selig figured it would be a battle to secure public financing as part of the package needed to build a new ballpark, but the fight became bloodier and more personal than even he imagined. The Brewers sought to fund a good portion of the facility with a five-county sales tax that many residents opposed. The state legislature would have to sign off on that plan, which led to considerable political posturing. After much haggling and wrangling, a stadium plan passed on October 6, 1995, but not without considerable drama.

A state senate session in Madison, Wisconsin, lapsed into the wee hours of the morning as supporters and detractors debated each other with fury and passion. When senator George Petak of Racine switched his vote from nay to yea, the bill passed by a 16–15 margin. After voters from his district removed him from office with a recall campaign, Petak would suffer consequences for changing his mind. To Brewers fans, fearful that the team might leave for greener pastures, however, Petak was a hero. "He paid a price for it, but I think most people now believe he did the right thing," Selig said. "Without a new ballpark, the Brewers had no chance to survive in Milwaukee. That became quite evident."

Selig had become interim commissioner of baseball during the fight to build Miller Park. He appointed his daughter, Wendy Selig-Prieb, as team president, and much of her life revolved around getting the stadium project passed, sometimes at the expense of getting dragged through the mud publicly by opponents. "There was a lot of suffering and heartache involved in making Miller Park a reality," Selig said. "We never realized going into it just how ugly the fight would become. There were personal attacks and a lot of bad behavior. But we knew what had to be done, and we were not going to lose sight of the goal."

The following March, Miller Brewing Co. announced it would pay $41.2 million over 20 years for the naming rights to the new ballpark, which would have an innovative retractable roof. To the dismay of those who wanted it downtown, Miller Park would be built on a lot adjacent to County Stadium.

Plans called for Miller Park to open for the 2000 season. But on July 14, 1999, a tragic accident occurred when a 467-foot crane called Big Blue collapsed while raising a large section of the roof infrastructure. Ironworkers Jeffrey Wischer, William DeGrave, and Jerome Starr were killed in that collapse. The damage was estimated at $100 million and set the project back a full year.

Selig had just returned from the All-Star Game in Boston, an uplifting event in which legendary slugger Ted Williams was feted. As Selig turned on the television in his downtown office to watch coverage of the accident, he couldn't believe his eyes. Tears began to stream down his face. "It was one of the saddest days of my life," he said.

After paying a proper tribute to the fallen ironworkers, the Brewers and construction officials regrouped, cleaned up the extensive damage, and returned to building the ballpark. The opening of Miller Park was pushed back to the 2001 season.

With the bitter funding battle and the tragic crane accident behind them, the Brewers played their first game in their new baseball palace on April 6, 2001. County Stadium, which had served both the Milwaukee Braves and Brewers for three decades, had been razed. "Well, we're home," Brewers shortstop Mark Loretta announced to the overflow crowd during pregame ceremonies.

With flashbulbs going off throughout the ballpark, president George W. Bush and Selig tossed out ceremonial first pitches. A crowd of 42,024 took in the festivities and then watched the Brewers pull out a tense 5–4 victory against the Cincinnati Reds. With the retractable roof closed, nobody noticed or felt the chilly, rainy weather. It was a new day in the history of the franchise, which remained rooted in Milwaukee thanks to the much-anticipated birth of Miller Park.

It's All About the Roof

During the battle to put together financing for the building of Miller Park, one high-ranking Wisconsin politician told a Brewers contingent that there would be no roof because it would drive the cost of the project too high. That delegation stood up and walked out of the room.

Members of the group wondered: had he ever gone outside in Wisconsin in April?

The Brewers weren't going to build the ballpark without the roof. Much of their attendance was contingent on group sales from outer reaches of the state, and even the most rabid fans aren't inclined to take a two-hour bus ride to Milwaukee, if the game is being threatened by bad weather.

So a retractable roof indeed was included in the project. The unique, fan-shaped design proved a bit problematic in extreme weather. The seals, covered by rubber gaskets, don't always hold up under heavy rain, causing leaks in different parts of the ballpark.

But in general, the roof does its job, keeping fans comfortable and dry during what passes for spring and fall in Wisconsin. (Summer usually lasts from July 4 to August 1, folks like to say.) And without question, it is the reason the Brewers have been able to draw fans at a level that a small city otherwise could only dream about.

The Brewers drew more than 3 million in attendance for the first time in 2008 and repeated that commendable achievement in 2009 and 2011. Having a playoff-caliber team didn't hurt, but climate control is recognized as a leading factor by all involved.

As for those original opponents of the roof, Selig rightly says, "Where are they now? You never hear from them."

7 In the Beginning

April Fool's Day in 1970 was no joke for baseball fans in Milwaukee. Major League Baseball was coming back to the city. In a Seattle bankruptcy court on April 1, 1970, judge Sidney Volinn ruled that the Seattle Pilots were to be sold to a group in Milwaukee led by Bud Selig and Ed Fitzgerald. When that gavel slammed down, the Brewers were born.

But there was no time to break out the party favors. The start of the regular season was less than a week away, and the Pilots equipment trucks had already left spring training in Tempe, Arizona, and headed for Las Vegas, where the drivers awaited word of Judge Volinn's decision. If the bankruptcy bid was denied, the trucks would head northwest to Seattle. If the club was sold, the drivers would head for the upper Midwest and Milwaukee.

Off to Wisconsin they went. The banner headline in the *Milwaukee Journal* the next day proclaimed, "We're Big League Again."

The Brewers would open the '70 season at home on April 7 against the California Angels. There was no time to have new uniforms made, so seamstresses went to work, ripping off the Pilots name and logo from each jersey. "Brewers" was stitched on, and a big yellow "M" went on the caps. The Navy-themed "scrambled eggs" design remained on the bills of the caps because it would be too time-consuming to remove them.

When the team arrived in Milwaukee late in the evening on Sunday, April 5, they were stunned at the reception they received. Fans were jubilant over having a team to replace the Braves, who departed for Atlanta five years earlier. Several thousand greeted the

Seated under the franchise's iconic ball-in-glove logo, Bud Selig deserves the credit for getting a Major League Baseball team to Milwaukee.

team at the airport, surprising players who weren't used to that kind of support in Seattle.

Two days later, manager Dave Bristol's team took the field at County Stadium under a bright, sunny sky with temperatures in the 50s, a balmy day in Milwaukee for that time of the year. A crowd of 37,237 showed up to watch the Brewers absorb a 12–0 beating at the hands of the Angels, who didn't mind spoiling the party. Even Selig, who would live and die with each game as the principal owner of the Brewers, wasn't upset over the outcome. "It was the only game that I didn't care if we won or lost," he said. "I was just so happy to have baseball back in Milwaukee."

It was a remarkable few days that left heads spinning, both in the clubhouse and the front office. And it was the culmination of five years of hard work by Selig and his group, who had explored every possible avenue to acquire a major league club.

At one point, Selig thought he had purchased the Chicago White Sox. Brothers John and Arthur Allyn, the owners of the club, agreed to play nine "home" games in Milwaukee in 1968 and 11 more in 1969, and Selig began negotiating to buy the Sox, who were not drawing well at Comiskey Park. Selig had a handshake agreement with Arthur Allyn to buy the team, only to have John Allyn step in and nix the deal. Disappointed, Arthur Allyn sold his shares of the team to his brother, and the White Sox remained in Chicago. "I can't tell you how disappointed I was," Selig said. "I thought that was our last chance."

Then came word that the Pilots, after only one year in Seattle, were in big trouble. They drew only 677,944 fans in 1969 to Sick's Stadium, a former minor league facility that had been expanded. Owners Dewey and Max Soriano were falling in debt and looking for a way out.

The Sorianos tried numerous ways to inject new cash into the club's operation without success. Seeing an opportunity they hadn't expected, Selig's group jumped in and began secretly negotiating to buy the Pilots. During the '69 World Series, the group known as Brewers, Inc., worked out an agreement to buy the team for $10.8 million and move it to Milwaukee.

Not so fast, said American League officials, who weren't keen on the Pilots leaving Seattle after only one season. A meeting was scheduled in March 1970 to vote on the matter, while the state of Washington filed an injunction to prevent the team from relocating. Selig's deal appeared to be falling apart.

But the Sorianos wanted out and responded by filing for bankruptcy, turning the matter over to the courts. Volinn ruled the team indeed was insolvent and ordered it be sold to Selig's group at the agreed-upon price. Word came on the evening before April 1 that the Pilots would become the Brewers.

And that was certainly no joke.

8 On the Mark

In January 2004 the Brewers surprised many people by announcing the team was for sale. The time was right, they said. Bud Selig, the principal owner who had run the team from its inception in 1970, had moved on to bigger and better things as Major League Baseball commissioner. His daughter, team president Wendy Selig-Prieb, was put in charge of the daily operations of the Brewers. She succeeded in getting the team into a much-needed new facility, Miller Park, and also set the course for on-the-field improvement by hiring general manager Doug Melvin after a disastrous 106-loss season in 2002.

But it was time for new blood to run the franchise, and the search began for a prospective owner. Over several months two men rose to the top of the list—Mark Attanasio and Daniel Gilbert. Attanasio was a Los Angeles money manager, and Gilbert was the chairman and founder of Quicken Loans.

Attanasio was more than a smart businessman. He also was a passionate baseball fan who grew up in the Bronx adoring the New York Yankees. When the opportunity came to buy the Brewers, he jumped at the chance, even though it would mean frequent travel from his home in L.A.

Attanasio put together a group that offered to purchase the Brewers for $223 million. He was chosen by club executives over Gilbert, who would go on to buy the NBA's Cleveland Cavaliers. Over time, it became apparent that the Brewers had made the right choice because Attanasio transformed the franchise into a winner over just a few years.

He was approved as new principal owner of the Brewers on January 13, 2005 at an ownership meeting in Scottsdale, Arizona. The sale by the Selig family ended the run of the longest-standing ownership group in MLB at the time. "There's no question it's the end of an era," Wendy Selig-Prieb said after that meeting. "But I have the unequivocal belief that this is the right time. The final piece was finding the right owner."

Attanasio indeed was the right man at the right time for the franchise. In his first year, he boosted the team's payroll from $27 million to $40 million. He moved it higher with each year until it reached $100 million in 2012, an unimaginable level for a small-market franchise.

His immediate goals were to produce a consistent winner and be fan-friendly in every way. And Attanasio succeeded on both fronts. The Brewers finally broke through to the playoffs in 2008, ending a 26-year drought. That year, they reached the 3-million mark in home attendance for the first time and would repeat that remarkable accomplishment in two of the next three seasons.

Attanasio constantly put his money where his mouth was. He gave Melvin the resources in 2008 to trade for Cleveland Indians ace CC Sabathia, who led the club to the playoffs. He stretched the payroll before the 2011 season to acquire pitchers Zack Greinke and Shaun Marcum, who helped the club win its first National League Central crown and establish a franchise record with 96 victories. "What I really want is to provide the best live entertainment experience at our stadium, be a leader in the community, and be the best possible team we can be on the field," Attanasio said after taking over as owner. "We want to be a consistent winner year after year. I'm going to hold myself to a very high standard."

He was true to his word, committing the finances necessary to push the Brewers into a contending mode. Attanasio continued to spend for improvements at Miller Park, making the facility more accommodating with each season. An interactive tribute to the team's founder, "The Selig Experience," opened in 2015. Before the 2017 season, the stadium's entire concessions operation was overhauled at a cost of some $20 million. Attanasio and his wife, Debbie, became leaders in the community, establishing Brewers Charities, Inc., which was devoted to improving the lives of Milwaukee people in need. And in the 2018 offseason, he opened the coffers to sign Lorenzo Cain and trade for Christian Yelich.

So the Yankees fan from the Bronx and West Coast resident/businessman proved to be exactly what a struggling team in the Midwest needed. What seemed to be strange bedfellows at the outset evolved into a perfect symbiosis. "Mark has been the perfect owner for the Milwaukee Brewers," Selig said. "He is a wonderful human being and a great owner. What he has done in such a short time is extraordinary. Everyone in baseball is so impressed."

9 It Took All 162

It came down to Game No. 162. Win and be assured of at least a tie for the National League wild-card berth. Lose and possibly go home.

That was the challenge the Brewers faced on September 29, 2008 at Miller Park as they took the field against the hated Chicago Cubs. Having already clinched the NL Central and with nothing to play for, the Cubs rested several regular players. The Brewers, on the other hand, entered the day tied with the New York Mets for the lone wild-card spot.

All that was at stake for the Brewers were 25 seasons of playoff futility. They hadn't tasted postseason play since the 1982 club went to the franchise's only World Series. An overflow crowd of 45,299 fans anxiously filed into the ballpark with fingers crossed that it would be a special day.

The Brewers felt good about one thing. Pitcher CC Sabathia, the midseason acquisition who put them in position to make the playoffs, was starting that day. The workhorse lefty was pitching on short rest for the third consecutive time, sacrificing his big body for the good of the team. Continuing his stretch of dominance, Sabathia held the Cubs to just one run, a tainted score in the second inning set up by first baseman Prince Fielder's error. But for the longest time, it appeared that one run would be enough to beat the Brewers, who couldn't get anything going at the plate.

The Brewers needed an assist, and Cubs reliever Michael Wuertz gave them one in the seventh inning, walking Craig Counsell with the bases loaded to force in the tying run. It was still 1–1 when Ryan Braun stepped in the batter's box in the eighth inning with a runner aboard and one down. Down the stretch,

Braun had shown considerable flair, socking game-winning homers to keep his club in contention. And he delivered one more time.

Getting all of a first-pitch fastball from veteran righty Bob Howry, the Brewers All-Star left fielder smashed a home run deep into the bleachers in left, resulting in a deafening roar from the home crowd. Braun pumped his fist as he rounded the bases and then did a little skip as he crossed the plate. "I just got caught up in the emotion," he said. "It's really difficult to describe. Just the emotion—from the crowd, from my teammates, the coaches. It was unbelievable."

Now, it was up to Sabathia to finish off the Cubs, and that's exactly what he did. Showing no weariness from his arduous work schedule down the stretch, Sabathia induced Derrek Lee to ground into a double play on his 122nd pitch to close the 3–1 victory. Sabathia punched the air with his fist and let out a mighty roar as Miller Park filled with joyous noise.

But the mission was not yet accomplished. The Brewers needed the Mets to lose at home to the Florida Marlins to secure the wild-card berth. Otherwise there would be a one-game showdown the next day in New York.

In a surreal scene, the final two innings of the Mets-Marlins game was shown on Miller Park's large video screen. Brewers fans stayed to see if the Mets would complete a final-week collapse. Players watched for a while and then retreated to the clubhouse for the final outs. The Mets complied, losing 4–2, touching off a wild celebration in both the clubhouse and stands, with players eventually pouring out to party with the crowd as confetti floated down from the rafters. "I like parties. If they're every 26 years, I guess that makes them more exciting," said Robin Yount, the 1982 MVP who joined the 2008 team for the final two weeks as bench coach when Dale Sveum took over for fired manager Ned Yost. "It's unbelievable," said Counsell, the Milwaukee native who was well aware of the franchise's long postseason drought.

Right in the middle of the celebration, wearing goggles to protect his eyes from the stinging, yet wonderful sprays of champagne, was team owner Mark Attanasio. When his group purchased the club before the 2005 season, Attanasio said his objective was to win and put the Brewers back into the playoffs. Three years later, that goal had been reached. "I can't express how I'm feeling," Attanasio said. "I'm so proud to be part of this effort, the whole group. It's great to be able to do this for the city. Four years [as owner] seems like 20 years, so I can imagine what 26 years feels like."

The Brewers finally had emerged from the baseball wilderness. The team and the city partied like it was 1982.

10 On Top Again, At Last

The Brewers enjoyed their long-awaited return to the playoffs in 2008 as a wild-card team, but as the 2011 season progressed, they had a bigger goal in mind: their first division championship since claiming the American League East on the final day of the 1982 season.

As the Brewers took the field at Miller Park to take on the Florida Marlins on September 23, their magic number for clinching the National League Central had shrunk to two. A sellout crowd of 44,584 packed the stands in hopes of watching a Brewers victory as well as having second-place St. Louis lose at home to the lowly Chicago Cubs.

Sure enough, it happened almost as if it had been scripted. With Ryan Braun supplying yet another dramatic home run, the Brewers topped the Marlins 4–1. Some 25 minutes later, the Cubs beat the Cardinals 5–1, dropping Milwaukee's magic number to zero. "I thought the first time was spectacular, and it would never be quite like that again," proclaimed team owner Mark Attanasio in a champagne-drenched clubhouse. "Well, this is like it but even better."

Attanasio referred to the final day of the 2008 season, when the Brewers topped the Cubs at Miller Park on an eighth-inning home run by Braun and then rooted for the Marlins to beat the New York Mets and give Milwaukee the wild card. This time, in an eerily reminiscent scene, the Brewers defeated the Marlins and then cheered for the Cubs. "It was really weird," said a hoarse Braun, barely able to speak above the din in the home clubhouse afterward. "It was identical to 2008. The game felt exactly the same. The atmosphere, the environment felt identical. It was the same score going into the eighth inning."

Just as they did three years earlier when the Marlins beat the Mets, the players watched the end of the Cubs-Cardinals game in the clubhouse before retreating back to the field to party with their raucous fans. Celebration music blared over the audio system as "2011 NL Central Champions" flashed over and over on the giant scoreboard beyond center field.

As players mingled on the field, Braun held high a boxing-style championship belt he ordered before spring training. That belt remained in the Brewers clubhouse all season, a symbol of the team's quest to win its first division crown since moving to the NL in 1998.

Under new manager Ron Roenicke, the team went on an amazing second-half surge, winning 27 of 32 games during one stretch to separate it from the rest of the pack in the division. The Brewers would finish with a franchise-record 96 victories, making the season even more special. "The one thing that stuck out with this team was our mentality that started in spring training," said veteran lefty Randy Wolf. "We had the saying, 'Championship

'11.' There was no question what the goal was. It wasn't like we hoped we could do it. We knew we could do it."

Realizing after the 2010 season that the Brewers' starting pitching wasn't good enough, general manager Doug Melvin traded many of the organization's prospects for Kansas City Royals ace Zack Greinke and Toronto Blue Jays right-hander Shaun Marcum. Those additions brought the pitching staff up to par with the potent offense led by sluggers Prince Fielder and Braun.

Melvin made another stunning move at midseason when he acquired New York Mets closer Francisco Rodriguez to serve as set-up man for John Axford, who was emerging as one of the top finishers in the game. With "K-Rod" and "Ax man" closing down the final two innings with machine-like precision, the Brewers did not lose a game during the second half of the season when they were leading after seven innings.

All of which put the Brewers in position to close the deal on September 23. With the score tied 1–1 through seven innings, the game evolved into a pitcher's duel. There was an anxious buzz in Miller Park, as the home faithful wondered who would step up and seize the moment. Since coming to the majors in 2007, Braun had long established his flair for the dramatic.

He would do so again.

After a one-out double by Corey Hart and a walk by Nyjer Morgan, Braun stepped in against Marlins reliever Clay Hensley and crushed a home run to center, a no-doubter that electrified the crowd and prompted the Brewers star to raise his bat in triumph as he began his home run trot. Axford closed out the Marlins in the ninth, and everyone waited for the Cubs, normally a hated division rival, to do the Brewers a favor in St. Louis. "This is what you live for as a team," Braun said. "There's nothing better. This is why you play the game."

11 Pick Your Favorite Moniker

When the Brewers acquired outfielder Nyjer Morgan from the Washington Nationals at the end of spring training in 2011, they didn't just add one player—they acquired multiple personalities. The flamboyant and excitable Morgan referred to himself at various times as Tony Plush (aka T. Plush), Tony Hush (on rare quiet occasions), Tony Gumbel, Tony Tombstone (his Western persona), and countless other colorful monikers.

On one of the biggest nights in Brewers history, Morgan would cement his place in team lore as Tony Clutch.

It was Game 5 of the 2011 National League Division Series against the Arizona Diamondbacks at Miller Park. There was considerable nervousness in Brewer Nation, and for good reason. The Brewers took a 2–0 lead at home in the five-game series only to go to Phoenix and get plastered in Games 3 and 4 by scores of 8–1 and 10–6, respectively.

Game 5 featured a reprise of the Game 1 pitching duel between the teams' aces, the Brewers' Yovani Gallardo and the Diamondbacks' Ian Kennedy. Gallardo out-pitched Kennedy in the opener, a 4–1 victory for the Brewers. Sure enough, the pitchers dominated the action again. The Brewers managed to give closer John Axford a ninth inning, 2–1 lead, which made the home fans feel safe. After all, Axford had converted a club-record 43 consecutive saves since his last failure, which was way back on April 18 in Philadelphia.

But nobody's perfect. The Diamondbacks rallied to tie the score against Axford, silencing the crowd. Axford was fortunate to hold the damage to one run, and when the Brewers failed to respond in the bottom of the ninth, the game went into extra innings. With a berth in the NLCS on the line, Axford came back with a strong 10th inning to keep the game deadlocked, giving the Brewers a second chance at a walk-off victory. Arizona went to its closer, J.J. Putz, who like Axford had enjoyed a sensational season. Craig Counsell lined out to right, but center fielder Carlos Gomez, who entered the game as a defensive replacement in the eighth, stroked a single to left.

The speedy Gomez then swiped second, putting the potential winning run in scoring position for Morgan, a .304 hitter during the regular season who had been held to two hits during the NLDS. With the count at 2–2, Putz fired a 94-mph fastball that Morgan bounced back up the middle and into center field.

Knowing there was no way Gomez was going to be thrown out at the plate, the Brewers stormed out of the dugout, some nearly getting there before the runner. Others made a beeline for the ebullient Morgan, lifting him in the air. "I knew that nobody was going to stop me," Gomez said. "They weren't going to throw me out at the plate."

As usual, Morgan had a unique way to describe the hit that gave the Brewers their first playoff series victory since 1982. "All I wanted to do was hit the ball and tickle it into the outfield," he said. "It's all how you finish, not how you start. Of course, I started off slow, but Plush is always going to finish strong."

Later that evening the St. Louis Cardinals would upset the Philadelphia Phillies 1–0 in Game 5 of that NLDS, giving the Brewers home-field advantage in the NLCS against the Cardinals. Alas, they would bow out in six games to their division rivals, who would go on to an improbable World Series crown by knocking off the Texas Rangers in a seven-game thriller.

But on this night, Morgan, the Brewers, and their fans would party long and hard. Beyond the tremendous excitement and joy, there was a feeling of relief that the NLDS did not get away from them after the Diamondbacks came back to even the series. "If we would have lost today's game, I think everything we accomplished all year would have been meaningless to most of us," Brewers slugger Ryan Braun said. "It would have all been for naught."

Known for somewhat crazed sound bites and his well-documented multiple personalities, Morgan was considered a circus act by many, especially those who saw him only from afar. Past scrapes on the field with opponents while playing with the Pittsburgh Pirates and Nationals contributed to that mixed viewpoint. Morgan proved to be a big part of the team, however, delivering key hits on the field and keeping teammates loose in the clubhouse with his fun-loving antics. "We wouldn't be where we are without his contributions," Braun said. "I told you, he's Tony Clutch."

12 Easter Sunday

There were only 29,357 fans in the County Stadium stands on Easter Sunday 1987, but at least three times that many claimed to be there on that bright and crisp afternoon. The surprising Brewers had won the first 11 games of the season, and no American League club had ever won its opening dozen.

As the game progressed, the Brewers could get nothing going against the Texas Rangers, who went to the bottom of the ninth with a 4–1 lead. Those in attendance were getting the idea that this would be the day the magic ended. Still, as the Brewers returned to the dugout for their final at-bat, the home fans stood and cheered as one, trying to jump-start their club.

But no one could have imagined the lightning bolts that were about to strike out of the blue sky.

Glenn Braggs got things off to an innocuous start by drawing a walk from Rangers reliever Mitch Williams, whose erratic nature earned him the nickname "Wild Thing." After a single by Greg Brock, Cecil Cooper flied out to center, bringing to the plate left fielder Rob Deer.

Deer was an all-or-nothing slugger, a powerful man built like a football player and known among his teammates as "Rooster" because of his flowing mane of red hair. When he got hold of a pitch, he could hit the ball a mile, but Deer also was known for prodigious strikeout totals. (He led the league four times in that category, including a whopping 186 in '87.)

Aware that Deer was prone to waving at breaking balls without making much contact, Texas manager Bobby Valentine summoned right-hander Greg Harris, a curveball specialist. And sure enough, Harris started off Deer with a first pitch hammer, which Deer missed with a mighty cut. No dummy, Harris came back with another curve, but this time Deer didn't miss.

Getting all of the hanger, he sent the ball on a towering arc toward the left-field bleachers, causing everyone on hand to watch it in awe. If not for a stiff breeze blowing in from left, the ball would have gone all the way over the stands. As it was, it landed in the upper reaches as fans scrambled for the ball that tied the game 4–4.

Just like that, County Stadium was up for grabs. Owner Bud Selig clapped so hard that he almost fractured his fingers. As Deer rounded first base, he thrust his right fist in the air. That pose was plastered on the cover of *Sports Illustrated* a few days later.

But the game wasn't over, though some, who claimed to be there that day, still talk about Deer winning the game with his home run. A shaken Harris recovered to strike out B.J. Surhoff, but Jim Gantner worked him for a walk, putting the winning run on base with two down.

Dale Sveum, the No. 9 hitter who went on to a wonderful season, worked the count to 3–2 before crushing a fastball over the bullpen in right-center for a two-run homer that gave the Brewers a miraculous 6–4 triumph and an unblemished 12–0 record.

No one wanted to go home that day. Sveum was summoned for two curtain calls and accompanied Deer for a third. It was the most magical day of a magic time in club annals, one that stretched to 13 consecutive victories before the Brewers finally tasted defeat. "It was one of those days you'll never forget," Deer said. "I was just glad to be a part of it."

On the 25th anniversary of that glorious day in 2012, former catcher Bill Schroeder—now a Brewers television analyst—recalled the events as if they happened yesterday. "It's hard to believe that was 25 years ago," he said. "People still talk about it. I guess they always will. Some things are just meant to be."

To this day, whenever Brewers fans gather to discuss the highlights of franchise history, the phrase "Easter Sunday" is inevitably brought up. One need not say anything more. The year is understood. And someone almost assuredly will claim to have been there that remarkable day.

We'll just have to take their word for it.

13. 3,000 Reasons to Smile

Throughout his career, Robin Yount displayed both consistency and a flair for the dramatic. On September 9, 1992, both of those traits would take center stage as he stepped to the plate in the seventh inning at County Stadium to face Cleveland Indians right-hander Jose Mesa.

A crowd of 47,589 stood as one, many with cameras in hand, wondering if this would be the magic moment. Yount entered the game with 2,999 career hits, one away from the magic plateau that certainly would guarantee a plaque in Cooperstown, New York.

But there was a sense of nervousness, as well. This was the final game of the homestand, and fans wondered if Yount was destined to collect No. 3,000 on the road. That anxiety level rose when Yount went hitless in his first three at-bats against Mesa, grounding out in the first inning and striking out swinging in the third and fourth.

After the second strikeout, the usually stoic Yount uncharacteristically threw his bat and helmet to the ground. He was disgusted with himself, realizing he was pressing to reach the landmark hit. "It was time to get into the ballgame and play baseball," he said.

When Yount came to the plate for the fourth time, he went right to work, fouling off Mesa's first pitch. On the next pitch, he used the inside-out swing that had worked so well throughout his career, lining a single to right field. He had done it—3,000 hits. Cameras flashed throughout the ballpark like thousands of fireflies, and the roar of the crowd was deafening.

Yount had barely retreated to first base before getting mobbed by teammates, led by longtime friends, Paul Molitor and Jim Gantner. He was lifted onto their shoulders. Somewhat embarrassed by the attention, Yount waved to the adoring crowd. "That was as exciting a moment as probably I ever had," he said. "It was a great feeling. You don't get feelings like that very often. It was something I was going to let last as long as I could because, like I said, it doesn't happen too often."

As the celebration continued, film clips of Yount's life and career were shown on the video board, beginning with his days as a Little League pitcher. Yount had accomplished something only 16 other major leaguers had. "All along I said it was no big deal. It was just going to be another hit," said the always humble Yount. "Well,

Hall of Famer Robin Yount joins an exclusive club with this single on September 9, 1992.

obviously, it turned out not to be just another hit. The way the fans got into the whole thing here, all the excitement behind it. It really turned into a lot more than I was thinking it was going to be."

Yount collected his first hit as a teenage shortstop in 1974. Now, a veteran center fielder and two-time MVP, he delivered once again before the home crowd, allowing them to share the moment. The night, however, did not end on a happy note for Yount, the

What's Your Name Again?

Brewers manager Tom Trebelhorn spent his off-seasons dabbling as a teacher in Portland, Oregon, so he certainly knew how to spell. And when it came to Robin Yount, no player was more recognizable in the history of the franchise.

Yet in one of those brain farts you seldom see from a skipper, Trebelhorn turned in a lineup on August 28, 1988, with Yount's name included twice. Yount was listed batting third in center field and also fifth as the designated hitter. Trebelhorn intended for Mike Young—acquired days earlier and in the starting lineup for the first time—to serve as DH, but instead of a "g" at the end of his name, he put a "t."

The Brewers were playing at home against the Detroit Tigers, and legendary skipper Sparky Anderson never missed a beat. Accordingly, he noticed immediately that Trebelhorn had put Yount's name on the lineup card twice.

Anderson remained mum when Yount lined out to second with two outs in the first inning against Doyle Alexander. But when Young stepped to the plate with one down in the bottom of the second, Anderson popped out of the visiting dugout to point out to home-plate umpire Mike Reilly that the lineup card said "Yount" in that spot.

Reilly summoned Trebelhorn to show him the error, and after 20 minutes of debate, Yount was ruled to be out of the game. An embarrassed Trebelhorn argued until he was ejected from the game. A furious Yount stood on the top of the dugout steps and screamed across the field at Anderson, gesturing angrily over what he considered pettiness on the part of the Tigers manager.

The good news for the Brewers was that, even without Yount, they rallied from a 9–4 deficit to win the game 12–10. Young did little to help, going 0–3 with a walk.

Brewers, and their fans. The Indians rallied late to take a 5–4 lead and won the game when Yount lined out to short for the third out in the bottom of the ninth.

True to form, Yount's enthusiasm was tempered by the game's outcome, particularly with the Brewers trying to stay in the playoff hunt. Always a team player, he would have given back his 3,000[th] hit and waited for another day if the game had gone the Brewers' way. "This was a big ballgame for us," the disappointed hero told reporters after the game. "We can't afford to lose too many more ballgames. We have a chance to win the division."

The Brewers would not make the playoffs that season. But those who were in the stands at County Stadium on September 9 would never forget the excitement, the atmosphere, or the history they witnessed that evening as Yount came through one more time.

14 Fits Like a Glove (and Ball)

From their inception in 1970 through the 1977 season, the Brewers' logo was "Barrel Man," a hitter in the shape of a beer barrel swinging a bat (with a nose that conjured up images of the Tin Man in *The Wizard of Oz*). During that period, the team's caps featured a large yellow "M," not the Barrel Man logo. But that image had run its course, and the club was ready to move on to a new logo for the 1978 season.

An open-to-the-public contest was held to pick a new design, and some 2,000 entries were submitted during October and November 1977. The winner of the $2,000 first prize was Tom Meindel, an art history student at the University of Wisconsin-Eau Claire who submitted an ingenious image. Using the lower case letters "m" and "b" for Milwaukee Brewers, Meindel designed what became known as the "ball-in-glove" logo, a baseball mitt with a ball in the center of the "b."

The logo became one of the most recognizable in sports and was featured prominently on the Brewers' baseball caps. It became a hot seller among the team's loyal fans, who snapped up caps, T-shirts, jerseys, and anything they could find featuring the new design.

As any club marketing person will tell you, the more alternatives you present to fans, the more the cash register rings. But sometimes change is not all that great. To celebrate their 25th year of existence, the Brewers decided to drop the popular "ball-in-glove" logo in 1994 for a new design. They switched to an interlocking "M" and "B" in the center of a baseball-diamond shape with crisscrossing baseball bats. The color green also was incorporated into the team's logo for the first time.

To say the least, fans were underwhelmed. To many, the interlocking "M" and "B" smacked of the interlocking "N" and "D" of the University of Notre Dame. The club's loyal fan base didn't understand why the ball-in-glove had been mothballed, and it soon became evident that the interlocking letters on the new logo would not last. By 1997 the team had switch to a simple capital "M" on their baseball caps.

Coinciding with the anticipated opening of Miller Park (a crane accident delayed the opening for a year) in 2000, the block "M" was replaced with a script "M" with a head of barley underlining it. The change was an improvement over its predecessors, but many fans yearned for a return to the ball-in-glove logo—if not permanently, then at least on a part-time basis.

After new owner Mark Attanasio took over in 2005, the team's marketing department no longer could ignore the wishes of its fans. The Brewers introduced Retro Sundays, during which the players would wear uniforms with the beloved ball-in-glove logo.

The design re-emerged in the merchandising of the club, and fans flocked to the team's stores to snap up apparel featuring the old logo.

The retro day later was changed to Fridays, which remains a well-received marketing ploy. On any given day at Miller Park, you will see far more fans sporting the retro ball-in-glove logo on their apparel than the official logo introduced in 2000. That new logo has a cursive "Brewers" written across a baseball, which is encircled by a blue rim that says "Milwaukee" on the top and has barley on the bottom.

New is not always better, which is why Tom Meindel's design remains the favorite among the Brewers' expanding fan base. It goes deeper than being the logo the club wore during its World Series campaign in 1982. For Brewers fans, it's merely the most ingenious and popular design in the club's history. Call it "retro," if you like. But as is often the case in clothing, what once was old becomes new again. Well, not new, but you get the idea.

15 Do or Die

When the Brewers arrived in Baltimore for the final series of the 1982 season, they were feeling pretty good about themselves. They had built a three-game lead over the Orioles in the American League East, meaning they had to win just once in the four games to clinch the division title and their first full-season playoff berth. (They won the second half of the strike-split season in 1981 and then lost to the New York Yankees in five games.)

The Brewers, however, suffered a mini-collapse in Baltimore, losing the first three games—including a makeup doubleheader—by the combined score of 26–7. If Harvey Kuenn's club didn't win on the final day of the season, it would be known forever as one of the biggest choke jobs in major league history.

Despite those do-or-die stakes, there was no sense of panic in the Memorial Stadium visiting clubhouse. Third baseman Sal Bando did a veteran thing the previous evening, taking out a large group of players to eat dinner at a restaurant in Baltimore's Little Italy. It was an effort to ease the tension, pull the team back together, and have some fun before the most important regular season game in franchise history. "Sal was buying. That in itself was an event," said right-hander Don Sutton, who started the final game against the Orioles. "I figured if that miracle could happen on Saturday night, another one could take place on Sunday."

Sutton had been acquired in an astute late-season trade by general manager Harry Dalton, who sent Kevin Bass, Frank DiPino, and Mike Madden to Houston to add a proven winner as a final piece to the puzzle. The future Hall of Famer certainly did his part, going 3–1 with a 3.47 ERA in six starts.

The Orioles would counter in the season finale with another Cooperstown, New York-bound pitcher, Jim Palmer. With the Brewers reeling, Baltimore's fans figured Palmer would finish the job and put the longtime East power into the playoffs against the California Angels.

What the Orioles, their fans, and most others didn't know was that Sutton almost missed his start that day. He arrived in town suffering from some kind of virus and requested an injection of antibiotics. But Sutton suffered an allergic reaction to the medication and broke out in hives, forcing trainers to give him a shot of cortisone.

Sutton, though, was feeling better by Sunday morning and was ready to go. He reported to the trainer's room to get his right big toe and left heel taped, measures he had used for weeks to provide support for nagging problems. As Sutton sat on the trainer's table, shortstop Robin Yount stuck his head in the door and delivered a succinct message. "Don't make us score five runs to get even, and we'll kick [Palmer's] butt," vowed Yount, who later would play a role as big as Sutton in the outcome of the game.

The stoic Yount was hardly a rah-rah type player, so the message had the desired effect on Sutton. It made him focus even more on the task at hand, and when gametime came, Sutton and his teammates were ready. But there would be one last message before the Brewers took the field. Team owner Bud Selig, after tossing and turning all night and thinking it over, asked Kuenn if he could address the club. He, too, had a simple message. "I just told them I was proud of them and thanked them for everything," Selig recalled. "I said, 'Go out there and have some fun.'"

And that's exactly what the Brewers did. Palmer and the Orioles never had a chance, as Yount socked two home runs and a triple, and Sutton held Baltimore's potent lineup in check. With two runners on and the Brewers on top 5–2, left fielder Ben Oglivie snuffed an eighth-inning rally with a sliding catch in the corner to rob Joe Nolan of an extra-base hit. The Brewers blew open the game with a five-run ninth inning.

Their resounding 10–2 triumph touched off a wild celebration in their clubhouse. "It was bedlam, absolute bedlam," Sutton said. "I felt so privileged and gratified to have the ball the last day and have it turn out so well. I felt like I wasn't just pitching for the Brewers. I was pitching for the whole state of Wisconsin."

Back home, the rabid baseball fans of that state were partying just as hard. The celebrations carried long into the night at every corner tavern. The Brewers were AL East champs.

16 A Little Body English Never Hurts

After winning their first division title on the final day of the 1982 season in Baltimore, the Brewers barely had time to exhale before heading west to take on the California Angels for the American League pennant. Before they knew it, they were down 2–0 in the best-of-five series. "The series in Baltimore was so emotional," said shortstop Robin Yount, who socked two homers off Orioles pitcher Jim Palmer on that memorable final day. "We flew clear across the country to California and came out flat. We didn't do much in those first two games. But all it takes is one win, and then you never know."

Re-energized by a raucous home crowd of 50,135 at County Stadium, the Brewers got that win in Game 3, holding on for a 5–3 victory behind veteran right-hander Don Sutton. Acquired in a master stroke by general manager Harry Dalton for the playoff push, Sutton prevented the Brewers from completely collapsing in Baltimore by outdueling Palmer on the last day of the regular season.

Now the Brewers had a foot in the door. There would be no Angels sweep, and the momentum shifted just a bit. Then the Brewers manhandled lefty Tommy John in Game 4 and romped to a 9–5 victory that left the Angels dazed and set up a series-deciding Game 5. "When we tied the series, the pressure was squarely on their shoulders," said first baseman Cecil Cooper, who would have a date with destiny the following day.

No team had come back from a 0–2 hole in a best-of-five playoff format, but an overflow crowd of 54,968 squeezed into County Stadium for the series finale, hoping for something special.

And they weren't disappointed. The Angels made those fans nervous, however, taking a 3–2 lead into the bottom of the seventh inning.

With one out, Charlie Moore reached on an infield single, which Angels second baseman Bobby Grich nearly caught on the fly. Jim Gantner followed with a sharp single up the middle. Reliever Luis Sanchez retired Paul Molitor on a pop fly, but Yount drew a walk to load the bases.

Up to the plate stepped Cooper, who was having a miserable series. He had only two hits in 19 at-bats. Earlier in the game, Cooper misplayed a bunt that led to the Angels' go-ahead run, and he also struck out to strand two runners in the fifth.

As Cooper dug into the batter's box, the home fans bellowed with their customary chant: "Coooop! Cooooop!" Angels manager Gene Mauch had left-hander Andy Hassler warming up in the bullpen, and everyone on the Brewers side, including the left-handed Cooper, figured a pitching change was coming. But in a decision that led to much second guessing, Mauch stuck with Sanchez, who was only in his second major league year.

That decision appeared wise when Sanchez quickly got two strikes on Cooper, who now had to protect the plate. Sanchez tried to slip a fastball past Cooper on the outside corner, but the slugger reached out and punched it into left field.

For a moment, it appeared the ball would hang in the air long enough for Angels left fielder Brian Downing to charge in and make the catch. As he broke from the box, Cooper followed the path of the baseball and motioned furiously with both hands, imploring it to get down.

The ball listened, dropping safely to the ground for a single. Moore scooted home from third, and Gantner came around from second, sliding in with the go-ahead run that turned County Stadium upside down with excitement. "All I was trying to do was put the ball in play," Cooper said. "When I saw that thing starting to sink, that's what you dream about. The noise was deafening, unbelievable. I was more grateful than anything because I had a chance to put us ahead a couple of innings before and didn't do it. The only thing was that it wasn't the bottom of the ninth. That would have been the perfect scenario."

That precarious one-run lead would hold up, but not before some ninth-inning drama. Angels pinch-hitter Ron Jackson led off with a single off lefty Bob McClure, prompting Brewers manager Harvey Kuenn to switch to Pete Ladd, a big raw right-hander who had spent much of that season in the minors.

Bob Boone sacrificed pinch-runner Rob Wilfong to second, putting the potential tying run in scoring position. Downing grounded out to third with Wilfong holding. The Brewers were one out from clinching the pennant, but it wasn't just any hitter standing between them and glory. Up to the plate stepped Rod Carew, a future Hall of Famer who seemingly could conjure up a hit whenever necessary.

With everyone in the stands and dugouts holding their collective breath, Carew pounced out of his trademark crouch and lined a one-hop smash right to Yount at short, who made the toss to Cooper. The veteran with the game-winning RBI raised both arms in triumph as the Brewers piled onto the infield in celebration.

The Brewers were going to their first—and to this day only—World Series.

17 Team Streak of '87

I had the honor of dubbing the 1987 Brewers club "Team Streak," a description that stuck like glue. It seemed to make perfect sense, considering how things quickly evolved for that roller-coaster bunch.

The Brewers began the season 13–0, the first American League team to do so, tying the 1982 Atlanta Braves for the best start ever. It was a magical run that included the only no-hitter in club history by Juan Nieves and a remarkable comeback victory on Easter Sunday.

That amazing streak came to an end at Chicago's Comiskey Park when the White Sox defeated Mark Ciardi, who made only one more appearance in the major leagues before moving on to a career as a male model and Hollywood producer. (You can't make this stuff up.)

There was absolutely no way to see this remarkable year coming. Nobody was paying much attention to the Brewers during spring training as they continued the transition from the long-gone glory days of the early '80s.

B.J. Surhoff, the first player taken in the 1985 draft and from the University of North Carolina, took over behind the plate. Greg Brock was the new first baseman. Dale Sveum was inserted at short-stop, a position that suffered from constant turnover once Robin Yount moved to center field. Power-hitting prospect Glenn Braggs was the new right fielder, with incumbent Rob Deer shifting to left.

The Brewers drew defending AL champion Boston in the opening series at County Stadium, which under normal circum-stances would have been a daunting assignment. But the Red Sox broke camp with their pitching in disarray, as evidenced by Bob

Paul Molitor and his 39-game hitting streak in 1987 symbolize Team Streak, a moniker coined by the author. (Getty Images)

Stanley drawing the Opening Day assignment. The Brewers pulled out a couple of close decisions to sweep that series and then hit the road to do likewise in Texas and Baltimore. Nieves punctuated the sweep of the Orioles with his no-hitter.

Then it was back to Milwaukee where the Brewers put an exclamation mark on a sweep of the Texas Rangers with their Easter miracle. Deer and Sveum socked ninth-inning homers to wipe out a three-run deficit and make it an even dozen victories without defeat.

The Brewers soon would go on a streak of a different kind. After boosting their record to 20–3 and threatening to run away with the AL East, they completely collapsed, losing 12 games in a row. To this day, the '87 Brewers are the only big league team to have winning streaks and losing streaks of at least 12 games in the same season.

By the All-Star break, the Brewers had frittered away all of their fantastic start, stumbling to a 42–43 record. On the first day of the second half, yet another remarkable streak began. Oft-injured Paul Molitor came off the disabled list and started a 39-game hitting streak, the longest in the AL since Joe DiMaggio's revered 56-gamer in 1941. Lefty Teddy Higuera also went streaking, pitching 32 consecutive scoreless innings to set a club record.

And so it went. With "Team Streak" rolling once again, the Brewers finished with a 49–28 record in the second half and 91–71 overall. Alas, that was only good enough for third place in the AL East, leaving Brewers fans to ponder what might have been without that early 12-game slide. "It was probably the greatest season a team has ever had without going to the playoffs," Sveum said.

18 Go Tailgating Before a Game

For countless members of Brewer Nation, attending a baseball game at Miller Park is only part of the experience. The real fun begins hours beforehand when fans set up tailgating parties throughout the vast expanse of parking lots around the ballpark. We're not talking about pulling out a tiny Weber grill and tossing on a few hot dogs and munching on some chips. In essence, Brewers fans are "professional" tailgaters, leaving no bratwurst unturned in making the pregame activity a true social event.

For starters, don't even think about showing up without a cooler of beer. That beverage is a requisite for tailgating, coming at a much more reasonable price than you'll be paying a vendor inside the ballpark.

Second on the list is providing the appropriate heat for your meat of choice. If you don't have the coals hot enough—or if you're smart, a dependable propane source—forget it. It's all about getting the carnivores the brat, hot dog, steak, chicken, or fish, in their mouths as soon as possible.

And despite the nomenclature, few folks are sitting and eating on the tailgates of their cars. Veterans of the culture know to bring tables and chairs—make that a lot of chairs. And if you really want to spruce up the environment, a table cloth and matching napkins provide a nice touch. Candlesticks and bottles of wine? Why not? Let's class up the joint a bit!

The parking lots around Miller Park generally open three hours prior to the start of games. But long before that time arrives, cars line up by the dozens with anxious tailgaters looking to land the premium spots.

Check Out the Kids Next Door

After Miller Park was finished in 2001 and the Brewers tore down adjacent County Stadium, they didn't just put up a parking deck or toss down a bunch of sod. They used that lot to build Helfaer Field, a gorgeous Little League/softball facility that seats more than 700 people and cost $3.1 million.

The Evan and Marion Helfaer Foundation donated $2.1 million of the cost, with the baseball district footing the rest of the bill. Evan Helfaer was an original investor in the Brewers when they were bought out of bankruptcy in Seattle in 1970.

The beautiful miniature stadium includes 502 bleacher seats and 220 concourse seats. The outfield fence is six feet high and 200 feet from home plate with 60-foot base paths meeting both youth baseball and softball standards. The foul poles from County Stadium were transferred to Helfaer, and along the left-field concourse is a marker that designates where home plate was in the old ballpark. The natural-turf surface has irrigation and drainage systems similar to those at Miller Park. Helfaer is used from spring to fall, allowing area youth to play on the site where the Milwaukee Braves and Brewers once cavorted.

The field is big league in many other areas, including the sound system, concession stands, stadium lights, scorer's table, restrooms, and pavilions located down the left-field and right-field lines for picnics and other activities. Beyond renting the facility for youth games, adults can reserve it for tailgating parties and other festive occasions. Beginning in 2012, fans attending Brewers games on Sundays were invited to visit Helfaer Field and play catch there at no charge.

Often before Brewers games, early-arriving fans and tailgaters wander over to Helfaer Field and watch the kids play. Who knows? Perhaps there's a future big leaguer, maybe even a future Brewer, on the field that day.

At the groundbreaking for the facility, then-Brewers president Wendy Selig-Prieb said, "Helfaer Field will be the premier youth ballpark in the country. This ballpark will provide an important bridge to our rich baseball past, as well as a special bridge to the future, as our children and their children learn to play the game of baseball here."

To allow everyone equal access to what has become a Brewers tradition, there are some rules everyone must follow. First of all, one parking space per tailgating expedition (or, if you're in cahoots with adjacent parties, feel free to cross over the white lines).

The Brewers also provide for large tailgating parties in pavilions, which are located across the Menomonee River from the Klement's Sausage Haus. Designated areas for larger parties can be found in the Uecker and Yount parking lots.

Most importantly, contain your flames. Gas/propane units with fuel valve turnoffs are mandated, and only self-contained charcoal units are permitted. In other words, no campfires and marshmallow roasts. Coal bins are provided for disposing of hot charcoal.

Longtime veterans of Brewers games still recall the night at old County Stadium when a van was incinerated in the parking lot beyond center field, creating a fireball and smoke plume that was seen for miles. Before entering the stadium, some—foolish or perhaps tipsy—tailgaters decided to slide their grill under their vehicle to keep it protected. Oops!

Former team owner Bud Selig was well aware of the passion of Brewers tailgaters and how important that activity was to their baseball experience in Milwaukee. It was one of the main reasons he fought against building Miller Park downtown where parking lots would be few and far between and spread out over several blocks. Tailgating in a parking deck on the fifth floor? Selig knew that would be a detriment to attendance.

That factor loomed large in building the new ballpark adjacent to the old one, allowing expansive parking lots already in place to continue to be used for tailgating purposes. The lots, of course, are open to the elements, unlike games played under the retractable roof of Miller Park, but Milwaukee tailgaters are a hardy bunch, willing to wear layers of clothing to experience outdoor dining, Brewers style.

So there's good reason why seats in Miller Park are often half-full at best when the first pitch is thrown. The game itself is merely Part II of the experience of attending a Brewers contest. And for many there is also a Part III—more tailgating after the last out.

As tailgaters like to say, you can never have too much of a good thing.

19 Harvey's Wallbangers

Through the first two months of the 1982 season, the Brewers were struggling, frustrating both fans and club officials. There was too much talent on the team to be foundering like this, so general manager Harry Dalton figured it was time for someone else to sit in the manager's chair.

Dalton made the difficult yet necessary decision to replace Buck Rodgers, who did not have the support of veterans on the club, with venerable hitting coach Harvey Kuenn. It was a switch that suddenly lit a fire under the previously rudderless club.

The Brewers were in Seattle on June 2 when the change was made. When the players reported to the clubhouse, there was a notice of a pregame meeting. Kuenn gathered his players together for a chat, which did not challenge Lincoln's Gettysburg address in either eloquence or length. "There's just two things I want you to know," Kuenn said. "No. 1, I don't like meetings. No. 2, this meeting is over. You guys go out and play."

And that's exactly what the Brewers did. Unlike Rodgers, who preferred a hands-on approach, Kuenn was an old-school skipper who made out the lineup and got out of the way. He knew there was enough talent to make a run at the top of the American League East, and his players didn't let him down. The club was still laden with power, which is why it was easy to transition from the earlier days of "Bambi's Bombers" under previous manager George Bamberger to the more appropriate "Harvey's Wallbangers." You just don't get team nicknames like that anymore.

The Brewers immediately went on a long-ball binge, socking 35 home runs over a sensational 15-game stretch. They won 20 of 27 games in June and jumped right into the thick of the playoff race, playing like Dalton expected all along. Kuenn had no ego whatsoever, eagerly passing along the praise to his players.

No player prospered more under the guidance of Kuenn than shortstop Robin Yount, who at age 26 was already an eight-year veteran. Yount often referred to Kuenn as a "second father," and the two formed a tight bond as the former AL batting champ schooled his pupil on how to get the most out of his offensive talent. "Harvey taught me how to play the game," Yount said "It was more than just hitting the baseball. He told us to play the game hard all of the time, which is the way I felt the game should be played, also. I respected him so much that whatever he said, I took it to heart."

Yount would go on to bat .331 with 29 home runs and 114 RBIs, leading the league with 210 hits, 367 total bases, and a .578 slugging percentage. When the Brewers went on to claim the AL East title in Baltimore on the last day of the season, Yount became the obvious choice as the league's Most Valuable Player.

Known for his toughness as well as his skill, Yount saw the same quality in Kuenn. He respected the way Kuenn handled personal adversity with nary a complaint. The Brewers manager endured a series of health problems that included heart bypass surgery; kidney and stomach ailments; and a circulation problem in his right leg that forced doctors to amputate it in 1980.

Sitting on the Hot Seat

Harvey Kuenn remains one of the most beloved managers in Brewers history, piloting the club to its only World Series in 1982. But Kuenn managed only 276 games for Milwaukee, not even close to the longest service time among Brewers skippers.

Here's a look at the men who managed the most games for the Brewers, only three of whom emerged with winning records:

Manager	Years	Games	Wins-Losses	Pct.
Phil Garner	1992–99	1,180	563–617	.477
Ned Yost	2003–08	959	457–502	.477
Tom Trebelhorn	1986–91	819	422–397	.515
George Bamberger	1978–80, 1985–86	728	377–351	.518
Ron Roenicke	2011–15	673	342–331	.508

Equipped with a prosthetic leg, Kuenn would limp out to the mound to make pitching changes, taking his sweet time. He didn't let that hindrance stop him from getting in the face of umpires, either, with an ever-present chaw of tobacco in one cheek.

Kuenn was an immediate favorite of Brewers fans because, in essence, he was one of their own. He was born in the Milwaukee suburb of West Allis, just down the road from County Stadium. Along with his wife, Audrey, he operated a motel and Cesar's, a popular local dive that did brisk business during the Brewers' surge to the AL pennant and World Series in '82.

The team embodied the grit and never-say-die attitude of their manager. After losing the first three games of a season-ending series in Baltimore to allow the Orioles to tie them for the division lead, the Brewers rolled to victory on the final day behind Don Sutton and Yount to claim the AL East. Down two games to none in the best-of-five ALCS against the California Angels, the Brewers rallied to win the next three games and earn a trip to the World Series.

Ahead three games to two in the Fall Classic, "Harvey's Wallbangers" finally ran out of luck, dropping the final two games in St. Louis.

When the club collapsed at the end of the '83 season, Dalton made a difficult choice, dismissing Kuenn and replacing him with Rene Lachemann. Even if his tenure as manager was a short one, Kuenn became a beloved figure in Brewers lore.

True to form, Kuenn went out with no complaints or bitter feelings. He was the right man at the right time in 1982, allowing a talented bunch of veterans to reach their full potential.

20 Bambi's Bombers

Before the Brewers had "Harvey's Wallbangers," they had "Bambi's Bombers." When George Bamberger was hired as manager before the 1978 season, his baseball background was as a former pitcher and pitching coach. But having served on the staff of legendary Baltimore Orioles manager Earl Weaver, "Bambi" also developed an affinity for Weaver's favorite play—the three-run homer.

Thus it was with great glee that Bamberger inherited a club with considerable power led by slugger Gorman Thomas. Bamberger and Thomas hit it off immediately, and the manager let the free-swinging center fielder know that he was staying in the lineup, no matter how many times he struck out. With the likes of Cecil Cooper, Larry Hisle, Sixto Lezcano, Don Money, Sal Bando, and Thomas in the batting order, the Brewers regularly bombed opponents into submission. So it was only fitting that the club soon took on the nickname "Bambi's Bombers."

Having a Grand Opener (Twice)

Hitting a grand slam on Opening Day is something a player remembers for the rest of his life. But what about hitting two and both at home, no less?

Sixto Lezcano became the first—and only—player in major league history to hit two grand slams on Opening Day, connecting on April 7, 1978 against the Baltimore Orioles and April 10, 1980 against the Boston Red Sox.

Lezcano's second homer was even more memorable because it came in walk-off fashion. After Carl Yastrzemski and Butch Hobson homered in the top of the ninth off Jim Slaton to tie the score at five, Lezcano connected with two outs in the bottom of the inning off Red Sox reliever Dick Drago, electrifying a sell-out crowd of 53,313. While pitching for the California Angels five years earlier, that same reliever had surrendered Hank Aaron's final home run.

Lezcano blasted a two-run shot in the fourth inning off Boston starter Dennis Eckersley, so the slam gave him a remarkable six-RBIs day. But it would prove to be Lezcano's last opener with the Brewers. After the season, he was one of four players traded to the St. Louis Cardinals in a blockbuster deal, which netted Pete Vuckovich, Rollie Fingers, and Ted Simmons for Milwaukee.

A year later, Lezcano was part of another major trade. He and Garry Templeton were sent to the San Diego Padres in exchange for Ozzie Smith, who became a Hall of Fame shortstop for the Cardinals.

After nine seasons of losing, including 95-loss campaigns the two previous years, the Brewers started to win under Bamberger, who made out the lineup every night and then stepped out of the way and watched the fireworks. Milwaukee won 93 games in '78, beginning the turnaround that would result in a World Series appearance four years later.

Brewers fans took to the exciting turn of events, resulting in an attendance of 1.6 million, a boost of nearly 500,000 from the previous season. Bamberger was named American League Manager of the Year for piloting the club to its best season yet.

The winning continued as the Brewers went 95–66 in 1979, finishing second behind Weaver's Orioles. Thomas led the league with 45 home runs, and more than 1.9 million fans clicked the turnstiles at County Stadium. "The reason we won is George gave people a chance to play," Thomas said. "He let you play, even if you failed for awhile. I got a chance to play every day. At first, he hit me ninth, but that's a hell of a lot better than 10th. If it wasn't for George, I wouldn't have had a career."

Sadly, Bamberger's time at the helm of the Brewers was short-lived. Before the start of the 1980 season, he suffered a heart attack in Arizona and underwent bypass surgery. "Bambi" turned over the reins of the club to Buck Rodgers until June.

Bamberger wanted Brewers fans to know he was with them in spirit. From his home in Florida, he taped a video message that was played at County Stadium on Opening Day: "I'd like to thank the fans. I'd like to wish the ballplayers much success. We've got very capable coaches who know their business." Then, showing how well he knew the Milwaukee fans, Bamberger smiled and said, "So sit back, enjoy the game, and have a beer on me."

The crowd erupted into applause and chanted "Bambi! Bambi! Bambi!" It was an unrehearsed display of their love for their missing skipper.

The offensive onslaught continued that year as Thomas, Cooper, and Ben Oglivie each compiled more than 100 RBIs. But the Brewers slipped a bit, winning only 86 games and finishing third. At the end of the season, Bamberger cited health reasons for stepping down as manager. But "Bambi" wasn't done with the Brewers. When the Brewers stumbled after their '82 World Series appearance, general manager Harry Dalton brought Bamberger back for an encore three years later. His second stay was a short one, ending in retirement from baseball before the end of the 1986 season.

During spring training in '86, Bamberger showed he had not lost his affinity for home run hitters. When an unknown player showed up in camp in Chandler, Arizona, and began socking balls out of sight during batting practice, Bamberger asked the beat writers covering the club, "Who the [fuck] is that guy?"

"That's Rob Deer," the skipper was informed.

"Well, he's on the [fucking] team," Bamberger said.

And, sure enough, Deer headed north with the Brewers at the end of spring training, destined to take part in several memorable events in years to come.

21 The Three Amigos

In the modern age of free agency, it's rare that a player stays with one team for 15 years. It's rarer still that two players would be teammates for that long. But three players on the same club for that length of time?

Fuggedaboutit.

That made the enduring relationship of Robin Yount, Paul Molitor, and Jim Gantner all the more special. They played together for 15 seasons in Milwaukee until Molitor departed as a free agent after the 1992 season. The manner in which they became teammates made that association even more remarkable.

A few days before the Brewers were to open spring training in 1978, Yount, who was attracted to anything that went fast, was motoring around on his dirt bike on some sand dunes outside of Phoenix. He got a bit too adventurous, however, and before he knew it, Yount was sailing off a cliff and landing with a crash. He somehow escaped with only a foot injury, but there would be no baseball for a while.

The budding young shortstop hid the injury from club officials as long as he could, staying away from camp. Rumors began circulating that Yount was contemplating a career change to professional golf. The truth finally came out, and the Brewers began preparing to open the season without No. 19.

General manager Harry Dalton and manager George Bamberger decided to turn over the shortstop position to Molitor, a first-round draft pick the previous year who had only 64 games of minor league experience. The Brewers had taken a similar chance a few years earlier with Yount, so why not try to catch lightning in a bottle again? That same spring, Gantner emerged to make the roster as a utility infielder. Not possessing the same skill set as Yount and Molitor, Gantner was a scrappy overachiever who grew up in tiny Eden, Wisconsin, and attended the University of Wisconsin-Oshkosh, a Division III school.

There was no way to know at the time that Yount, Molitor, and Gantner would go on to set a record for the number of years that three big leaguers played together. A shoulder injury eventually forced Yount to switch from shortstop to center field. Molitor would move to third base and later become a designated hitter, mostly for health reasons. Gantner emerged as the team's everyday second baseman, known for his gritty play on the field and his humorous misadventures with the English language off of it.

Though the three players had distinctly different personalities, they soon bonded and became the faces of the franchise. They hung out before and after games, playing cards with the same competitiveness that made them successful on the baseball diamond. "We'd get in disagreements," Gantner said. "Paulie was always good for throwing the whole deck of cards. If he was losing, he'd throw the whole deck and say, 'There, we're done.'"

Yount and Molitor became offensive machines, each eventually reaching 3,000 career hits and earning berths in the Hall of Fame in Cooperstown, New York. Gantner was a solid contributor, as

Man of Many Names (and Words)

No player in the Brewers clubhouse in the late 1970s and 1980s had more nicknames than second baseman Jim Gantner.

Because of his hard-nosed style of play, many teammates called him "Dog." Teammate Gorman Thomas, who thought Gantner moved and talked like the cartoon character "Gumby," started calling him by that name. Reliever Rollie Fingers came up with the nickname "Klinger" after the hilarious, cross-dressing character on the TV show, *M*A*S*H*.

Beyond his many monikers, Gantner kept teammates in stitches with his gift for malapropisms. He was sort of a baseball version of Norm Crosby, meaning one thing but saying another. Unlike Crosby, however, Gantner didn't do it on purpose.

Asked one spring what he had done over the winter, Gantner replied, "I went hunting in one of those Canadian proverbs."

Another time, when told that an opposing pitcher could throw with either arm, Gantner exclaimed, "He's amphibious!"

Then, there was the time Gantner tutored a young infielder during a workout, imploring him to "stay up on the palms of your feet!"

"You never knew what Gumby would say next," Thomas said. "Half the time we had no idea what he was talking about."

well, but more in a blue-collar mold that made him a fan favorite of working-class Milwaukee fans, who affectionately referred to their second baseman as "Gumby."

Gantner didn't have the foot speed of his longtime teammates but gave no quarter on the field. He'd take ferocious hits at second base while hanging in to turn a double play, but he would pay dearly for that spunk with two knee surgeries. Fundamentally sound, he became one of the best-fielding second basemen in the league without receiving Gold Glove recognition.

Molitor and Gantner both took their cues from Yount, the unselfish team player who never bragged about his accomplishments or engaged in self-promotion. Yount's stoic, one-day-at-time approach to baseball made him a true professional who turned the page after every game and looked forward to the next. He was the moral and competitive compass of the club, and Molitor and Gantner learned more from watching him than listening to any coach.

One by one, the other veterans of the '82 World Series team peeled away, but Yount, Molitor, and Gantner stayed, even through the tough times that followed. Molitor was often injured in the early years of his career, missing the equivalent of three full seasons. Yet he always returned better than ever.

Yount nearly broke up the trio after the 1989 season when the California Angels recruited the free agent. Frustrated over the losing seasons that followed the glory of 1982, he was ready to jump ship when owner Bud Selig traveled to Yount's home in the Phoenix area to make a personal plea to stay with the Brewers. Yount relented and would never wear another uniform during his 20 seasons in the big leagues.

The game's economics changed in the early '90s, making it tougher for small-market clubs such as the Brewers to keep their top talent. After a successful 1992 season in which Milwaukee won 92 games, Molitor received an offer from the Toronto Blue Jays that the Brewers couldn't match and was gone. Unlike his cherished former teammates, he would make it back to the World Series the next season, as the Blue Jays repeated as champions.

Gantner's career with the Brewers also came to an end that winter as he opted to retire before the '93 season. A year later, Yount made the same decision, ending a magnificent career that guaranteed him iconic status in the history of the franchise. "That was special for us to play together all those years," Ganter said. "You'll never see that again—three guys playing together for 15 years. The game is different now."

22 Rollie Saves the Day

When the San Diego Padres sent Rollie Fingers to the St. Louis Cardinals in an 11-player trade on December 8, 1980, the veteran reliever figured his stay would be short with his new club. The next day St. Louis general manager Whitey Herzog acquired another closer, Bruce Sutter, from the Chicago Cubs. "I knew something was going to happen," Fingers said. "They would have to either trade Sutter or me somewhere."

Four days later, Fingers was flipped to the Brewers in a seven-player swap that also brought right-hander Pete Vuckovich and catcher Ted Simmons to Milwaukee.

Though the '81 campaign was split in half by a labor strike, Fingers put together a season that was unlike any other by a relief pitcher in major league history. Not only did he win the Cy Young Award, he captured American League MVP honors, as well. For good measure, he also claimed the Rolaids Relief Man Award and was Fireman of the Year.

How dominant was Fingers in 1981? He led the majors with 28 saves, compiled a miniscule 1.04 ERA, walked only 13 batters in 78 innings, and allowed only one earned run at home all season. In the games he earned saves, the man with the handlebar mustache didn't allow an earned run in 41 innings.

Oddly enough, the first game back after the strike was the All-Star Game in Cleveland, and Fingers was tagged with the loss. "Other than that, it was one of those years when nothing went wrong," Fingers said. "It was one of those fantasy years. The guys made the plays behind me."

Fingers' performance was the difference in the Brewers finally breaking through to the postseason for the first time. They claimed the second-half title in the AL East but bowed out to the New York Yankees in five games in the mini-playoffs, following the odd strike-shortened season.

The Brewers knew they were getting a reliever who could handle high-pressure games. Fingers was a key figure on the Oakland A's teams that won three World Series in a row from 1972–'74, claiming MVP honors in the last championship round. During the '70s, he compiled 209 saves, and in those days, closers often worked multiple innings, not the one-inning room-service calls of today's game.

Although reliever Rollie Fingers won a Cy Young Award and an MVP with Milwaukee, he is best known for his iconic mustache. (Getty Images)

Unfortunately for Fingers and the Brewers, he injured his arm on September 2, 1982 in the first game of a doubleheader in Cleveland. He didn't pitch again the rest of the season and was unavailable for postseason competition. The Brewers lost the World Series in seven games to St. Louis, and many believe the outcome would have been different had Fingers been able to pitch.

After sitting out the 1983 season with that arm injury, he bounced back with a bad team in 1984, collecting 23 saves and a 1.96 ERA in 33 appearances. Late in that season, however, he ruptured a disc in his back pitching against the Yankees and was never quite the same. He retired after going 1–6 with a 5.04 ERA and 17 saves in 47 appearances in 1985.

Recalling Fingers' first season with the Brewers in '81, second baseman Jim Gantner said, "It was the best pitching I ever saw. I only saw him throw one pitch down the middle all year, and he blamed me. We were in Boston, and Rollie had the bases loaded with two outs. Dwight Evans was up with a 3–0 count, and I was thinking, 'I hope he doesn't throw him a meat pitch right down the middle.' Sure enough, he threw one, and Evans hit a grand slam.

"After the game, I told Rollie, 'He's one of the best 3–0 hitters in the game.' He blamed me for the home run. He said, 'You should have come in and told me that. I'm new in the league. It's your fault he hit a grand slam. I could have just walked him and only cost us one run.'"

As amazing as Fingers was that season, it only made sense to blame someone else for the rare failure.

23 Mollie Makes the Hall

When Paul Molitor was elected to the Baseball Hall of Fame in 2004, there was some question at first as to which team he would represent in Cooperstown, New York. Would the Brewers get their second Hall of Famer, joining Robin Yount? Would Molitor go in representing the Toronto Blue Jays, for whom he was a World Series MVP in 1993? Or perhaps his hometown Minnesota Twins, the team with which he collected his milestone 3,000[th] hit and would later manage?

With the first 15 years of his brilliant 21-year career spent with Milwaukee, it was rightly decided that he would represent the Brewers on his Hall of Fame plaque.

During his acceptance speech, "Mollie" made it quite clear that Yount's influence was paramount in his evolution into a Hall of Fame player. Molitor recalled his first major league camp in 1978 when he made the club as a shortstop due to an injury to Yount. "I went through some pretty ugly days early in camp," said Molitor, a first-round draft pick the previous year. "There was even one day when [coach] Frank Howard asked me if the scout was drunk when he signed me. But somehow I made the Opening Day roster, largely due to an injury to Robin. It was the beginning of a very memorable 15 years in Milwaukee.

"One of the best parts about my time in Milwaukee was that Robin Yount and Jim Gantner were my teammates the entire time I was there. What can I say about Robin? I learned so much from Robin. Although we were contemporaries in age, he had played in the big leagues four years before I got there. Robin had a simple philosophy about playing: 'What can I do to help my team win today?' And believe me, there were a lot of things that Robin Yount could do to help his team win. I'm honored to follow him into the Hall as the second player to wear a Brewers hat on his plaque."

Molitor, of course, would play shortstop only briefly, with Yount returning to assume that role. There would be some action at second base, but Molitor eventually settled in at third base, and when injuries took their toll on his legs and diminished his speed, he became a designated hitter in every sense of the role. Few players could hit like Molitor, who used his lightning quick bat to put together a club-record 39-game hitting streak in 1987.

There were some misplaced hard feelings among Brewers fans when Molitor left for Toronto via free agency after the 1992 season. They didn't understand that the game's economics were working against small-market clubs keeping marquee players. He heard some boos upon return trips to County Stadium, but time eventually healed all wounds. Peace was made on both sides, with the Brewers retiring Molitor's No. 4 in '99, just as they had done with Yount's No. 19 five years earlier.

The Hits Parade

Paul Molitor accumulated 2,281 of his 3,319 career hits while playing for the Brewers, placing him second on the club's all-time list. Robin Yount, another member of the 3,000-hit club, accumulated all 3,142 of his hits during his 20-year career in Milwaukee.

Here is a look at the Brewers' all-time leaders in hits with the club, entering 2018:

Robin Yount	3,142
Paul Molitor	2,281
Cecil Cooper	1,815
Ryan Braun	1,699
Jim Gantner	1,696
Geoff Jenkins	1,221
Don Money	1,168
Ben Oglivie	1,144
B.J. Surhoff	1,064
Charlie Moore	1,029

Milwaukee would always hold a special place in his heart, Molitor promised. "The baseball memories are great, but when you think about it, the people memories are even better," said Molitor, who was joined by Dennis Eckersley as inductees into the Hall that year. Echoing the remarks made by Yount five years earlier during his acceptance speech, Molitor noted that he did not play the game to get into the Hall of Fame. "My dreams never took me to Cooperstown," Molitor said. "Like most of these [Hall of Fame members] and probably all of them, I didn't play the game to get here. I played the game because I loved it.

"That being said, it's the Hall of Fame. It's that magical place; it's that place that transcends time. Baseball is respectful, traditional, simple, and pure."

24 Braun Wins 2011 MVP

Ryan Braun was not about to pretend that November 22, 2011 was just another day. The Baseball Writers Association of America (BBWAA) was scheduled to announce the National League Most Valuable Player Award, and the Brewers All-Star left fielder was considered the favorite. Too anxious to sleep in, Braun awoke early and went for a drive along the Pacific Ocean to pass the time. He returned to his home in Malibu, California, and relaxed—as much as possible, anyway—with both his cell phone and house phone nearby. "I didn't know exactly what time I would be getting a phone call," he said, "if I was fortunate enough to win the award."

Shortly after 10 AM PST, the call came from Jack O'Connell, secretary-treasurer of the BBWAA. Braun was the 2011 NL MVP.

Ryan Braun rejoices after hitting one of his 33 home runs during his 2011 MVP season, though his achievements were tainted when he was suspended two years later for PED use during that banner campaign.

Much to his surprise, Braun won the award easily over runner-up Matt Kemp of the Los Angeles Dodgers and teammate Prince Fielder, who also had a big hand in the Brewers claiming their first NL Central title that year. The 28-year-old Braun received 20 of 32 first-place votes and was second on the other 12 ballots for a total of 388 points.

Kemp, who made a run at baseball's Triple Crown for a team that finished third in the NL West, received 10 first-place votes and 332 points. Fielder garnered one first-place vote and finished with 229 points. Two BBWAA members in each NL city cast ballots, with 14 points awarded for first place, nine for second, eight for third, and so on.

Braun became the third player in Brewers history to claim an MVP award, following reliever Rollie Fingers in the strike-split 1981 season and Robin Yount, who won as a shortstop in 1982 and as a center fielder in 1989. Hank Aaron won the award in 1957 when the Braves were in Milwaukee for the city's only other baseball MVP.

Braun batted .332 with 33 home runs, 111 RBIs, and 33 stolen bases in 150 games. He led the NL with a .597 slugging percentage, 77 extra-base hits, and .994 OPS (on-base plus slugging percentage), and batted .351 with runners in scoring position. He was a driving force in the Brewers' push to the division title, socking a three-run homer on September 23 to beat the Florida Marlins and clinch that crown. He was named the NL Player of the Month for September as the Brewers surged to a franchise-record 96 victories, and that clutch hitting down the stretch might have sealed the MVP award.

With Kemp having a statistically better year, though not by a large margin, Braun conceded that playing for a first-place team gave him a decided edge in the balloting. "Honestly, that's the one thing that separated us," Braun said. "His numbers are slightly better than mine. I feel fortunate to be able to be on a better team. That's the one separation. It's an individual award, but it's also part of being on a special team. Matt's one of the best players in the game. The season he had will always go down as one of the greatest in Dodgers history. If he had won the MVP, I certainly couldn't have argued with it. He had a phenomenal year.

"This is beyond my wildest dreams to be in this position at this stage of my career. It's an incredibly prestigious award. It's a special group of guys to be mentioned with. Whenever you win an award like this, forever next to your name it will say, 'MVP.'"

Earlier that season, Braun signed a five-year, $105 million contract extension that committed him to the Brewers through 2020 with a mutual option for 2021, in essence making him a lifetime

Brewer. He then went out and had one of the greatest years in franchise history.

Braun joined Tommy Harper (1969) as the only players in the franchise with 30/30 seasons (homers and steals). He became the first Brewer to knock in at least 100 runs in four consecutive seasons, joining Robin Yount (1982–'84) as the only Brewers with three consecutive 100-run seasons. Last but not least, Braun became the first player in the franchise with three 100-RBIs/100-run seasons. "If you honestly assess why I won the award," Braun said, "my teammates deserve a ton of credit, my coaches deserve a ton of credit, our ownership group and management group deserve a ton of credit because I think ultimately the reason I won is because they put a better team around me."

It didn't come out until a few weeks later, but Braun was harboring a dark secret, which would shock Brewer Nation as well as the rest of the baseball world. He had tested positive in early October at the outset of the playoffs for a banned substance, synthetic testosterone, and news of that test was leaked to the media instead of remaining confidential as intended in the MLB drug program. Braun vehemently insisted he was innocent and that the test had gone awry in some fashion, prompting an immediate appeal on his part.

There were debates about whether Braun should be allowed to keep the MVP award if found guilty of using a banned substance. Braun was temporarily redeemed when he appealed the test and was exonerated by arbitrator Shyam Das to avoid a 50-game suspension. But he later admitted guilt by accepting a 2013 suspension, which forced him to miss the season's final 65 games. Accordingly, many considered the MVP award tainted.

25 Hank, the Ballpark Pup

Anyone who knows Brewers third-base coach Ed Sedar, who has a family pet named Squirt, knows he is a dog lover. So when a mangy, dirty, slightly injured stray wandered into the team's spring training complex in Phoenix a few days after camp began in February 2014, it was hardly surprising that the gregarious Sedar reached out a hand.

In that hand was a link of sausage. "Every dog loves sausage," Sedar said.

An instant bond was formed, and the team's new, unofficial mascot wasn't about to go back on the streets. Soon dubbed "Hank" after the great slugger Hank Aaron, who finished his career with the Brewers, the dog was cleaned up, fattened up, and quickly became a target of affection from uniformed personnel and staff. Hank made himself quite at home in the team's clubhouse, quickly becoming the sensation of camp.

Thanks to social media and reporters who knew a good story when they saw one, Hank's heartwarming tale became known back in Milwaukee and across the nation. The Brewers took full advantage of Hank's growing popularity, dressing him in a tiny team jersey and posting daily updates of his activities on their web site. A four-legged star was born, surpassing levels usually achieved only by players.

Soon, the inevitable question was asked: what would happen to Hank when the Brewers broke camp and headed back to Milwaukee to start the season? There was no way he was going to be left behind, and no one stepped forward in the Phoenix area to claim him as their pet (not legitimately anyway). Working with the Wisconsin Humane Society, the Brewers arranged for Hank to be adopted by a club executive and transported back to a new home in Milwaukee.

But Hank's celebrity status could not be denied. Knowing a good thing when they saw it, the Brewers rolled out an extensive line of merchandise with his image and a new, fuller name: "Hank, the Ballpark Pup." Fans lined up at Miller Park for autograph signings (actually "pawtographs") and photo opportunities. Everybody wanted to meet Hank, hug him, and revel in his feel-good story. Lassie never had it so good.

Hank made an appearance at Miller Park on Opening Day, drawing loud applause. He had bobbleheads made in his image for giveaway promotions and was available for fan visits at his custom-made doghouse on the main concourse. Only the Brewers know how much money Hank put in the team's coffers, but suffice it to say he was a profitable pup. To the team's credit, 20 percent of all retail sales of Hank items were donated to the Wisconsin Humane Society with hopes of paying it forward with more adoption stories.

In January of 2015, Hank was named "Dog of the Year" at the CW Network's "World Dog Awards" in Los Angeles. The award was intended for the canine who made the biggest impact on pop culture the previous year, and Hank had few peers in that regard. He has yet to have his paw prints installed on the Hollywood Walk of Fame, but there's always hope.

In recent years, the Brewers scaled back Hank's appearances and allowed him to live the good life of family dog. They were prompted to bring him back on stage in March 2016 after a blogger published what he called satire, claiming Hank had died and was replaced by the Brewers with a look-alike. The team actually called a press conference to debunk that theory, presenting a notarized letter from a veterinarian who had inserted a microchip in Hank after he arrived in Milwaukee. Hank was alive. All was well in the world. You can't make this stuff up.

26 The Only No-No

Bill Schroeder still shakes his head when recalling the night in Baltimore when he caught Juan Nieves' no-hitter. How in the world could you allow no hits when the only pitch you could really command was the fastball? "Juan had trouble getting his other pitches over," Schroeder said. "By the fifth or sixth inning, we decided to stick with the fastball. He had a pretty good one that night."

Schroeder wasn't slated to be behind the plate that night, but No. 1 catcher B.J. Surhoff had undergone a root canal earlier in the day and wasn't up to playing. During batting practice, manager Tom Trebelhorn told Schroeder to have his gear ready.

There was no reason to expect anything special from Nieves that night. A talented but unproven 22-year-old lefty, he was in his second season in the majors and had struggled in his previous outing, an 11–8 slugfest in Texas.

The Brewers had bolted to an 8-0 start and would go on to a record 13–0 beginning, but that meant nothing to baseball fans in Baltimore. It was a cold, damp, and misty evening, and only 11,407 bothered to show up for the game on April 15. Perhaps they were too consumed by getting their taxes mailed that day.

As almost always happens as a no-hitter evolves, there were some defensive gems in the early innings that no one considered important at the time. Jim Paciorek, a seldom-used backup, charged in from deep left field to make a diving catch of Eddie Murray's shallow pop fly in the second inning. Third baseman Paul Molitor gloved line drives off the bats of Cal Ripken Jr. and Floyd Rayford in the fourth and fifth innings, respectively.

Clinging to a 1–0 lead for much of the game, the Brewers broke it open with two runs in the seventh and three in the ninth.

Was Sabathia Robbed?

Many folks in Brewer Nation believe CC Sabathia should have joined Juan Nieves to make it a two-man, no-hit club for the Brewers. On August 31, 2008 in Pittsburgh, the only hit Sabathia allowed in a complete-game shutout was a disputed one that left the Pirates' official scorer under fire.

Leading off the bottom of the fifth inning, Andy LaRoche tapped a soft roller toward Sabathia. The hulking lefty moved in and had time to make the play, but instead of using his glove to scoop up the ball, Sabathia tried to pick it up bare-handed and dropped it.

Bob Webb, an official scorer for 20 seasons, ruled the ball was hit so slowly that LaRoche—hardly known for his speed—would have beaten it out. Brewers assistant media relations director John Steinmiller, realizing Sabathia had no-hit stuff that day, implored Webb to check the replay and reverse his call, but the scorer wouldn't budge.

Sure enough, Sabathia allowed no more hits that day, leaving manager Ned Yost fuming over Webb's ruling. "That's a stinking no-hitter we all got cheated from," Yost said. "I feel horrible for CC. Whoever the scorekeeper was absolutely denied Major League Baseball a nice no-hitter right there. That's a joke. That wasn't even close."

The Brewers felt so strongly that Sabathia was cheated that they sent a DVD of the play to the commissioner's office, seeking a reversal of the ruling. But MLB officials weren't about to open Pandora's box by awarding a no-hitter after the fact, and Webb's decision was upheld.

Sabathia had to settle for a one-hitter, leaving Nieves' gem on April 15, 1987 in Baltimore as the Brewers' only no-hitter. "That's sad. It really is sad," said Yost, who would be fired a few weeks later after a prolonged collapse threatened the Brewers' playoff status.

With the game no longer in doubt, a buzz started as the Orioles' hit column on the Memorial Stadium scoreboard still registered a zero.

Nieves quickly dispatched Ken Gerhart and Rick Burleson in the bottom of the ninth while teammates in the dugout nervously leaned forward in unison and crossed their fingers. Nieves pitched around Ripken after falling behind in the count, walking him to bring the switch-hitting Murray, on his way to 3,000 career hits and a berth in the Hall of Fame, to the plate.

Schroeder called for a first-pitch fastball and Murray, batting from the right side, sent a slicing drive the other way into the gap in right-center. Off the bat, it appeared Nieves was destined for the cruel fate of so many pitchers in major league history who lost their chance for a place in the record book on the final out.

Robin Yount, the former All-Star shortstop who transitioned to center field after ongoing issues with his throwing shoulder, had other ideas. Shaded toward left, Yount took off as everyone in Brewers road gray held their collective breath. At the last second, when it appeared the ball would land safely on the outfield turf, Yount launched himself into a fully stretched-out dive, cradling the ball in his glove before smacking the ground. "I might have been able to catch it without diving, but it seemed like the best thing to do," Yount said. "I probably made it look harder than it actually was. I just wanted to make sure I caught it."

A joyous, yet disbelieving Nieves was mobbed on the mound by his teammates. For a few minutes, the Brewers' 9–0 start to the season was pushed to the background. No Brewers pitcher had thrown a no-hitter until that night, and somewhat remarkably, none has done so since. "It's hard to believe that's still the only no-hitter for the Brewers," said Nieves, whose promising career would be cut short only a few years later by shoulder woes. "Every April 15, I think about that night."

So does Schroeder, who later returned to Milwaukee to serve as the Brewers television analyst. "They say the best pitch in baseball is still the fastball," Schroeder said. "That was Juan's best pitch that night. We decided to keep throwing it."

27 Wrong Time to Be Unarmed

The good news was that the Brewers beat the Cubs on the final day of the 2008 season to claim the National League wild-card berth. The bad news was that the starting rotation was in disarray as the Brewers prepared to face the powerful Philadelphia Phillies in the Division Series.

Right-hander Ben Sheets, plagued by injuries throughout his career, was out with an elbow injury suffered in the final weeks of the season. CC Sabathia, acquired at midseason from the Cleveland Indians in a brilliant trade by general manager Doug Melvin, would not be available to pitch until Game 2, and then it would be for the fourth consecutive time on short rest. Veteran righty Jeff Suppan pitched miserably throughout September and had been roughed up over the past three years (0–4, 6.93 ERA) by the Phillies.

So who would start Game 1 against Phillies ace Cole Hamels? With few viable options, interim manager Dale Sveum, who replaced fired skipper Ned Yost with 12 games remaining, selected 22-year-old right-hander Yovani Gallardo. Never mind that Gallardo missed most of the season after undergoing surgery to repair a torn ACL in his right knee.

Gallardo was injured on a freak play in a May 1 game against the Chicago Cubs at Wrigley Field, colliding with base runner Reed Johnson near first base. He sat out nearly five months before returning for one start in the final week against the Pittsburgh Pirates, throwing four strong innings.

No pitcher had started Game 1 of a playoff series coming off only four regular-season outings, but Gallardo wasn't intimidated by the surroundings. "You've got to go out there and look at it like a regular baseball game and not try to do anything extra," Gallardo said. "We play 162 games, so it's just one extra game."

He pitched four gritty innings, allowing no earned runs. It was the three unearned runs that Gallardo surrendered, however, that resulted in a 3–1 loss to Hamels and the Phillies.

Second baseman Rickie Weeks was unable to handle a low throw from third baseman Bill Hall on a sacrifice bunt by Hamels in the third inning. Weeks' error led to a three-run rally, which included Chase Utley's weather-aided double that eluded center fielder Mike Cameron, normally a defensive stud. "Things like that, it's going to happen," Gallardo said of the Weeks error and Cameron misplay. "It's no excuse for letting your guard down. You still have to make pitches and get out of situations like that."

The Brewers counted on Sabathia to come through one more time in Game 2 and help them draw even in the series, but it was obvious early on that the big lefty was running on fumes after so many starts on short rest. It didn't help when Phillies pitcher Brett Myers, a notoriously poor hitter, worked Sabathia for a nine-pitch walk in the second inning, putting runners on first and third base. Two batters later, Shane Victorino hit a grand slam.

Philadelphia's five-run outburst led to the 5–2 victory that put the Brewers in a 0–2 hole in the best-of-five series. Sabathia was done after 3⅔ innings, but nobody was going to blame him for the loss given his yeoman duty down the stretch. "The man left everything out there on the field," reliever Seth McClung said. "You can't question anything he has done. He's the man we needed out there today."

When the series shifted to Milwaukee and the electric atmosphere at Miller Park, it was up to right-hander Dave Bush to keep the Brewers' hopes alive. Bush delivered, holding the potent Philly attack to five hits and one run during 5⅓ innings. The Brewers got to ageless lefty Jamie Moyer for two quick runs in the first on a sacrifice fly by Prince Fielder and an RBI single by J.J. Hardy.

Milwaukee added runs in the fifth (a sacrifice fly by Ryan Braun) and seventh (an RBI single by Jason Kendall) to take a 4–1 lead into the ninth.

All of that hard work was placed in dire jeopardy in the ninth when three consecutive singles off closer Salomon Torres loaded the bases for the Phillies with no outs. Torres had been one of the team's pleasant surprises after taking over in the early stages of the season for the struggling Eric Gagne, but he appeared on the verge of a collapse that would eliminate the Brewers in three games.

With the home fans growing increasingly nervous, the tide turned when Pedro Feliz swung at the first pitch from Torres and grounded into a 5–4–3 double play. The Brewers were happy to exchange a run for two outs, but the news got even better when Victorino was called for obstruction at second base on Craig Counsell's relay to first. By rule, the other runners had to return to second and third base, and when Carlos Ruiz tapped back to Torres for the final out, the Brewers had a 4–1 victory—their first postseason triumph since 1982. "I had no idea what was going on," Torres said. "I already considered that they had scored one run. When they put the runners back on base and took the run away, that was even better."

Sveum was now left to pick the lesser of two evils. He could either pitch Gallardo on short rest, a tough thing to do with a promising young pitcher who had missed most of the season, or go with Suppan, the fading veteran with a poor track record against the Phillies.

Sveum chose Suppan, and the results went according to the pitcher's history. Jimmy Rollins led off Game 4 with a home run, and the Phillies pounded Suppan for four more runs in the third inning, including homers by Pat Burrell and Jayson Werth. Right-hander Joe Blanton limited the Brewers to five hits and one run over six innings, and Philly rolled to a 6–2 victory that sent Milwaukee home for the winter.

Had the Brewers been able to somehow steal a win, they had Sabathia ready on full rest for Game 5 to go against Hamels. Alas, it wasn't meant to be, and the Brewers' first playoff experience in 26 years ended on a sour note. "I didn't say much [afterward]," Sveum said. "I just kind of said, 'Hell of a year. And don't hang your heads about nothing. You've got everything to be proud of, and you guys had one hell of a year.'"

28 Born to Be a Brewer

In essence, Craig Counsell was born to manage the Brewers. Craig's father, John, worked in the Brewers' front office from 1979 to 1987 and often brought his baseball-crazy son to County Stadium to hang out. Craig would go on to play six of his 16 major league seasons for Milwaukee, including the last five, before retiring. He then worked in the Brewers' front office as an assistant to general manager Doug Melvin.

So, it was hardly surprising, and maybe inevitable, that the Brewers saw no reason to go beyond the hallways of their front office when replacing manager Ron Roenicke one month into the 2015 season after an ugly 5–17 start. Melvin tabbed Counsell, giving him a three-year contract with the understanding that the major league roster would be torn down and rebuilt.

Counsell grew up in Whitefish Bay, a northern suburb of Milwaukee, and still makes his home there with wife, Michelle, and their four children. The village's Little League park, where Counsell played as a child, is named after him. Those local ties clearly played a role in his selection as manager, and he made it clear from the outset how much the job meant to him. "I've worked here as a player and in the front office," Counsell said at his introductory media session. "I've watched Brewers games for 35 years. I'm a Milwaukee Brewer. I've always felt that way. Baseball in this city is important to me. It's part of me. I feel a responsibility for it. I always have. And I'm proud to have that responsibility. The [Brewers] logo means something to me. My dad worked here. I was at County Stadium since I was 10. That means something to me. I think that just gets you more excited about it. It makes you work harder for it and at it because there is something more."

Counsell, who was 44 at the time of his hiring, became the 19th manager in franchise history but only the second with local ties. The late Harvey Kuenn, who led the Brewers to their only World Series in 1982, was a native of nearby West Allis and, like Counsell, popular with the local fans because he grew up as one of them.

It is often said that the best managers are those who had to work hard to succeed in the game and who didn't get by merely on natural talent. And Counsell certainly fit that mold. Drafted in the 11th round out of Notre Dame by the Colorado Rockies in 1992, Counsell figured out early on that the more versatile he became, the longer his career would last. Turning himself into a scrappy infielder who could start or play off the bench, he played in 1,624 games for five teams over 16 years.

Using an unorthodox, elongated batting stance with the bat held high over his head, Counsell batted only .255 during his career but was valuable because of his savvy and defensive versatility. He was the baseball version of Forrest Gump, finding himself with the right team at the right time. He was part of World Series championship teams in Florida in 1997 and Arizona in 2001, scoring the winning run in the 11th inning of Game 7 with the Marlins and figuring in the winning Game 7 rally for the Diamondbacks in their dramatic win against the New York Yankees. Upon being named manager of the Brewers, Counsell joked, "I think I'll be better at this than I was at playing."

But Melvin said that playing career was the perfect backdrop for Counsell to succeed as a manager. "It's all about preparation and getting the players prepared," Melvin said. "If they're prepared properly, they'll play the game at a high level. I think that he's ready for that because he was the type of player that prepared himself to be ready—[even] on the days he didn't play."

The Chicken Runs at Midnight

When uniformed personnel were allowed to put nicknames on the backs of their jerseys for the first MLB Players Weekend from August 25–27, 2017, Brewers manager Craig Counsell didn't have to think long to come up with his. He wore "The Chicken" on the back of his jersey and made sure to contact Rich Donnelly to let him know.

That gesture meant the world to Donnelly, who was third-base coach of the Florida Marlins in 1997 when Counsell scored the winning run in the 11th inning of Game 7 of the World Series against the Cleveland Indians. Six years earlier, Donnelly's 18-year-old daughter, Amy, died of a brain tumor but not before she coined a phrase that would forever stick with her father.

Back then, Donnelly coached third base for the Pittsburgh Pirates, and Amy would watch with interest as he cupped his hands to shout instructions to runners taking leads off second base. One day she asked, "Hey, Dad, what are you yelling at those guys, 'The chicken runs at midnight,' or something?'"

They both got a laugh out of that, and Donnelly tried to remember those good times when Amy died shortly afterward. Fast forward to that decisive Game 7, which the Marlins tied in the bottom of the ninth. In the 11th they loaded the bases with two down, and Counsell, a skinny, gangly infielder stood on third base as Edgar Renteria stepped to the plate.

Donnelly's sons, Tim and Mike, were in uniform as bat boys and had come to be close with the personable Counsell, whom they privately called "chicken" because of the way his left elbow stuck out from his unusual batting stance. Renteria delivered a ground single through the middle, and Counsell skipped home with the championship run, leaping as he touched the plate. As the Marlins celebrated on the field, Tim looked up at the stadium clock. It read: 12:00.

"Look, Dad!" Tim shouted to his father. "The chicken ran at midnight!"

So, the kid who used to hang around the Brewers grew up and eventually became their manager. A bit surreal, right? Not so, maintained Counsell. "It's a place where I feel like I've prepared myself to be," he said. "Surreal was playing. This is probably more where I thought I would end up. It's an honor and it's humbling, but I feel like this is what I was meant to do."

29 So We Meet Again

Ironically, it was the Brewers who gave their National League Central rivals, the St. Louis Cardinals, a foot in the door in getting back in the playoff hunt in 2011. The Cards were going nowhere, and the Brewers were rolling with a 10½ game lead in the NL Central at the end of August when St. Louis came to Miller Park and swept a three-game series.

The Brewers still had a safe 7½ game lead to take into September en route to their first division crown since 1982. But St. Louis had new life in the wild-card race after trailing Atlanta by 10½ games on August 25, and the Cards went on to win 23 of their final 32 games.

The Braves suffered a monumental collapse, losing 18 of their last 26 games, including the last five, to allow St. Louis to slip in as the NL wild card on a frantic final day of the season. At the time, the Brewers thought the Cards had done them a favor because St. Louis would have to go to Philadelphia to take on the heavily favored Phillies, while Milwaukee opened at home against the Arizona Diamondbacks.

St. Louis continued to beat the odds, however, eliminating Philly in five games. The finale featured a tremendous pitching duel between Roy Halladay and Chris Carpenter, who shut out the Phillies on three hits to claim a nail-biting 1–0 victory.

The Brewers dispatched the Diamondbacks, winning a Game 5 thriller that carried into extra innings. Just like that, the fierce Central Division foes would meet once again—this time for the NL pennant. It had been well established that the teams didn't like each other, with much gamesmanship taking place involving St. Louis manager Tony La Russa. "It's always under the surface," Cards outfielder Lance Berkman said. "So we'll see what happens. If everybody behaves themselves and we just play baseball, then I think it'll be fine."

And that's exactly what the teams did. The Brewers, who had the best home record (57–24) in the majors during the regular season, out-slugged the Cardinals in the opener to win 9–6. Ryan Braun, Prince Fielder, and Yuniesky Betancourt each socked homers with the latter two coming during a six-run outburst in the fifth inning against lefty Jaime Garcia and reliever Octavio Dotel.

But St. Louis shattered the Brewers' aura of home-field invincibility in Game 2, romping to a 12–3 victory. Cards slugger Albert Pujols was a one-man wrecking crew, hitting a homer and three doubles to knock in five runs. Brewers right-hander Shaun Marcum, who collapsed down the stretch after pitching brilliantly for most of the season, continued to struggle, getting tagged for seven hits—granted, some of them cheapies—and five runs in four innings. Marcum had been roughed up in the NL Division Series against Arizona, making him 1–4 with an 8.18 ERA over six outings. "I guess I pissed off the baseball gods or something," Marcum said about his late-season meltdown. "That's the way it's gone the last six weeks. There's nothing I can do about it. That's baseball."

With the series shifting to St. Louis, Game 3 offered a promising pitching matchup of Carpenter vs. Yovani Gallardo. But neither pitcher showed up with his best stuff. Gallardo proved more vulnerable, allowing four first-inning runs in the 4–3 loss as the Cardinals edged ahead in the series. It didn't help that substitute center fielder Mark Kotsay failed to track down a shallow fly by John Jay, which turned into an RBI double.

Carpenter allowed six hits and three walks in five innings but managed to hold the Brewers to the only three runs they scored. The feared pitching excellence came not from Carpenter—but the St. Louis bullpen, with four relievers combining to retire all 12 hitters they faced. "We know their bullpen is good," said Brewers manager Ron Roenicke, foreshadowing what would prove to be the difference in the series. "They have tremendous arms. They are throwing the ball well. They have done a great job for quite a while."

Down 2–1 in the seven-game series, the Brewers faced a desperate situation in Game 4. That put the burden on veteran lefty Randy Wolf, who was looking for redemption after being pounded for seven runs in three innings of Game 4 of the NLDS against Arizona. "The day after the Diamondbacks start, I didn't eat or shower," Wolf said. "I don't know if they call that depression, but it was tough to swallow."

Wolf's personal hygiene was put in no further jeopardy, however, as he rose to the occasion with seven strong innings against the Cardinals. The Brewers drew even in the series, assuring they would take the NLCS back to Milwaukee, no matter what happened in Game 5. "The goal was to make sure we get an opportunity to go back home and play Game 6," Braun said. "If we didn't get to do it, that would have meant our season was over."

Whether that assurance prompted the Brewers to lose focus or not, they turned in a sloppy performance in Game 5 that doomed them to a 7–1 loss and a 3–2 hole in the series. The Brewers had overcome a substandard defense during the regular season with superior pitching and timely hitting, but there would be no answer for this four-error nightmare.

The victim of the shoddy defense was right-hander Zack Greinke, who didn't help matters by failing to record a strikeout. During the season, he accumulated 201 of them, seemingly able to summon one whenever necessary. On this night when balls were put in play, not enough were fielded by the Brewers. "Obviously we didn't play our best game, and they took advantage of it," said third baseman Jerry Hairston Jr., who allowed a sharp grounder by pitcher Jaime Garcia to go through his legs in the second inning for a two-run error. "We didn't play our game tonight, but we've got to bounce back. We worked extremely hard for home-field [advantage], and let's hope it works in our favor."

The security of returning home for Game 6, however, was greatly tempered by one factor. The scheduled starter was Marcum, who had been out of form for weeks and was pounded in his two previous postseason starts. There was little reason to expect a turnaround at that point, but Roenicke stuck by his pitcher. "I have confidence that Shaun will bounce back and give us a good start," Roenicke said. "It's the right move for our team."

The Brewers manager could not have been more wrong. Marcum set the tone for a dismal night by surrendering four runs in the first, the only inning he would pitch. St. Louis continued to pound the Brewers' fragile bullpen, claiming a 12–6 victory that propelled them to what would become an unlikely and thrilling World Series title.

The Brewers, hoping to advance to the Fall Classic for only the second time in franchise history, were left to ponder what might have been. Things looked so promising after Game 4, but an otherwise fantastic season ended with two clunkers. The Cardinals scored 11 first-inning runs in the six games against a faltering rotation, forcing the Brewers to play from behind each time out. "We didn't reach the ultimate goal, which is to get to the World Series," said Roenicke, who was roundly second-guessed for going with Marcum. "We fell two games shy of that. [But] I'm happy with our season. I'm happy with a bunch of guys. I was certainly blessed to be able to manage not just a great team but a great bunch of young men."

30 Listach: Right Time, Right Place

Pat Listach was not slated to play for the Brewers in 1992—certainly not at the start of the season. The speedy shortstop was assigned to Triple A Denver near the end of spring training, with the major league club set to open with Bill Spiers at that position.

But shortly before the Triple A club was slated to break camp in Arizona and head to Denver, Listach got an unexpected telephone call. "They told me, 'You're in the big leagues,'" he said.

Unbeknownst to Listach, Spiers was stricken with an ailing back and would open the season on the disabled list. Listach was thrust into the starting lineup, but new manager Phil Garner and club officials had no idea what to expect. They merely hoped he would keep his head above water.

As it turned out, the 5'9" Listach was the perfect triggerman for Garner's daring style of offensive play. The Brewers unleashed a running game never before seen in the American League, a circuit accustomed to power-based offenses befitting the use of the designated hitter.

When the smoke had cleared on the base paths that season, Listach had accumulated 54 steals, a Brewers record at the time. (Tommy Harper swiped 73 for the Seattle Pilots in 1969 before the club relocated to Milwaukee.) The team romped to a league-best 256 stolen bases and finished 92–70, chasing the eventual World Series champion Toronto Blue Jays in the AL East until the final weekend of the season. "We were a scrappy team," Listach said. "When Phil came in, he told us to play the game the right way and play hard. It became contagious, and we became a team that really made things happen on the bases."

In 149 games that season, Listach batted .290 with 19 doubles, six triples, 47 RBIs, and his 54 steals. He became the first Brewer to be elected Rookie of the Year by the Baseball Writers Association of America, topping Cleveland Indians center fielder Kenny Lofton, who led the league with 66 steals and batted .285 and was considered by many to be the better player. (Ryan Braun would become the Brewers' second ROY in 2007.)

Lofton went on to a long and prosperous career, but Listach would not be able to follow that same path. He was sidelined the following year with an ailing knee that robbed him of his primary skill, speed. He eventually needed surgery for the painful patellar tendinitis, played in only 16 games in 1994, and was never the same. "It took away what I did best, but there was nothing I could do about it," he said. "It's just something that happened."

By 1997, Listach was done as a major league player. But he was determined to stay in the game he loved and embarked on a career of managing and coaching in the minor leagues. Listach resurfaced in the major leagues in 2009 as a coach with the Washington Nationals before moving on to the Chicago Cubs staff. In 2012 he served as the Cubs' third-base coach but was dismissed after the season.

Though his playing career didn't pan out in the long run as expected, Listach still looks back with fondness on that '92 season when a previously unknown player sparked an exciting season from a hustling club with larceny in its collective hearts. "That was a fun year," Listach said. "Phil pretty much turned us loose and gave us the green light to go whenever we could. Nobody had seen that style of ball in the American League. We caused a lot of havoc for pitchers. [Toronto's] David Cone didn't even have a slide-step until we stole a bunch of bases against him.

"It's an honor to know I was the Brewers' first Rookie of the Year. A lot of great players came before me in Milwaukee. I was just in the right place at the right time."

31 Parting Is Sweet Sorrow

The unheralded Brewers surprised many pundits with an exciting 1992 season when they won 92 games under new manager Phil Garner. Though it wasn't enough to make the postseason, Brewers fans were encouraged by the down-to-the-wire competitive nature of the club and hopeful of more good things the next season.

But the game's economics were changing, taking a turn for the worse for small-market clubs such as the Brewers. It soon became evident to team owner Bud Selig and general manager Sal Bando that they couldn't afford to keep all of their players without going deep in the red.

At the center of that internal debate was Paul Molitor, one of the team's true stars and an offensive force known as "the Ignitor" for his ability to trigger rallies. At 36, Molitor was toward the end of his career, but the infielder-turned-designated hitter was still productive and quite popular among Brewers fans.

When the Brewers made a salary offer to Molitor for less than he made the previous season, it was viewed for what it was—a token offer made in part to appease the fan base. He quickly declined it and looked to the free-agent market, where a very interested Toronto Blue Jays team was courting him behind the scenes.

When the winter meetings began in Louisville, Kentucky, in early December, it had become evident that Molitor's days in Milwaukee were numbered. Hopeful fans kept their fingers crossed that a last-second deal could be reached, but that proved unrealistic. Instead the Blue Jays swooped in with a stunning three-year, $13 million contract. That agreement was announced moments after the Brewers offered Molitor arbitration, a move that did nothing more than guarantee draft-pick compensation for the Type A free agent. "I was as stunned as anyone," insisted Bando when Toronto's deal was announced.

After 15 years of playing for the Brewers, including a trip to the World Series in 1982 and a special bond with teammates Robin Yount and Jim Gantner, Molitor was leaving town. He coveted another shot at a championship and figured the Blue Jays had a strong chance to repeat after winning it all in 1992. "I can't begin to tell you how difficult it is to leave here," said Molitor after Toronto announced the agreement. "You play somewhere for 15 years and a big part of you, no matter what happens in other negotiations, tells you to remain here. But I had to kind of step away from that and take a more objective look at it, and it became a rather easy decision after a while. But there's going to be a transition period here for myself physically, as well as the emotional separation from a town and team I feel real close to."

The decision proved a wise one for Molitor. Toronto repeated as World Series champions, with Molitor earning MVP honors after the Philadelphia Phillies were dispatched on Joe Carter's home run in Game 6.

Back in Milwaukee, Bando became a lightning rod among angry fans who blamed him for allowing Molitor to leave. Bando tried to explain the game's economics for teams such as the Brewers, but he made the mistake of calling Molitor "only a designated hitter," which played poorly with both players and fans. "When they say they're being cheated, my argument is, if we don't have it, we can't spend it," Bando said of the team's finances. "The positive thing to come out of this situation, the Paul Molitor situation, is that it is a wake-up call toward the economic problems we have in a small market."

Molitor eventually moved on to Minnesota to play for his hometown team, the Twins, where he reached 3,000 career hits. Some fans considered him a traitor for leaving, no matter what the Brewers offered him, and Molitor often was booed when he returned to County Stadium.

Eventually, those hard feelings subsided, and the prodigal son was welcomed back to have his No. 4 retired by the Brewers. When Molitor was elected to the Hall of Fame, he went in as a Brewer, joining Yount as the only players in franchise history to be so honored.

It took a dozen years for the Brewers to recover from stripping down that 1992 club, including the loss of right-hander Chris Bosio. They wouldn't finish .500 again until 2005, and many of the club's fans remained bitter about the loss of Molitor and the team's descent into the baseball wilderness that followed.

Slip Slidin' Away

The original Bernie Brewer was a man, not a mascot. In June 1970 with the Brewers still finding their way in Milwaukee as a born-again club bought out of bankruptcy in Seattle, 69-year-old Milt Mason decided it was time to force the issue at the gate. Mason said he would sit in a trailer atop the scoreboard at County Stadium until the team drew a crowd of 40,000.

It took some 40 days for Mason to be freed from his perch. On August 16, a Bat Day promotion drew 44,387 fans, allowing Mason to punctuate the Brewers' 4–3 victory against the Cleveland

Indians with a slide down a rope. Mason passed away three years later but was recognized by then as the original Bernie Brewer.

In 1973, Bernie Brewer became the team's official mascot, sporting an oversized mustache and wearing lederhosen in true alpine fashion. In the most unique home run celebration in the major leagues, Bernie would emerge from his beer-barreled chalet and go down a slide into a huge beer mug. His lederhosen took on a bit of a shine from constant sliding in the late '70s and early '80s when power-packed Brewers clubs known as "Bambi's Bombers" and "Harvey's Wallbangers" mashed one home run after another.

Bernie became the center of a mini-controversy when Texas Rangers manager Whitey Herzog accused him of stealing signs and relaying them to the Brewers players. That tempest in a beer mug soon passed, thankfully.

Later, Bernie was joined by a female counterpart, Bonnie Brewer, who used a broom to sweep the bases clean between innings and would playfully swat the rear end of the opposing team's third-base coach before running off. Alas, Bonnie's act did not catch on, and she later disappeared.

As so often happens in the world, Bernie Brewer became the victim of urban renewal in 1984. The team rebuilt the center-field bleachers at County Stadium, replacing his chalet with a new sound-system tower. Bernie was sent into retirement, with the giant beer mug and chalet stored in the bowels of the stadium.

By popular demand, Bernie was brought out of retirement in 1993 when fans voted overwhelmingly for his return to action. This time, he came back as a cartoonish character, with an enlarged foam head, huge yellow mustache, and full costume. The chalet was rebuilt and placed atop the outfield bleachers in left center, and Bernie again began sliding into his beer mug to celebrate home runs.

When the Brewers opened Miller Park, their new retractable-domed baseball palace in 2001, Bernie's surroundings changed

Bernie Brewer, Milwaukee's beloved, yet cartoonish mascot, scoots down his slide to celebrate a Brewers home run. (Getty Images)

drastically. Instead of a chalet, he was given his own dugout in a lofty perch beyond the left-field foul pole. His landing spot was changed from a giant beer mug to a platform in the shape of home plate, later renamed the "Kalahari Splash Zone," sponsored by a popular water resort in Wisconsin Dells. Bernie now pops up at the end of his slide to wave a big Brewers flag in celebration.

Now there's a lot going on in that left-field corner when a Brewer hits a home run at Miller Park. Not only does Bernie Brewer emerge from his dugout to slide down a curvy yellow slide into his splash zone, Hall of Fame broadcaster Bob Uecker's

Visit Bernie's Original Chalet

Bernie Brewer actually resided in two different chalets over a period of years. His original beer-barreled chalet was replaced in 1984 by a sound-system tower, with Bernie going into retirement. Nine years later, Bernie re-emerged in a new chalet, relocated from the center-field bleachers to left-center.

The second chalet was placed out of service when Miller Park opened in 2001, and Bernie moved to his dugout perch down the left-field line. Both the original chalet and its replacement can be found at Lakefront Brewery in downtown Milwaukee.

The original chalet was auctioned off and purchased by former Brewers bat boy Bill La Macchia Jr. for about $5,000. La Macchia wanted the chalet as a sentimental memento of his days with the club and asked to keep it at Lakefront Brewery, according to Russ Klisch, owner of that establishment.

After County Stadium closed following the 2000 season, Klisch also purchased the second chalet, along with the original oversized beer mug that Bernie slid into, for $18,000. "They didn't want to auction that one," Klisch said, "because they wanted it to be in a place where it would be used properly."

Today, the first chalet and beer mug sit outside the brewery/restaurant, while the newer one is inside. Due to liability concerns, the slide is not attached to the mug, so don't even think about replicating Bernie Brewer's signature home run celebration. As consolation, fans can have their photos taken with them during brewery tours.

signature home run call, "Get up, get up, get outta here, GONE!" lights up in neon.

As might be expected, Bernie Brewer is very fan friendly, often stopping to pose for pictures with paying customers. Just don't try to strike up a conversation with him. For whatever reason, it was decided that Bernie would stay mute, acting out his emotions without speech—sort of the Charlie Chaplin approach to being a team mascot.

33 Wheelin' and Dealin'

The Brewers were finally turning the corner as a franchise as the 1980s began, but they needed something extra to put them over the top. General manager Harry Dalton realized the team could use more of a veteran presence and engineered a trade with the St. Louis Cardinals to acquire right-hander Pete Vuckovich, reliever Rollie Fingers, and catcher Ted Simmons, all bona fide stars in the big leagues.

To acquire that trio on December 12, 1980, Dalton had to surrender outfielders Sixto Lezcano and David Green, as well as pitchers Lary Sorensen and Dave LaPoint. Lezcano was one of the most popular Brewers, and Green was considered a top prospect with a huge upside. But you have to give up something to get something, so Dalton pulled the trigger on the trade. "[Green] was on the list of people we wouldn't trade," said Dalton, who swapped proposals with cagey St. Louis general manager Whitey Herzog. "It got to the point where we had a deal on paper, but they still wanted David Green. I had a little buyer's remorse afterward. I wondered if I had done the right thing."

As it turned out, Dalton acquired two future Cy Young Award winners. Fingers claimed that award and the American League MVP during the strike-split 1981 season by leading the majors with 28 saves and helping the Brewers to the playoffs for the first time. Vuckovich was voted the Cy Young winner the following season for leading Milwaukee to the World Series.

The Brewers clinched the second-half championship of the split '81 season on the penultimate day of the season with a 2–1 victory against the Detroit Tigers. Vuckovich outdueled Tigers ace Jack Morris before Fingers got the win, guaranteeing Milwaukee would finally taste postseason play.

In 1981 the gritty Vuckovich, who would do whatever it takes to succeed on the mound, led the AL with 14 victories and in winning percentage (14–4, .778). Fingers was simply the best closer in the game. Simmons batted only .216 but hit 14 homers with 61 RBIs in 100 games while doing yeoman work behind the plate. "Rollie dominated that year," second baseman Jim Gantner said. "The key was getting him and Vuckie and 'Simba' [Simmons] in that trade. They got us over the hump."

The Brewers were matched up in the first round of the playoffs against the mighty New York Yankees, a team that Milwaukee fans grew to hate. They pushed the pinstripers to the full five games before bowing out, but it proved to be a valuable experience the club used as a springboard to win the AL pennant in '82. "You have to get over that first hurdle," first baseman Cecil Cooper said. "Then you know you belong. You could see that growth process taking place."

Vuckovich and Fingers would fall victim to arm injuries, making their stays in Milwaukee shorter than expected. Simmons also would move on a few years later, but not before solidifying the catching position and handling a veteran pitching staff exactly as expected.

And what about David Green, the player the Cardinals had to have in the deal? The big slugger never realized his potential, battling alcohol problems that negated his tremendous physical skills. He would play in only 489 major league games, accumulating just 374 career hits. The savvy Dalton knew a prospect was exactly that—a player with potential who might or might not do big things.

But established stars seldom let you down. And it was the blockbuster deal that netted Vuckovich, Fingers, and Simmons, which finally stamped the Brewers' ticket to the postseason.

Final Piece to the Puzzle

The blockbuster trade with the St. Louis Cardinals that netted Rollie Fingers, Pete Vuckovich, and Ted Simmons prior to the 1981 season helped put the Brewers over the top. But as the 1982 season progressed, general manager Harry Dalton suspected he needed one more piece to make it to the World Series.

On August 30, one day before the deadline, Dalton mortgaged a little of the club's future by sending outfielder Kevin Bass and pitchers Frank DiPino and Mike Madden to the Houston Astros for Don Sutton. The veteran right-hander's best years were behind him, but Sutton still had some gas left in his tank, and his acquisition proved huge for the Brewers.

The 37-year-old Sutton went 4–1 with a 3.29 ERA in seven starts, the biggest one coming on the final day of the season when he outdueled Baltimore's Jim Palmer in a winner-take-all showdown for the American League East crown. He had done exactly what he was acquired to do—pitch the Brewers into the postseason.

Sutton also came up big in Game 3 of the AL Championship Series against the California Angels, helping the Brewers stave off elimination before finally running out of gas in the World Series against St. Louis. The Sutton deal still ranks as one of the best late-season pickups in club history. "I can't think of another six weeks in my career," he said, "that meant as much to me and still does as my six weeks in Milwaukee."

34 A Bold Move for CC

When word began circulating in early July 2008 that the Brewers were talking to the Cleveland Indians about a possible trade for left-hander CC Sabathia, many considered it sheer speculation. Small-market clubs such as Milwaukee don't outbid the big boys for the likes of the reigning American League Cy Young Award winner, right?

Wrong.

In one of the boldest moves in club history, general manager Doug Melvin—with the blessing of team owner Mark Attanasio—decided to do whatever it took to acquire Sabathia, a pitching behemoth who was underperforming a bit (6–8, 3.83 ERA) for an Indians team going nowhere. The Brewers hadn't been to the postseason in 26 years, and Melvin figured Sabathia might be the final piece to the puzzle.

But pitchers of that ilk do not come cheap. The Indians quickly made it known that they wouldn't consider moving Sabathia unless the Brewers included their top prospect, outfielder/first baseman Matt LaPorta, a 2007 first-round draft pick.

Melvin soon agreed to include LaPorta—with one important caveat. The Indians had to do the deal now. No shopping around the Brewers offer to other clubs. No waffling, no changing the players involved. Do it today, or the deal is off the table.

It was Sunday, July 6, and Melvin reasoned that by getting the deal done immediately, he could get two starts out of Sabathia before the All-Star break and get a jump on other clubs seeking help via trades. The Brewers had climbed to a season-high 10 games over .500 earlier in the day, and Melvin hoped that adding Sabathia to

Burly 6'7" pitcher CC Sabathia anchors the Milwaukee rotation during its 2008 playoff run.

a staff led by ace Ben Sheets would put the club over the top. "We thought CC could be a difference maker," Melvin said.

The deal quickly came together, with the Brewers throwing in minor league pitchers Zach Jackson and Rob Bryson, as well as a "player to be named later," who turned out to be another top prospect, center fielder Michael Brantley.

Sabathia won both of his starts before the break, but he was just scratching the surface. In one of the most brilliant half-seasons by an acquired pitcher in major league history, Sabathia put the Brewers on his broad shoulders and lifted them to the National League wild-card berth. In 17 starts Sabathia went a remarkable 11–2 with a 1.65 ERA. Despite being with the Brewers for only half a season, he led the league with seven complete games and three shutouts. More important, with the playoffs on the line in the final weeks of the season, the 6'7", 300-pound giant of a man put his arm and upcoming free agency on the line by agreeing to pitch on short rest four consecutive times.

With Sheets sidelined by his ailing elbow, the Brewers rotation was thinned by injuries. On the final day of the season with the Brewers tied with the New York Mets for the wild-card lead, Sabathia delivered one more time. He went the distance in a 3–1 victory against the rival Chicago Cubs at Miller Park, allowing only four hits and an unearned run.

Shortly after that game ended, the Mets lost to the Florida Marlins, and the wild-card berth belonged to the Brewers, ending their long and agonizing playoff drought. Running on fumes at that point, Sabathia—again pitching on short rest—lost in Game 2 of the NL Division Series against the eventual World Series champion Philadelphia Phillies.

But in terms of a trade making an impact, it was mission accomplished for Melvin and the Brewers. They knew they'd probably lose their big ace to free agency, and sure enough, the New York Yankees blew away the Brewers' offer of five years and some

$100 million with a seven-year, $162 million deal that made it an easy decision for Sabathia to leave.

Attanasio showed he was willing to make a financial commitment merely to acquire Sabathia. By picking up nearly half of his $11 million salary, the Brewers allowed their payroll to approach $90 million, a high-water mark in franchise history at the time.

There were never any regrets on the Brewers' part for making the deal, and rightfully so. Label Sabathia a half-season "rental" or whatever term you prefer, but he gave the Brewers and their long-suffering fans one of the most memorable stretches in franchise history, touching off a wild celebration at Miller Park after the wild-card was clinched. "That trade did what we hoped it would do," Melvin said. "We thought CC might be the final piece to getting us to the playoffs, and he was. You have to give up something to acquire a pitcher of that caliber. But we'll never have regrets over making that trade. That was a big season for the franchise."

The following season, Sabathia would lead the Yankees to their first World Series crown in eight years, showing he could make an impact on the biggest stage, as well. But he retained a soft spot in his heart for that glorious period in Milwaukee, and Brewers fans will forever feel likewise.

35 Sing "Roll Out the Barrel"

At ballparks throughout the country, it is customary for fans to stand during the seventh-inning stretch and sing, "Take Me Out to the Ballgame." In Milwaukee, however, that tune is merely a prelude to the signature song of Brewer Nation, "Roll Out the Barrel."

The song's actual title is the "Beer Barrel Polka," which Czech musician Jaromir Vejvoda originally composed without lyrics in 1927. It became an international sensation in the late '30s, and the version recorded by German bandleader Will Glahe hit No. 1 on the Hit Parade in the United States in 1939.

The authors of the English lyrics were Lew Brown and Wladimir Timm, but only one verse of an otherwise lengthy tune is sung by fans at Brewers games:

Roll out the barrel, we'll have a barrel of fun
Roll out the barrel, we've got the blues on the run
Zing, boom tararrel, ring out a song of good cheer
Now's the time to roll the barrel, for the gang's all here

All of which raises the oft-asked question—what exactly is "tararrel?" Well, other than being a word that conveniently rhymes with barrel, it appears open to interpretation. According to Wikipedia and other random sources, the word was used in Europe in the late '30s and denotes a source of pride, something you would cheer for and celebrate.

No one knows exactly when "Roll Out the Barrel" was first played during the seventh-inning stretch for Brewers games, but it has become as much a tradition as drinking beer and eating brats. With Milwaukee's rich Polish heritage, it makes sense that a polka tune would be a big hit at the ballpark and remain a constant.

The song is something of a state song in Wisconsin and also is played at University of Wisconsin and Green Bay Packers games, among other events. Many famous recording artists gave their take on it over the years, including the Andrews Sisters, Glenn Miller Orchestra, Mitch Miller, and Bobby Vinton. It even became the signature song of flamboyant entertainer Liberace, who just happened to be born in West Allis, a Milwaukee suburb down the road from Miller Park.

The Frankie Yankovic version is the one often heard at sporting events these days, but whatever your preference, it's a song that unites all Brewers fans during the seventh-inning stretch and a tradition that you won't experience in any other major league ballpark.

36 A Change of Direction

General manager Harry Dalton was the architect of the Milwaukee clubs that finally broke through to the winning side in the late 1970s and on to the World Series in 1982. After team owner Bud Selig hired him away from the California Angels in 1977, Dalton proceeded to make one astute personnel move after another.

Dalton orchestrated the blockbuster trade before the 1981 season that brought Pete Vuckovich, Ted Simmons, and Rollie Fingers to Milwaukee from the St. Louis Cardinals, providing the missing pieces to a championship club. He added pitcher Don Sutton late in 1982 to push the Brewers over the top as the American League East champ and pennant winner.

But as the decade of the '80s wound to a close, the Brewers were foundering. Manager Tom Trebelhorn piloted "Team Streak" to 91 victories in 1987, and the Brewers won 87 games the next season before falling back to an 81–81 campaign in '89. There was major slippage in 1990 when the Brewers finished with a 74–88 record.

As often happens in the game, Dalton inexplicably lost the magic touch he once had in making personnel moves. Shortly after retaining pitcher Teddy Higuera with a $13.1 million contract, Higuera blew out his shoulder and basically was done. The much-heralded free-agent signing of first baseman Franklin Stubbs became a colossal flop.

Toward the end of the '91 season, there were indications that Selig had become restless with the direction of the club under Dalton. The Brewers would rally in September to finish with 83 victories, but the decision already had been made to overhaul the team's baseball operation.

Dalton was kicked upstairs to an advisory position as senior vice president, and former Brewers third baseman Sal Bando was named the new general manager. "It's something of a bittersweet moment for me," said Dalton, whose close relationship with Selig had become somewhat strained, making him realize a change was in the offing. "I would be less than candid if I told you I was particularly thrilled about no longer being the general manager of this team, but I am very, very pleased about remaining with the team."

Bando had been with the organization since leaving the Oakland A's as a free agent in 1976. When he retired as a player after the '81 season, he was named a special assistant to Dalton. "I'm excited about the challenge," Bando said. "I do feel that there are some areas where I may lack experience, but we'll have competent and able people. But in other areas, I feel that I'm very experienced. I hope that however long my tenure is as general manager that I can experience part of the success that Harry Dalton has had as general manager."

The early signs were certainly favorable. As one of Bando's first acts, he dismissed Trebelhorn as manager. Bando hired Phil Garner as a first-time manager, and he piloted the Brewers to an unexpectedly strong season in 1992, chasing the eventual champion Toronto Blue Jays to the wire in the AL East before settling for a 92–70 record.

That success, however, would be short-lived. With the game's economics starting to work decisively against small-market clubs, the Brewers would descend into the baseball wilderness for the

Lonely at the Top

During the early years of the franchise, the Brewers changed general managers more often than some folks change the sheets on their beds. When the team was transplanted from Seattle to Milwaukee in 1970, Marvin Milkes came with them as GM.

After only one season, the Brewers switched to legendary Frank "Trader" Lane, who was nearly 75 and about traded out. Lane also would last only one year, giving way to Jim Wilson in 1972. Wilson had some familiarity with County Stadium, having thrown a no-hitter there for the Milwaukee Braves in 1954, the first in franchise history.

A mere two years later, the Brewers promoted scouting director Jim Baumer to replace Wilson, who became chief of the Major League Scouting Bureau. Baumer's claim to fame was acquiring first baseman Cecil Cooper from the Boston Red Sox after the 1976 season, but the Brewers continued to struggle on the field, and after their eighth consecutive losing season in 1977, he was replaced by Harry Dalton.

Baumer was part of what was called the "Saturday Night Massacre" on November 20, with manager Alex Grammas and director of player development Al Widmar also getting the boot. Dalton proved to be the ironman of Brewers GMs, holding that position for 14 seasons.

remainder of the '90s, never putting together another winning record. Baseball would be torn apart by the labor wars of 1994–'95, and it would be well into the next century before the Brewers returned to contending mode.

Bando named Bruce Manno as his top assistant and selected Al Goldis to be his scouting director. Goldis would remain in that post less than two years before moving on to the Chicago White Sox.

Selig admitted it was painful to push Dalton aside after the years of fine work he did for the Brewers, but he felt the game had passed by his GM to a certain extent. "I have great regard for him both as a friend and as a professional," Selig said. "But I think he's really satisfied with the arrangement, and I am, too. It's important. I have great, deep feeling for him and I always will. I think we're just adjusting to the times. I don't think we were behind the times in any way, shape, or manner. I think a constant adjustment to the changing environment, which is what we've done here today, is necessary if you want to continue to be successful."

37 Off with Their Heads

For several seasons, Phil Garner had been tilting at windmills. The Brewers manager was not given much to work with after 1992, his first season with the club. The Brewers went a surprising 92–70 under their fiery new skipper that year, but subsequent budget cuts resulted in the stripping of much of the team's talent, including Paul Molitor, who bolted for Toronto as a free agent.

A succession of losing seasons followed, though many observers thought Garner coaxed the most out of thin clubs, which went 80–82 in 1996 and 78–83 in 1997. The Brewers slipped to 74–88 in 1998, and a seventh consecutive losing season seemed inevitable in '99.

Garner rallied his overmatched troops as often as possible during the first half of that season. After falling 10 games below .500 (28–38) on June 18, the Brewers put together their best stretch of baseball and evened their record at 47–47 on July 18.

The hot streak quickly fizzled, however. The team's top run producer, right fielder Jeromy Burnitz, was sidelined with a hand injury, and the pitching staff began to wilt. A lackluster 8–5 loss to Colorado on August 11 ended a dismal homestand in which the Brewers went 4–8 to fall to 52–60 for the season.

With fans getting increasingly restless, general manager Sal Bando met with club president Wendy Selig-Prieb and told her it was time for a managerial change. Then, much to the shock of Selig-Prieb, Bando informed her that he planned to resign, as well. She tried to talk Bando out of it, but he was firm in his decision. He had come in with Garner after the 1991 season when GM Harry Dalton was reassigned and manager Tom Trebelhorn was dismissed. Bando considered himself and Garner a package deal and felt it best that they go out together.

In a press conference the next day, Garner took the high road out of town, handling the situation with dignity and class. He didn't point fingers at anyone else. He didn't complain about the lack of talent he futilely tried to turn into winners. Garner merely said he didn't get the job done and understood why fans were down on the club. "The fans are frustrated," he said. "We've gone seven years without putting a winning ballclub out there. That's a fair amount of time for the frustration to build up."

Garner's dedication to the ballclub was never questioned. Even in the worst of times, he spoke optimistically about his team and the prospects for improvement in the future, though deep down he knew the deck was stacked against the Brewers. Garner, who could have slipped out of town without entertaining questions from the media, spoke openly and honestly about the club's situation, even referring to the Brewers as "we" despite having a pink slip in hand. Before leaving the premises, he paid visits to other front office personnel to say good-bye and thank them for their support over the years.

Hitting coach Jim Lefebvre was named interim manager for the final month and a half of a season that ended with a 74–87 record. Before that season was done, Dean Taylor was hired as Milwaukee's new general manager, and he selected Davey Lopes as Garner's replacement.

The new regime would have no more luck than the Bando-Garner tandem in turning around the club, and both Taylor and Lopes would be gone before the 2002 season was complete.

38 Back to Their NL Roots

When Major League Baseball awarded two new franchises in 1995—the Arizona Diamondbacks in the National League and the Tampa Bay Devil Rays in the American League—it created a scheduling issue. With an odd number of 15 teams in each league, two teams would have to be off every day, or interleague play would have to be extended to a year-round affair. (MLB wasn't ready for interleague play throughout the season but changed its mind when the Houston Astros agreed to switch to the AL for the 2013 season.)

The decision was made that one team would have to switch leagues when the new franchises began play in 1998. But which team would make that unprecedented move? Concerned with negative reaction from their fan bases, many owners immediately dismissed the notion.

Commissioner Bud Selig, who grew up in Milwaukee a rabid fan of the Braves and was heartbroken when they departed for Atlanta after 13 seasons, was intrigued by the proposition of moving the team, he once operated, to the NL. He knew the city's baseball roots were in the senior circuit and that fans probably would welcome the move. Selig also realized that a budding rival, the Chicago Cubs and their beloved Wrigley Field, sat 90 miles to the south.

As the former owner of the club, Selig was wary of a conflict of interest, so he wasn't about to decree that the Brewers would make the move. He first offered the option to the Kansas City Royals, who were struggling and possibly in need of a change of scenery. The Royals passed, however, leaving it to the Brewers, who quickly

Please Forward the Mail

Before moving from the American League to the National League in 1998, the Brewers bounced around from division to division.

Upon their inception in 1970, the Brewers began play in the AL West, geography be damned. It was merely a function of picking up the schedule of the Seattle Pilots, who became the Brewers when bought out of bankruptcy only days before the '70 season began.

The Brewers didn't stay in the West for long. In 1972 when the Washington Senators moved to Texas and became the Rangers, the Brewers were shifted to the AL East, where they had to battle the powerful franchises of the New York Yankees, Baltimore Orioles, Boston Red Sox, and Detroit Tigers (and later Toronto Blue Jays).

When baseball was realigned in 1994, the Brewers were reassigned to the AL Central, finally a more appropriate geographic location. It also meant the Brewers were the only team to play in three divisions in the AL. That season was shortened by a labor strike, so Milwaukee did not get to compete for the division crown until '95.

The Brewers' big move came prior to the '98 season when they made the unprecedented transition of switching leagues. They were assigned to the NL Central, which became MLB's only six-team division, but the number dropped to five when the Houston Astros moved to the AL West in 2013.

said yes. The franchise had polled their fan base about switching leagues, and the response was overwhelmingly positive.

On November 6, 1997, MLB announced that the Brewers would move from the AL Central to the NL Central, forming a new six-team division. The Detroit Tigers agreed to move from the AL East to the AL Central to replace the Brewers in that division. On the day of the announcement, Selig said, "Somebody had to take the first step. Will this be good for the Brewers? Absolutely. There's no question about it. There are a series of things that make this very compelling. But the game itself will be better. And, as [former Detroit owner] John Fetzer taught me, it you do in the end what's in the best interests of the game, the best interests of the Milwaukee club will also be served."

Selig admittedly was nervous about the perception that he might be showing favoritism to his former club by moving the Brewers to the NL. "I felt an enormous amount of pressure," he said. "It was a very traumatic time for me."

That nervousness subsided when MLB's realignment committee sent an unsolicited letter to Selig, urging him to sign off on Milwaukee's move. And as Selig suspected, it became a very positive thing for the Brewers in conjunction with the opening of their new facility, Miller Park, in 2001. The club's fortunes on the field had sagged in the mid to late 1990s, but the change of leagues and opening of a new ballpark provided a much-needed energy boost.

As anticipated, the rivalry with the Cubs quickly blossomed. Brewers fans did whatever they could to procure tickets at the Friendly Confines whenever the clubs met in Chicago. And Cubs fans, unable to purchase home tickets for those series, soon began snapping up large quantities of seats at Miller Park, leading some to dub it "Wrigley Field North."

The lesson, as always, be careful what you wish for. The move to the NL did not result in immediate success on the field for the Brewers. A losing streak, which already stood at five seasons at the time of the switch, extended to 12 years before they finally achieved a .500 record in 2005. It would be three more years before the Brewers claimed their first NL playoff berth as the wild-card team. Three years later, in 2011, they finally won their first NL Central crown.

But there have been no regrets about the historic switch of leagues. The Brewers' attendance reached the 3 million mark three out of four years from 2008–2011. The NL fit the club and its fans like a pair of comfortable slippers. Those who rued the day that the Braves bolted for Atlanta were at least partially appeased about the return to the NL.

As they say, what goes around, comes around.

39 Stearns and the Youth Movement

Baseball can be a monkey-see, monkey-do industry, so when the trend of hiring young Ivy League types as general managers caught fire in the second decade of the century, there was no stopping it. Thus, when the Brewers began their search for a new GM in 2015, candidates with degrees from Harvard or Princeton had a distinct advantage.

The Brewers found their man—young man, that is—in David Stearns, who at 30 was less than half the age of outgoing GM, 63-year-old Doug Melvin. A 2007 Harvard graduate with a degree in political science, Stearns was born in 1985, three years after Milwaukee's lone trip to the World Series. As odd as it might have sounded, team owner Mark Attanasio cited Stearns' extensive baseball background in introducing him. "We focused on his experience," Attanasio said. "His experience is quite impressive. The fact that he was able to achieve all of that at comparatively young age is only a benefit and testament to his work ethic and drive."

Despite his tender age, Stearns indeed had been around the baseball block a few times. Before graduating from college, he already had worked as an intern with the Pittsburgh Pirates. After graduation he worked briefly in the Arizona Fall League and then for his hometown New York Mets. Stearns later took a job in Major League Baseball's central office in New York, where he learned the behind-the-scenes workings of the game while cultivating contacts with various clubs.

Stearns got back in the competitive side of baseball with a one-year stint as director of baseball operations for the Cleveland Indians before being hired by Houston Astros GM Jeff Luhnow as his assistant, helping with the challenge of rebuilding that team.

Now, he would get to lead his own rebuild with the Brewers, who already had hired a new manager (Craig Counsell replaced Ron Roenicke) and were trading veteran players for prospects.

The Brewers interviewed many qualified candidates, including their own internal candidate, scouting director Ray Montgomery. The Brewers quickly realized each person was eminently qualified for the job, prompting team chief operating officer Rick Schlesinger to ask Attanasio at one point, "How thin do we want to slice the baloney?"

The interview committee eventually selected Stearns, whose first day on the job came after the 2015 regular season ended. When asked what separated Stearns from the others, Attanasio admitted it wasn't something you could write down on paper. "He just felt right," said Attanasio, who knew there was too much at stake to make the wrong choice. "This is where it gets a little off the scorecard. We had a lot of internal conversation about what we needed. By definition any of the candidates we interviewed only had the highest level of professional accomplishment and respect from our organization."

Melvin, a lifelong baseball man, was hired to oversee a similar large-scale rebuilding project after the low point in franchise history in 2002. That team lost 106 games, leading to the firing of GM Dean Taylor (manager Davey Lopes was dumped a couple of weeks into the season). Under Melvin the Brewers snapped a 26-year playoff drought by claiming the 2008 National League wild-card and captured their first National League Central crown three years later. But the 2014 team collapsed badly over the final five weeks, finishing in third place after leading the division for 150 days. When the '15 team staggered to a 5–17 start, it became evident it was time to blow it up and start over again.

Having worked in Houston to return that team to respectability, Stearns knew there were no shortcuts in the process and that every box had to be checked along the way. "Each situation is unique," he said. "This situation is different. This is not the same team, the same structure, the same city. I would expect this type of process to be different. The philosophy of building a sustainable playoff team is not a secret. You need to acquire, develop, and keep controllable, young talent."

"Acquire, develop and keep controllable, young talent" would become Stearn's oft-repeated mantra. He accelerated the rebuild that offseason, turning over 20 spots on the 40-man roster, an unprecedented housecleaning. In nearly every deal, he tried to get more players back than he sent away with an eye on building depth of talent. Asked if he thought it possible for the Brewers to do something they had yet to accomplish—win a World Series, Stearns said, "I would not have come here if I did not think it was possible to win a World Series in Milwaukee."

40 Hammerin' Hank Comes Full Circle

Hank Aaron became a professional baseball player in the state of Wisconsin. After helping the Indianapolis Clowns win the Negro League World Series at the tender age of 18, he accepted a $10,000 signing bonus from the Boston Braves in 1952. The Braves assigned Aaron to their affiliate in Eau Claire, Wisconsin, a Class C entry in the Northern League. Playing in the infield, he broke his habit of hitting cross-handed and was a unanimous choice as that circuit's Rookie of the Year, batting .336 with nine homers and 61 RBIs.

In 1953, the year the Braves moved from Boston to Milwaukee, Aaron was assigned to Jacksonville, Florida, a Class A affiliate in the South Atlantic League. Despite enduring the cruelty of racial segregation there, he persevered to be league MVP. He then was sent to winter ball in Puerto Rico to transition to playing the outfield, a landmark decision in his career.

When Braves left fielder Bobby Thomson fractured an ankle sliding into second base during spring training in 1954, the door was opened for Aaron to enter the major leagues. A Hall of Fame career began that would see him play a dozen years in Milwaukee

Last But Not Least

There was no way to know that Hank Aaron would never hit another home run after July 20, 1976. On that day, the Brewers played the California Angels at County Stadium. In front of a sparse crowd of 10,134, it was just another game in the long 162-game season between two last-place clubs.

Angels reliever Dick Drago was working his third inning of relief when George "Boomer" Scott belted a homer with two out in the seventh, bringing Aaron to the plate. Drago hung a first-pitch slider to Aaron, who even at his advanced age still had wrists quick enough to turn on a mistake pitch, knocking it over the left-field fence. "The thing about hitters," Drago said, "the last thing to go is their bat speed."

It was the 10th homer of the season for Aaron and No. 755 of his career. With 76 games remaining on the Brewers' schedule, one figured "The Hammer" would add to that total. But he played sparingly over the final two months, as manager Alex Grammas gave younger players more action with a nod toward the future.

The baseball from Aaron's final homer was retrieved by Richard Arndt, a member of the grounds crew. Arndt supposedly offered to return the ball to Aaron on the condition that he met the home run king in person, but for whatever reason, that request was denied.

Arndt was fired the next day for refusing to hand over the baseball, and as the story goes, was even docked $5 from his final paycheck to pay for the baseball. Aaron later wrote in his autobiography that he offered $10,000 to Arndt for the ball, but Arndt wouldn't sell it.

Years later, Arndt sold the ball, which he discreetly had Aaron sign at an autograph show, for $650,000 at an auction, reportedly. Aaron's record of 755 home runs was eclipsed in 2007 by San Francisco Giant Barry Bonds, but many still view Aaron as baseball's all-time home run king because of strong suspicions of Bonds' steroid use.

before the team relocated to Atlanta, where Aaron would go on to surpass Babe Ruth's seemingly unbreakable record of 714 home runs.

Growing up in Milwaukee as a huge Braves fan, Bud Selig idolized the future home run king. Thus it only made sense that when Selig later came to own the Brewers, he would hatch the idea of bringing Aaron back to the city where his big league career was born.

By 1974, Selig was looking for something to give his budding yet foundering franchise some promotional juice. Aaron obviously was nearing the end of his brilliant career and no longer an elite player, but Selig wanted to get "The Hammer" into a Brewers uniform.

During the '74 World Series, Selig traveled to Atlanta to meet with Aaron and Braves chairman Bill Bartholomay. Negotiations picked up steam, and a deal was struck on November 2. The Brewers sent outfielder Davey May and a player to be named later (minor league pitcher Roger Alexander) to the Braves for Aaron. "Getting Hank to come back and wear a Brewers uniform was remarkable," Selig said. "And Hank was excited about it, too."

On April 11, 1975, a frigid 37-degree day in Milwaukee, the Brewers held "Welcome Home, Henry Day" at County Stadium. A crowd of 48,160 showed up to welcome baseball royalty back to the city, and Aaron assumed the foreign role of designated hitter during a 6–2 victory against the Cleveland Indians.

Young players on the team, including 19-year-old shortstop Robin Yount, could barely believe they were sharing the same clubhouse with baseball's all-time home run king. "It was tough not to be in awe of him," Yount said. "Obviously, he wasn't the same player as he was earlier in his career, but he was still Hank Aaron."

It soon became obvious that the 41-year-old Aaron was only a shadow of the dominant offensive force that terrorized National League pitching for so many years. He batted only .234 that year with 12 home runs and 60 RBIs, but his return to Milwaukee was still a tour de force for the Brewers, who set a club record by drawing more than 1.2 million fans.

Aaron's skills continued to deteriorate in 1976, so it was no surprise when he announced his retirement, effective at the end of the season. Aaron played little after the All-Star break, giving way to younger players. He saw action in only 85 games, batting .229 with 10 home runs and 35 RBIs. But Aaron's return further cemented his ties to Milwaukee, a city he considers his second home, and his relationship with Selig progressed to a life-long bond.

Aaron joined Rollie Fingers, Paul Molitor, and Yount in the inaugural class of the Miller Park Walk of Fame in 2001. Statues of him stand outside of that ballpark, as well as Turner Field in Atlanta. At Selig's urging, Major League Baseball initiated the Hank Aaron Award in 1999, which is given annually to the top offensive performers in both leagues. "The people here in Milwaukee and Wisconsin molded me into the person I am today," Aaron said in an interview with the *Milwaukee Journal Sentinel* in May 2012. "I was a young kid when I came here, unfamiliar with everything. I met so many good friends, people who were dear to my heart and taught me what life was all about, other than just baseball."

The Brewers further honored the baseball legend with the Hank Aaron State Trail that connects Miller Park with the lakefront, some seven miles away. The HAST, which opened in 2000, winds through the Menomonee Valley and emerges not far from the Klement's Sausage Haus in the ballpark's east lot. One can take a pedestrian bridge across the river for the final yards into the parking lot.

Beginning at Lakeshore State Park near the Henry W. Maier Festival Grounds (think Summerfest) and heading west through the historic Third Ward, the well-used trail provides an ideal travel route for bicyclists, walkers, runners, and inline skaters. Along the route are markers that relate the cultural, industrial, and natural history of the valley. Trail art has been placed strategically along the route to pay tribute to the state's Native Americans, who first populated the area. The trail later was extended beyond the ballpark and into West Allis for a total distance of approximately 12 miles.

41 County Stadium, the Old Gray Lady

In terms of sheer aesthetics, County Stadium was no beauty queen. Encased in gray, corrugated metal, it was built more for functionality than design. Nevertheless, Milwaukee's civic leaders showed great foresight in pushing through plans to build the ballpark merely on speculation that it might help them get a baseball team one day. With Major League Baseball having no expansion plans at the time, it took courage to build a facility with no known tenant.

Bud Selig, a teenaged baseball addict growing up in Milwaukee, would stand high atop Story Parkway and watch the worker bees scurrying about, building the facility that would come to be known as Milwaukee County Stadium. "I couldn't believe we were going to have a double-deck ballpark in Milwaukee, a major league stadium," said Selig, who 20 years later would bring a second big league team to the city.

The first phase of construction was competed in March 1953 at a cost of some $6 million. Stunningly, only two weeks passed before the Boston Braves announced they were coming to Milwaukee to set up shop in the new ballpark. Unhappy with second-fiddle status to the Red Sox in Boston, team owner Lou Perini took the Braves to what he considered greener pastures.

The team would be successful beyond anyone's wildest dreams in the shiny new facility. In 13 seasons in Milwaukee, the Braves never had a losing record—the only professional franchise to stay in one place that long and do nothing but win.

After barely missing out in 1956, the Braves made it to the World Series in '57 and knocked off the mighty New York Yankees in seven games. "Bushville Wins!" proclaimed the *Milwaukee Journal,* using the demeaning label some New Yorkers had pinned on the city. The Braves almost repeated that feat, losing in seven games to the Yankees in 1958.

Before Perini announced his decision to move the Braves, the city planned to move the minor league Brewers from old Borchert Field to County Stadium. That plan was scrapped when the opportunity arose to bring major league baseball to the city.

About 60,000 fans showed up when the Milwaukee Braves arrived at the train station and were paraded through downtown. Braves manager Charlie Grimm proclaimed it "the greatest reception any ball club received from any town." After drawing only 281,278 fans in their final season in Boston, the Braves surpassed 1.8 million in home attendance during their first year in Milwaukee, establishing a National League record. In what baseball officials called the "Milwaukee Miracle," the Braves attracted more than 2 million fans to County Stadium in each of the following four seasons.

Braves players were treated like kings in the city. Meals were on the house in restaurants, car dealerships provided "loaners," meat factories and dairies delivered the staples of life, and local breweries competed to have their suds associated with certain players.

As they say, all good things must come to an end, and that proved to be the case with the Braves, as well. Attendance began dropping precipitously in the early '60s, which many blamed on a new county ordinance, preventing fans from taking their own beer into the ballpark.

Perini decided to sell the team to a group of Chicago businessmen led by Bill Bartholomay, who soon had a deal in place to move

A *Major League* Ballpark

County Stadium became Cleveland's Municipal Stadium—thanks to the magic of Hollywood. The action scenes from baseball games in the 1989 hit movie, *Major League*, were shot in County Stadium, because it was cheaper, and the producers were unable to work around the schedules of the Indians and NFL's Cleveland Browns.

Every time a scene was shot, the interior of County Stadium would be transformed to replicate the Indians' home park. The color of the padding on the outfield walls was changed, signage and logos were replaced (you can still see a Miller Lite ad on the scoreboard shots), and volunteers were seated in the stands to pose as Cleveland fans.

While the film starred notable actors such as Charlie Sheen, Wesley Snipes, Corbin Bernsen, Dennis Haysbert, and Rene Russo, there were two casting choices that gave a distinct Milwaukee flavor to the film. Brewers radio voice Bob Uecker played Harry Doyle, the Indians' oft-inebriated and animated announcer. And former Brewers pitcher Pete Vuckovich played fictional Yankees slugger Clu Haywood, a brooding first baseman.

Scenes often were shot in the middle of the night after the Brewers finished playing a home game. As the Brewers would retreat to their clubhouse, out would emerge Sheen, Snipes, Bernsen, and Haysbert dressed in Cleveland Indians uniforms to play in County Stadium-turned-Municipal Stadium.

the Braves to Atlanta. After a lame duck 1965 season in which only 555,584 fans came to County Stadium, the team relocated to the South.

Other than a few Green Bay Packers games, County Stadium stood mostly dark over the next four years. Selig put together a group that worked feverishly to bring major league baseball back to Milwaukee, finally succeeding in buying the Seattle Pilots out of bankruptcy in 1970.

Though aging and occasionally springing leaks here and there, the old gray lady served the Brewers well for more than 30 years before being replaced by Miller Park in 2001. With iconic broadcaster Bob Uecker as the emcee and many former Braves and Brewers attending, there was a rousing sendoff for County Stadium at the end of the 2000 season. "You can ask yourself, 'Because of County Stadium, was Milwaukee and Wisconsin a better place to live?'" Selig said. "The answer is so clearly yes that it's not even worth debate."

42 A Hero Becomes a Goat

It's supposed to be a good thing when you deliver a game-winning hit in your home ballpark, right? Don't tell that to Rick Manning, who was booed by Brewers fans for doing exactly that on August 26, 1987 against the Cleveland Indians at County Stadium.

Brewers designated hitter Paul Molitor entered that contest with a club-record 39-game hitting streak, a wonder on many levels. For starters, it began in the first game after the All-Star break, with the future Hall of Famer coming off a three-week stay on the disabled list for a hamstring injury.

Molitor struggled with injuries throughout the first half of his career, and the DL stint was his second that year because of an ailing hamstring. But Molitor was a hitting machine with an uncomplicated short stroke, and he immediately went on an offensive binge when he returned to the lineup. It would evolve into the most torrid stretch of Molitor's prolific career. During that wondrous 39-game surge, he batted .415 with seven home runs and 33 RBIs. He was ridiculously good in the clutch, batting .525 with runners in scoring position, and he collected more than one hit on 19 occasions.

The Brewers, who had stumbled into the break with a 42–43 record after jumping out to records of 13–0 and 20–3, rode

Molitor like a thoroughbred, reeling off 25 victories during his hitting streak.

There was no reason to think that Molitor would be unable to make it an even 40 games in a row. On that fateful night of August 26, Cleveland started rookie pitcher John Farrell, who made his big league debut eight days earlier in relief against the Brewers and promptly surrendered a hit to Molitor, the first batter he faced.

This time around, Molitor was unable to solve Farrell. He struck out in the first inning, bounced into a double play in the third, grounded out to short in the sixth, and reached on an infield error in the eighth. By that stage, the modest crowd of 11,246 was beginning to stir, realizing Molitor's streak was in dire jeopardy. But with the teams playing to a scoreless tie through nine innings, there still was the chance that "Mollie" would come to the plate at least one more time.

Brewers lefty Teddy Higuera, masterful on this evening, pitched into the 10th, holding the Indians scoreless on a mere three hits. Farrell gave way in the bottom of the inning to closer Doug Jones, a change-up specialist who began his career in Milwaukee's system and would return to pitch for the Brewers 10 years later.

After Jones plunked slugger Rob Deer with a pitch, manager Tom Trebelhorn substituted speedy Mike "Tiny" Felder as a pinch-runner. Felder advanced to second on Ernie Riles' comebacker to Jones, prompting the Indians to issue an intentional walk to Dale Sveum to get to No. 9 hitter Juan Castillo.

Trebelhorn countered with Manning, a light-hitting veteran reserve outfielder but a left-handed hitter. With Molitor in the on-deck circle, awaiting another opportunity to keep alive his hitting streak, the last thing Brewers fans wanted was a winning hit by Manning. There were even cheers when Manning took a first-pitch strike, prompting the hitter to step out of the box. "I looked down at my uniform and said, 'Is this a Cleveland uniform or a

Milwaukee uniform?'" said Manning, who began his career with the Indians before being traded to the Brewers for Gorman Thomas in 1983, a swap that angered Brewers fans.

Manning gathered himself and found a change-up to his liking, slapping it up the middle past shortstop Julio Franco. Felder scored easily from second base to give the Brewers a 1–0 victory, eliciting a chorus of boos from home fans who wanted to see the streaking Molitor receive another at-bat.

Molitor joined the mob of teammates swarming Manning at first base, but the game's hero had mixed feelings. "I'm probably the only player ever to get a game-winning hit and get booed by the home fans," Manning said. "That might have been one of the strangest situations ever. It never crossed my mind that I would get booed. Your goal is to win the game. I did my job. I'm sure people wanted me to make an out. Then Paul could win the game with a hit and have a 40-game hitting streak."

Manning would retire after that season, hanging up his cleats after 13 years in the big leagues. But not before he experienced the odd feeling of getting booed for winning a game at home.

43 End of the Road for Stormin' Gorman

Gorman Thomas still calls it the saddest day of his baseball career.

He was relaxing at home on June 6, 1983, when his telephone rang. It was Brewers general manager Harry Dalton calling to inform Thomas he had been traded to the Cleveland Indians. "What?" Thomas replied incredulously, making Dalton repeat the message to make sure he wasn't dreaming. If so, it would've been a nightmare.

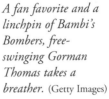

A fan favorite and a linchpin of Bambi's Bombers, free-swinging Gorman Thomas takes a breather. (Getty Images)

The Brewers' ultra-popular center fielder had been traded to Cleveland with pitcher Jamie Easterly and minor league hurler Ernie Camacho for another center fielder, Rick Manning, and pitcher Rick Waits. Thomas never asked Dalton to explain the thinking behind the deal.

The gruff slugger merely put the phone down and began to sob. "I was stunned, devastated," he said. "I never saw it coming. I don't know why I was traded. I know unequivocally that I never did anything that was inappropriate. Sure, they were getting somebody [Manning] who could run faster, but that was it. That ruined the rest of my career. It became just a job. I still played hard, but it was a job. I wanted to be in Milwaukee."

Rabid Brewers fans felt exactly they same. Many never forgave Dalton for trading away Thomas, though he had slowed down considerably and become much less productive. At the time of the trade, Thomas was hitting .183 with five home runs and 18 RBIs in 46 games.

The previous season, however, "Stormin' Gorman" socked 39 homers and drove in 112 runs, helping the Brewers make it to their first—and only—World Series. He was one of the most-feared sluggers in the game, and he was a player who would bust his butt every day, doing anything he could to help his team win.

Thomas had been with the Brewers since their inception. In fact, he was the franchise's very first No. 1 draft pick, getting selected by the expansion Seattle Pilots in 1969. Thomas never had heard of the Pilots, and when his mother told him he had been drafted, he thought she meant into military service. "We were in Vietnam," he said. "I thought the Seattle Pilots might be part of the Navy or Coast Guard."

The doomed Pilots played only one season in Seattle before being sold to Bud Selig's ownership group in Milwaukee. Thomas immediately won over the city's baseball fans with his all-out, wall-crashing hustle, as well as his tremendous power at the plate.

The Brewers were mostly dreadful in Thomas' early days with the club but eventually turned the corner in the late 1970s, and he played a huge role in that breakthrough. He was an all-or-nothing hitter prone to high strikeout totals but also capable of carrying the team on his back for weeks at a time. He wasn't particularly fast, but would sacrifice his body to make catches that didn't seem possible in center. "The fans liked me because I played hard," Thomas said. "I knew what it meant to get a chance. I played with reckless abandon. It wasn't something I thought about. It was just the way I was taught."

That style of play led to his rhyming nickname, and Thomas further endeared himself to fans by joining tailgate parties in the

County Stadium parking lots before games. "I'd have a Coke and a brat," he said. "Then I'd come back after the game and have a beer. It was no big deal. Some of the other guys did it."

Thomas, prone to committing devilish pranks, was also a popular figure with his teammates, particularly Pete Vuckovich. After the pitcher was acquired before the 1981 season, the two bonded, becoming nearly inseparable. A few years later, they opened a bar together in Milwaukee named "Stormin' and Vuke's."

In the years after the Brewers bowed to the Cardinals in seven games in the '82 World Series, Dalton began dismantling a team that had become a bit long in the tooth. It eventually became Thomas' turn to go, much to his chagrin, as well as his legion of devoted followers.

Thomas actually was traded twice by the Brewers. He was sent to Texas after the 1977 season, completing an earlier trade. The Brewers then purchased him back from the Rangers before the start of the 1978 spring training.

Although there was no reversing the 1983 deal, Dalton tried to capture lightning in a bottle during the 1986 season when he re-signed Thomas, who had been released by the Seattle Mariners. But there was no magic left in Thomas' bat, and he retired after batting only .179 with six homers in 44 games with the Brewers.

By then, Thomas had made peace with the trade to Cleveland. To this day, however, he considers himself a Milwaukee Brewer, through and through, and often is seen these days at Miller Park.

44 The Tie

It's a huge honor for any city to be awarded the All-Star Game. Accordingly, when Milwaukee was named the 2002 host, one year after the opening of Miller Park, Brewers officials were understandably giddy. But instead of becoming a Kodak moment to cherish forever, the game would become a punch line for ongoing jokes.

The event seemed cursed from the outset when torrential rains forced the Miller Park roof to be closed for what became a steamy Home Run Derby (won by the New York Yankees' Jason Giambi). The weather also ruined a previously scheduled outdoor gala on Milwaukee's lakefront.

When the game began, there was a scintillating moment in the first inning. San Francisco Giant Barry Bonds hit a shot to deep center for what appeared to be a sure National League home run. But the Minnesota Twins' Torii Hunter leaped and reached over the wall, robbing Bonds who playfully picked up Hunter off the ground as he took the field the next inning.

All-Star Games are often low-scoring showcases for the top pitchers, but this contest soon evolved into a slugfest. Bonds avenged his robbed homer by socking a two-run shot in the third inning to give the NL a 4–0 lead. The American League pecked away until a four-run outburst in the seventh put the visitors on top 6–5. Lance Berkman's two-run single in the bottom of the inning gave the lead back to the NL, but the AL responded with a run in the eighth to tie it.

That's when the problem began to surface. Because the All-Star Game had been handled like a glorified exhibition game for years, with managers trying to get as many players in the game as possible, the respective benches started to empty. When the game lapsed into

Commissioner Bud Selig tries to solve the debacle that became of the 2002 All-Star Game hosted by Milwaukee. The game ended in a 7–7 tie.

extra innings, AL manager Joe Torre and the NL's Bob Brenly were running out of players.

The NL's Vicente Padilla and AL's Freddy Garcia each pitched scoreless ball in the 10th and 11th innings, keeping the game tied. They were the last available pitchers on the 30-man rosters of each team, so during the middle of the 11th, Torre and Brenly met with commissioner Bud Selig in his field-level box to discuss the dilemma.

It was decided that if the NL didn't score in the bottom of the inning, the game would be called and ruled a tie. When Miller Park public address announcer Robb Edwards relayed that resolution to the crowd, boos rained down from the stands, along with chants of, "Let them play!"

Alas, the NL failed to score, and the game was stopped with the score 7–7. Major League Baseball did not award a Most Valuable Player of the game, and there was considerable grousing, as the 41,871 paying customers exited Miller Park.

"I think the fans got a great show, a great game," said Dodgers outfielder Shawn Green. "It was the best All-Star Game, as far as competitiveness, in a long time." That's not the way the general public saw it, however, and members of the media across the nation took their shots. Selig, who was notoriously photographed raising both hands in the air while talking to the umpires, was roundly criticized for the game ending in a deadlock. He was a true scapegoat because Torre and Brenly were to blame for running out of players through poor planning, not Selig.

The commissioner, however, was determined to have something good come of the debacle. By negotiating with the players' union, it was decided that the winner of future All-Star Games would receive home-field advantage in the World Series. Critics declared that format attached too much significance to the mid-season contest, but the leagues, with the aid of expanded rosters, began playing with a purpose instead of treating it as a meaningless showcase.

MLB began marketing the All-Star Game under the slogan, "This Time It Counts."

"They weren't playing the All-Star Game like a real game, and that bothered a lot of people in baseball," Selig said. "Former players would come up to me and say, 'It's not the same. You need to do something about it.' I like the format we have now. The players are into the game more, and it's more enjoyable for the fans. Something had to be done. It's no longer just an exhibition game. Now the game counts."

But not forever. Selig's successor as commissioner, Rob Manfred, abandoned that format in 2017 in favor of giving home-field advantage in the World Series to the team with the best record, a change for which many had clamored.

 A Rookie to Remember

By the time Ryan Braun was summoned to the big leagues for the first time on May 24, 2007, the other rookies in the National League had a two-month head start on him.

No problem.

Braun started hitting shortly after arriving from Triple A Nashville, Tennessee, and didn't stop. When the smoke off his bat had cleared, he had a .324 batting average, 34 home runs, 97 RBIs, 15 stolen bases, and a .634 slugging percentage, the highest by a rookie in major league history. Not bad for playing in only 113 games.

But would it be enough to make Braun only the second player in club history to win the Rookie of the Year Award as voted on by the Baseball Writers Association of America? Fifteen years had passed since shortstop Pat Listach came out of nowhere to claim that honor in 1992.

Colorado Rockies shortstop Troy Tulowitzki, selected two spots behind Braun (fifth) in the first round of the 2005 draft, also had a big first year—he led all NL rookies with 177 hits, 33 doubles, 104 runs, 292 total bases, and 99 RBIs.

Another factor possibly working against Braun was his shaky play at third base (26 errors) compared to Tulowitzki's league-leading .987 fielding percentage at shortstop. Tulowitzki's Rockies claimed a playoff berth, which often works in favor of candidates for individual awards.

In the closest vote since the current format was instituted in 1980, Braun edged Tulowitzki 128 points to 126. Braun collected 17 of 32 first-place votes, 14 for second, and one for third, while "Tulo" garnered 15 first-place votes and 17 seconds. "It's just incredible. It speaks to what Troy Tulowitzki did, also," said the 23-year-old Braun. "I knew Troy had a phenomenal year and helped get his team to the postseason. I knew that would be a factor in [the vote]. I figured it would be close. I had no idea if I would win."

Braun's slugging percentage was a whopping 155 points higher than Tulowitzki's .479 mark, and he also led all NL rookies in homers and extra-base hits (66). Braun's home run and RBI totals were the most ever by a Brewers rookie, topping the marks of 28 and 81, respectively, set by Prince Fielder one year earlier. His 34 homers also were the most ever by a Brewers third baseman, easily surpassing the 23 hit by Wes Helms in 2003. Not only was Braun the NL rookie of the month for June (.382, six home runs, 21 RBIs), he also claimed that honor for July (.345, 11 home runs, 25 RBIs) as well as NL Player of the Month.

The day he accepted that award, Braun told reporters he planned to work on his defense and vowed, "I'm going to be a good third baseman." But before his second major league season, Braun was shifted to left field, so he could concentrate on his offense and open up third base for Bill Hall, a move that didn't work in the long run for the latter. Braun, however, would go on to be a perennial All-Star in the outfield, thanks to uncanny offensive skills that were evident from the very start.

46 An Explosive Start

Everyone involved with the franchise eagerly anticipated the opening of the new spring training facility in Chandler, Arizona, in February of 1986. The team had trained on the other side of Phoenix in Sun City since 1973, but that facility had become obsolete with cramped quarters no longer suiting a major league club. When it opened, Compadre Stadium, with its unique sunken-bowl playing field, was considered the jewel of the Cactus League. But only a few days after the Brewers took occupancy, a tragedy literally shook the team to its core.

Unusually cold on the morning of February 27, it was decided to turn on the previously untested heating system. A worker was bleeding the gas line on the elevated heater in the coaches' dressing room when something sparked an explosion that sent a fireball through the clubhouse and collapsed the cinder-block walls.

Third-base coach Tony Muser was burned so badly that he was transferred to a trauma center in California and nearly died during the following days. The badly burned worker also was lucky to survive. When the wall between their offices caved in, manager

George Bamberger and general manager Harry Dalton were injured. Pitching coach Herm Starrette and bullpen coach Larry Haney also suffered burns, and a handful of players received minor burns and singed hair.

The explosion occurred right over the locker of hitting coach Frank Howard, a mountain of a man who surely would have taken the brunt of the blast had he been there. But, as usual, the hard-working Howard already was on the field, preparing to throw batting practice to his hitters. "This fireball came rolling down the hallway and into the clubhouse," said catcher Bill Schroeder, who along with pitcher Bill Wegman was slightly singed. "It was up high, so everybody ducked and hit the floor. We just wanted to get out of there."

Players scampered out of the clubhouse, rolling on the grass and making sure everybody was okay. Like a scene out of a disaster movie, the impact of the explosion was so great that it lifted the clubhouse roof off its moorings. It was a miracle that no one was killed that day.

Muser was forced to sit out the entire 1986 season, a development that changed the course of franchise history. Muser generally was considered to be the manager-in-waiting for George Bamberger, who was in his last season as the Brewers skipper. Instead, Tom Trebelhorn, a minor league coach in Milwaukee's system, took over for Muser at third base and became the next manager when Bamberger retired in the final weeks of the season.

The Brewers shook off the terrible incident and moved forward, and Muser would recover and go on to manage the Kansas City Royals from 1997–2002. Trebelhorn served as manager much longer than anyone could have anticipated, serving from the end of the '86 season through 1991, compiling three winning campaigns over that period.

One of Trebelhorn's clubs was the much-celebrated "Team Streak" of 1987 that began the year with a 13–0 record, lost 12 in a row soon afterward, and then rode the rollercoaster to a 91–71 finish, which included a 39-game hitting streak by Paul Molitor.

As for Compadre Stadium, it did not last nearly as long as expected as the Brewers spring training home. With a proliferation of new facilities popping up in the Valley of the Sun, Compadre Stadium soon became outdated. The Brewers sought improvements that were never made as priorities changed in Chandler, which went from a cow town to a boomtown seemingly overnight.

Developer John T. Long stepped into the lurch and offered the Brewers a new facility in the Maryvale section of Phoenix, and the team moved there in the spring of 1997. They trained in Compadre Stadium for only 11 years, but no one ever forgot the explosion that rocked the place at the very beginning. "We all felt sorry for what happened to Tony Muser, but we were fortunate that nobody died that day," Schroeder said. "It was the start of camp, so only pitchers and catchers were there. If the full roster had been there, it might have been different. You hate to even think about it."

47 Separating Your Shoulder Tearing Phonebooks and Other M*A*S*H Stories

Every team has had its fair share of unusual illnesses, injuries, and maladies over the course of its history. It goes with the territory when you have that many players year after year. When it comes to odd injuries and afflictions, however, few clubs can top the Brewers. At the top of that list is knuckleball pitcher Steve Sparks, whose trip to the disabled list in the spring of 1994 was unprecedented.

The Brewers had suffered through a tough season in '93, going from 92 victories the year before to 93 losses. Looking to inspire his players, general manager Sal Bando brought a group of California motivational speakers, who called themselves "Radical Reality," to spring camp. To show what could be done if properly motivated, a couple of musclemen tore apart thick telephone books with their bare hands as part of their presentation. After the show was over, Sparks decided to see if he could tear a phone book in half. He ended up separating his left (non-throwing) shoulder and landed on the disabled list. "This is one of the freakiest injuries I've seen," Brewers trainer John Adam said, "and a bit annoying because I had to look up a number later."

It was the seventh time the 28-year-old rookie had separated the shoulder, with one leading to surgery two years previously. Manager Phil Garner termed it "something that just happened," but Bando was none too pleased, saying, "It's not very intelligent, especially when he has a shaky left shoulder to begin with."

No tomfoolery was involved in late June 2006 when reliever Matt Wise was helping himself to a salad at the postgame buffet after a game against the Chicago Cubs at Wrigley Field. But Wise grabbed the serrated edge of the salad tongs instead of the handle and sliced open the middle finger on his pitching hand, which landed him on the DL. "I thought salads were supposed to be good for you," said Wise, trying to keep his sense of humor about the freak accident.

The Brewers' 2006 season already had been replete with weird injuries. Third baseman Corey Koskie suffered a concussion when he tumbled to the ground chasing a pop-up. Second baseman Rickie Weeks tore a tendon sheath in his right wrist merely "waggling" his bat while sitting on the bench. And after just missing a home run, infielder Jeff Cirillo bruised an ankle by slamming down his batting helmet. "We put injuries in two categories—there are accidental injuries and there are preventable injuries," general manager Doug Melvin said. "Injuries that happen on the field are accidental. You can't do anything about them."

Injuries on the basketball court, however, are a bit different. After the Brewers traded for Kansas City Royals ace Zack Greinke before the 2011 season, he wasn't looking so great in spring training. The team and Greinke eventually confessed that he had cracked a rib playing a game of pickup basketball at the outset of camp. Greinke would miss the first five weeks of the season. "I've been doing this for a couple of years now, and people have always said, 'You're going to get hurt,'" Greinke said. "It finally caught up to me, playing basketball. I had a lot of fun doing it, but it wasn't worth it."

Taking off a shoe should be no big deal, right? Reliever Will Smith suffered a torn lateral collateral ligament in his right knee near the end of spring training in 2016, merely trying to remove a baseball shoe. The problem was he tried doing it standing up—rather than sitting down—lost his balance, and felt a pop in the knee. "I was standing on one leg, trying to take the shoe off, and I pulled hard, and it stayed on. My knee just went up and popped," said Smith, who missed two months of that season and later was traded to the San Francisco Giants.

Shortstop Jean Segura had no idea he was in harm's way when he exited the Brewers' dugout and headed for the on-deck circle during a game in April 2014. He didn't see Ryan Braun, the third batter due up that inning, swinging a bat over his head on the top step of the dugout, and was hit on the side of his face, just below the eye. Segura needed stitches to close the wound but was fortunate to avoid a more serious injury. "Whenever you're involved in a situation like that, I think it puts life in perspective and you realize how insignificant baseball is," Braun said. "It could have been a lot worse or a lot worse places he could have been hit."

48 Keep Your Motor Runnin'

After losing a World Series, most teams disband and go home for the winter. When the Brewers lost the final two games of the 1982 Suds Series in St. Louis, however, club and city officials decided to fete the team's exciting, though ultimately disappointing season. After a parade through downtown Milwaukee on Wisconsin Avenue, the team returned to County Stadium for a rally to conclude the festivities. Discouraged by losing a World Series they led through five games, players had to be talked into attending the event. They were in no mood to celebrate, but their spirits were lifted by the raucous reception along the parade route.

No player was more downtrodden than Robin Yount, the team's excellent shortstop who was a few weeks away from being named the American League Most Valuable Player. Winning was everything to Yount, and he had pushed all of his emotional chips into the center of the table in hopes of winning the big pot. "I was devastated," Yount said. "We all play the game to win the World Series, and it seemed we had it within our grasp. We worked so hard to get there and then we weren't able to finish it off. It was very disappointing. I was really in no mood for a celebration."

Next to baseball, Yount's passion was riding motorcycles, and that day he rode one to the rally, parking it in the tunnel under County Stadium. When it came time for the players to take the field to be feted by their rabid fans, Pete Vuckovich, Gorman Thomas, and Ted Simmons presented a dare to Yount. That mischievous trio urged him to ride the motorcycle onto the field for his introduction.

Yount balked at the idea at first. But the more his teammates egged him on, the more he warmed to the stunt. As the players marched onto the field one by one to loud applause, it came time for Yount's name to be called. But to the puzzlement of all but the conspiring players, he was nowhere to be found.

Suddenly, the bullpen gates swung open, and out roared a leather-clad rider on a motorcycle with one fist raised in the air. When fans realized it was their beloved shortstop, the place went nuts. Yount took a lap around the outfield warning track, eventually making his way to home plate where he slammed on the brakes and jumped off the bike.

Yount's teammates thoroughly enjoyed the moment, breaking out in huge smiles and laughter, slapping one another on the back. It was a much-needed moment of levity and sheer delight that momentarily made them forget the recent events at Busch Stadium.

That spur-of-the-moment event highlighted the day's festivities and further cemented Yount in club lore. People still talk about the day "The Kid" roared onto the field, riding his unlicensed dirt bike.

No one was more shocked than team owner Bud Selig. When he realized his prized player was risking life and limb with a baseball version of Paul Revere's ride, Selig almost passed out. "I almost died," he said. "Here comes this figure, racing around like a mad man, and it turns out to be Robin. Nobody knew he was going to do it. I'm up there ready to faint, but the crowd loved it. It turned out to be one of the most memorable events of that year."

Yount, who had ridden some form of motorized bike since he was old enough to walk, never envisioned his stunt would become famous. He was just blowing off steam, trying to soothe the open wounds suffered by coming up just short in the World Series. "I was being a rebel, I guess," he said. "It all came out of a dare. I didn't really think much about any consequences. It turned out to be something that everybody remembered."

49 Listen to Ueck's Hall of Fame Speech

Inductees to the Baseball Hall of Fame in Cooperstown, New York, usually are given strict marching orders regarding their acceptance speeches. Get off the stage as quickly as possible. Keep your remarks brief. Don't exceed 10 minutes. For one thing, it is often brutally hot during the outdoor ceremonies in late July. The living Hall of Famers are introduced individually and seated on stage, so extended discourses make for a long and uncomfortable ceremony.

The guidelines regarding brevity were suspended on July 27, 2003, however, when iconic Brewers radio voice Bob Uecker accepted the Ford C. Frick Award for excellence in baseball broadcasting. Recognized as one of the funniest men on the planet, Uecker was told to take as much time as he wanted.

And "Mr. Baseball" came through in fine fashion, in essence delivering a stand-up act fit for a comedy club. The former baseball greats seated behind Uecker had tears of laughter rolling down their cheeks. With each punch line, they slapped each other on the back and delivered elbows to those seated adjacently. His induction speech became an instant Internet sensation, with avid fans calling up the audio and listening to each comment with glee.

Uecker began the hilarious speech by literally going back to the very start. "I was born and raised in Milwaukee, Wisconsin," he said. "Actually, I was born in Illinois. My mother and father were on an oleomargarine run to Chicago back in 1934 because we couldn't get colored margarine in Wisconsin. On the way home, my mother was with child—me—and the pain started, and my dad pulled off in an exit area, and that's where the event took place. It was a nativity-type setting, an exit light shining down and three truck drivers there. One was carrying butter, one had frankfurters, and the other guy was a retired baseball scout who told my folks that I probably had a chance to play somewhere down the line. I remember it being very cold; it was January. I didn't weigh very much. I think the birth certificate says 10 ounces. I was immediately wrapped in swaddling clothes and put in the back of a Chevy without a heater. And that was the start of this Cinderella story that you're hearing today."

Mr. Baseball, whose hilarious Hall of Fame speech left its members in stitches, announces a Brewers game during 2003.

And so it went. Uecker proceeded to detail his youth and how he became interested in sports. His first love was football, and he talked about throwing around the ol' pigskin with his dad. "I was very young, and he didn't know a lot about it," Uecker said. "He came from the old country. We tried to pass it and throw it and kick it, and we couldn't do it. It was very discouraging for him and me. We almost quit, and finally we had a nice enough neighbor who came over and put some air in it."

Uecker resorted to an oft-repeated but funny shtick, describing signing his first baseball contract with his hometown team. "I signed for $3,000 with the Braves of Milwaukee, which I'm sure a lot of you know, and my old man didn't have that kind of money to put out. But the Braves took it. I remember sitting around our kitchen table, counting all this money, coins out of jars, and I'm telling my dad, 'Let's forget this. I don't want to play.'

"He said, 'No, you are going to play baseball. We're going to have you make some money and we're going to live real good.' So I signed."

Uecker relived his days playing for legendary manager Gene Mauch. "I'd be sitting there and he'd say, 'Grab a bat and stop this rally.' Or he'd send me up there without a bat and tell me to try for a walk. Or look down at the third-base coach for a sign and have him turn his back on you."

On and on Uecker went, describing humiliating events of his career and life. It was a day at Cooperstown that folks involved with the Hall of Fame still talk about. So, do yourself a favor, especially if you're in a down mood and in need of a few laughs. Google the audio of Uecker's speech. At the very least, call up a transcript and read through one of the greatest acceptance speeches ever given in any venue.

50 The Express Rolls Through

It is not customary to go to the ballpark and root for the opposing team. But on July 31, 1990, a sold-out audience of 51,533 jammed into County Stadium, hoping to watch Texas pitcher Nolan Ryan make history. The Rangers ace was sitting on 299 career wins, having failed to reach the magic plateau of 300 in his first attempt against the New York Yankees. Now a traveling caravan of national media, the Brewers, and their fans gathered to see if the second time would be the charm. A national TV audience also tuned in to see if this would be Ryan's date with destiny.

The Ryan Express already had six notches on his no-hit belt and 5,211 strikeouts, guaranteeing him a spot in the Hall of Fame. But 300 victories would be the coup de grace to a remarkable career, a level that only 19 pitchers previously had reached.

At age 43, Ryan still had plenty of gas left in the tank, as the Brewers would discover, accumulating only six hits and one earned run against him over 7⅔ innings. Unable to command his curveball in the early going, Ryan went mainly to his fastball. His heater may no longer have been a 100-mph rocket, but it was still a force in the mid-90s. "I didn't have the command at the beginning that I had in the middle innings," Ryan said. "I had a better fastball and got ahead of them. That way I was able to throw my changeup and curveball [later]."

Given a 4–1 lead, Ryan smelled blood and held the Brewers hitless from the fifth through seventh innings. He failed to escape the eighth, mainly because two errors by second baseman Julio Franco led to a pair of runs for Milwaukee. Having thrown 146 pitches—something no modern-day pitcher would be allowed to do—Ryan was removed from the game, receiving a loud ovation from Brewers fans in recognition of what was about to be accomplished.

Standing on second base, veteran Brewers designated hitter Dave Parker clapped his hands as Ryan walked to the visiting dugout. "[The fans] gave him a standing ovation," Parker said. "I gave him one, too."

When the Rangers exploded for six runs in the ninth (Franco atoned for the errors with a grand slam), it locked up Ryan's 300th victory. "I'm relieved it's over with," Ryan said. "The last 15 days, emotionally, have been the toughest 15 days I've gone through. I really wanted to get it done [in my first attempt]. I didn't want this to be an ongoing deal. I'm probably one of the most boring people when it comes to celebration. My celebration will be to just let things return to normal and enjoy not having to face all the anxieties. I'm not one to reflect on my career and things. I'll wait until I retire, and then I'm sure I'll look back. But right now I'm going to get up in the morning and get ready for my next start. I want to help win as many games as possible."

On this particular evening, it was okay for the home fans to root for the other pitcher. And Ryan made it clear afterward that he appreciated the magnanimous gesture. "It was rewarding on a personal basis to hear the Milwaukee fans be so supportive tonight," he said. "The crowd that we had, I think that really speaks well of them as a baseball community and baseball fans. To me, the way I perceived it, was their way of saying they appreciated, I guess, my career and that they were supportive of me tonight.

"I'm sure a lot of them had mixed emotions. I'm sure a lot of them wanted me to win the 300th game, but the die-hard Brewer fans are very supportive of their ballclub. It was very special."

51 A Closer's Saving Grace

The 2010 season quickly became a disappointing one for Trevor Hoffman. Unlike the previous year, the veteran closer's first with the Brewers, Hoffman struggled in the early weeks. After the 42-year-old change-up specialist blew five of his first 10 save chances, Brewers manager Ken Macha switched to John Axford, a relatively untested but hard-throwing right-hander who quickly took to the closer role.

Without complaint, Hoffman became a set-up guy in the bullpen. But a huge banner on the concourse level of Miller Park constantly reminded Hoffman of his exile. It counted up to career save No. 600, a plateau that no Major League Baseball reliever had reached. With Hoffman no longer closing games, that banner remained stuck on No. 596 for weeks on end.

"It tested me in a lot of different areas, a lot of different ways," said Hoffman, who signed with the Brewers before the 2009 season when the San Diego Padres decided he no longer fit their plans.

But Hoffman kept working and got his game back together. Though he never used his health as an excuse for those early-season failures, a cortisone injection at the All-Star break did wonders for an ailing elbow. True to his classy nature, Hoffman held no grudges for being shuttled into second-banana status in the pen. To the contrary, he served as mentor to Axford, offering advice and support.

With Hoffman throwing the ball well again, Macha became more comfortable with the idea of using him to finish select games. "His work ethic and perseverance paid off," Macha said. "He had to grind it out to get there." The manager began looking for openings for Hoffman, who held up his end by converting saves 597, 598, and 599, putting him on the brink of that magic plateau.

On September 7, the Brewers took the field at Miller Park to play their National League Central rival, the St. Louis Cardinals. As is always the case regarding relief pitchers, there was no way to know ahead of time who would be needed and if a save situation would arise.

With the Brewers ahead 4–2 in the eighth inning, Macha and pitching coach Rick Peterson opted to use Axford, and he escaped a two-on, two-out jam by striking out Yadier Molina. If the save situation remained intact, the ninth would go to Hoffman.

By the time the bullpen door swung open and Hoffman emerged to his familiar AC/DC heavy-metal tune "Hells Bells" blaring over the sound system, the crowd of 33,149 was already on its feet. Colby Rasmus led off with a bloop hit, but pinch-hitter Randy Winn grounded into a double play. The decibel level in the stands soared as Hoffman faced another pinch-hitter, Aaron Miles.

Miles hit a routine grounder to shortstop Craig Counsell, the sure-handed Milwaukee native, who threw over to first, putting save No. 600 in the books. Hoffman immediately was mobbed by teammates in front of the mound and was carried off in triumph. Asked to explain how he persevered and made it to 600 saves, Hoffman said, "If you love the game, it's going to love you back."

In a special moment, Hoffman's wife, Tracy, and sons, Brody, Quinn, and Wyatt, emerged from the stands to embrace the emotional hero. Afterward he admitted to moments of doubt as to whether he'd get to 600 saves. "I was a player who was questioning if I had enough to get things done," he said.

The 2010 Brewers were a disappointing team during the second half of the season and never made it into the pennant race. But, on this cool September evening, the electricity generated by Hoffman's milestone made for a glorious scene at Miller Park.

Hoffman would retire after that season, and New York Yankees closer Mariano Rivera would pass him as the game's all-time saves leader the next year. But Brewers fans had the satisfaction of knowing they had watched a future Hall of Famer accomplish a special feat. (Hoffman was inducted into Cooperstown in 2018.) "You can't allow yourself to put the cart in front of the horse," Hoffman said. "You don't let your mind wonder that it's going to happen. I'm just thankful I've been given the opportunity to get there."

52 Yost Goes from the Penthouse to the Outhouse

On September 1, 2008, the Brewers were flying high. They had breezed through a 20–7 August to move 24 games above .500, and their first playoff berth in 26 years was in sight. The Brewers held a 5½-game lead in the National League wild-card race, a potential cushion in case they didn't catch the Chicago Cubs for the Central Division crown.

Then the bottom fell out.

The Brewers stumbled through a 3–7 homestand against the New York Mets, San Diego Padres, and Cincinnati Reds, and suddenly their playoff chances were in jeopardy. They traveled to Philadelphia for a four-game series against the Phillies, who were bearing down on them in the wild-card race.

Philly swept that series, including a doubleheader on Sunday. It was a lifeless performance by the reeling Brewers, allowing the Phillies to draw even in the pursuit of the wild-card. The next day was a scheduled off day in Chicago, a much-needed breather to regroup after two horrid weeks in which the Brewers lost 11 of 14 games.

But it would not be a day of rest for manager Ned Yost, who had taken over a moribund team in 2003 and helped guide it into a contender. Team owner Mark Attanasio traveled from Los Angeles to Chicago to meet with general manager Doug Melvin, and they decided to make a managerial change. Yost was summoned to Melvin's hotel suite where he was informed of his dismissal and the decision to replace him with third-base coach Dale Sveum.

It was a stunning, unprecedented move by a team in playoff contention and 16 games above .500 with only 12 games remaining in the season. Melvin, Attanasio, and Sveum addressed questions from the media, who had to hustle down from Milwaukee for the hastily scheduled press conference at the Chicago Westin. "I'm not sure I have all the answers," Melvin said. "I'm not sure this is the right one, either. I don't think any of us know, but I'm going to turn the managerial position over to Dale Sveum and hope we can kick start a ballclub that we feel has a lot of talent."

The Brewers also reassigned bench coach Ted Simmons. To replace him, Sveum called in a favor from one of his closest friends, franchise icon Robin Yount, who served as bench coach for Yost for one season in 2006.

Sveum admitted that the managerial shake-up this late in the season served as an intended wake-up call. "We're hoping it's a shock reaction to get [players] to perform up to their level," he said. "We're trying to send a shockwave through this team."

Some folks in baseball labeled it a panic move, but the Brewers turned aside that characterization. "It could be viewed that way," Melvin said. "In the end, we hope the message to the players is that we think we can turn it around. It does seem funny. It does seem odd to let someone go that has given his heart and soul to the organization. I didn't have any other options at this point. I didn't know what else to do, the way we were performing."

As might be imagined, Yost was stunned by the decision to dismiss him. Two weeks earlier, he was a candidate for NL Manager of the Year. Now he was out of a job with only a dozen games remaining and the Brewers still tied for the wild-card. "The timing of it surprised me," he said. "It's the nature of the business, but it's gotten a little strange. Two bad weeks [and you get fired]."

Yost was in his sixth season at the helm of the Brewers. The year before he was hired, they lost a franchise-record 106 games. The rebuilding club finished at .500 in 2005, the Brewers' first non-losing record since 1992. Two years later, they broke through with a winning record (83–79).

Yost figured to see that turnaround completed, but instead he went home to Georgia with his head spinning. "It's unfortunate that Ned's not able to follow this through," said Melvin, visibly upset over the turn of events. "He sacrificed wins and personal goals to try to develop those young players. We want to take that next big step."

The Brewers did take that step, but the change in managers hardly provided a miracle cure. With injuries thinning the pitching staff, Sveum guided the club to a 7–5 record over those final dozen games. On the final day of the season, it took a victory against the Cubs, who had already clinched the division, and a home loss by the New York Mets versus the Florida Marlins for the Brewers to claim the wild-card and end their long playoff drought. Even with their new manager, though, the Brewers' playoff run did not last past the opening series—the Phillies defeated them in four games. Yost would bounce back in a big way as manager in Kansas City, leading the Royals to consecutive World Series berths in 2014 and 2015, winning it all the second time around.

53 A Very Young 50

During his rookie season in 2006, first baseman Prince Fielder showed he could be an offensive force by socking 28 homers and driving in 81 runs. But Fielder stepped up his power game in a big way the next year.

It became obvious early on that Fielder was en route to a special '07 season on the home run front. At the All-Star break, he had 29 homers on the board as well as 70 RBIs, and his power surge helped keep the underdog Brewers in the playoff hunt in the National League Central.

With six games remaining in the season and Fielder sitting on 48 home runs, the Brewers took on the St. Louis Cardinals at Miller Park. Fielder went right to work, socking a two-run shot off Braden Looper in the first inning. Needing one more to reach the 50-homer plateau, Fielder launched another two-run shot off reliever Kip Wells in the seventh.

At 23 years and 139 days of age, Fielder became the youngest player in Major League Baseball history to sock 50 homers in a season. He topped the mark of the great Willie Mays, who was 24 years, 137 days when he reached 50 home runs in 1955. "That's an awesome feat," Fielder said when informed about topping Mays' accomplishment. "Now, my kids can know that one time their dad was pretty good."

On the subject of dads, Fielder had made it clear many times that he didn't like talking about his father, former big league slugger Cecil Fielder. The two had been estranged for years, the result of some financial misdeeds by the elder Fielder that drove a sizable wedge into the family. But on this night Prince admitted one of his primary goals was to escape from the shadow of his father

The Brewers' Biggest Boppers

Before leaving Milwaukee as a free agent after the 2011 season and signing a nine-year, $214 million deal with the Detroit Tigers, Prince Fielder accounted for the two highest single-season home run totals in franchise history. He also tied for the 10th highest total with 38 in 2011. A look at the Brewers' Top 10 in home run totals for one season:

	Home Runs	Year
1. Prince Fielder	50	2007
2. Prince Fielder	46	2009
3. Richie Sexson	45	2003
3. Richie Sexson	45	2001
3. Gorman Thomas	45	1979
6. Chris Carter	41	2016
6. Ryan Braun	41	2012
6. Ben Oglivie	41	1980
9. Gorman Thomas	39	1982
10. Prince Fielder	38	2011
10. Jeromy Burnitz	38	1998
10. Gorman Thomas	38	1980

for good. Asked for his 50th home run ball plans, Fielder said he only wanted to keep No. 52, should he reach that mark. "My dad had 51 [as a season high]," he said. "Then he can't say anything."

Fielder was not happy about comments his father made in a magazine article earlier in the year, claiming his son would not have been a first-round draft pick in 2002, had Cecil not paved the way. That interview only widened the rift between the two. "A lot of people said, 'That's the only reason I got drafted,'" Prince said. "That's what drives me. People said I was too big and all this, and the only reason I got drafted was because of the name. That's why I'm so passionate about playing. I don't mind people comparing me to him, but I'm a completely different player. One day I want people to mention my name and not have to mention his."

Fielder became the first Milwaukee big leaguer, including both Braves and Brewers, to hit 50 home runs in a season. Alas, he would not get to his goal of 52, going homerless over the club's final five games, including the final contest, which he sat out. Fielder, however, did receive one of the game's highest honors when he was named recipient of the Hank Aaron Award for NL offensive achievement. He was presented the award by Aaron himself prior to Game 4 of the World Series.

Fielder would go on to hit 230 home runs in just more than six seasons with the Brewers before leaving as a free agent with the Detroit Tigers, for whom his father starred, after the 2011 campaign. The closest he came to accumulating 50 again was in 2009 when he smacked 46 out of the park—the second highest total in club history—while leading the majors with 141 RBIs. Fielder was traded to the Texas Rangers before the 2014 season but was forced to retire two years later due to ongoing neck issues.

54 Coming Through in the Clutch Again

During his 20-year career with the Brewers, Robin Yount was known for coming up big when it mattered most. His clutch play earned him two MVP awards, countless other honors, and the respect of all who played for and against him. Yount, however, was not known as the most eloquent of speakers. If reporters avoided him after games, it suited him just fine. But when stepping to the podium on July 25, 1999 in Cooperstown, New York, to deliver his Hall of Fame acceptance speech, he came through in a completely different way.

Yount, who was inducted with good friend George Brett and strikeout king Nolan Ryan in one of the most impressive three-man classes in Hall of Fame history, knocked his speech out of the park. Speaking from the heart, Yount spoke of personal experiences, what baseball meant to him, and how he never dreamed that his career would take him to Cooperstown. He concluded his speech with this touching commentary: "Okay, now's the time I'm supposed to wake up from all this. I mean, it's okay. It's been a great dream. But if in fact, if this is reality, then with all due respect, Mr. [Lou] Gehrig, today I consider myself the luckiest man on the face of the earth."

Before taking his seat, Yount also paid tribute to the three iron-workers who died a couple of weeks earlier in a crane accident while helping build the retractable roof at new Miller Park. "As great a day as this is for us up here, we have to remember there are people out there who are hurting," Yount said. "We are often reminded how quickly things can be taken from us. My heart goes out to the families of the men who lost their lives in the construction of the new stadium in Milwaukee. The game of life can sometimes be too short, so play it with everything you've got."

Making Yount's speech even more impressive was the revelation that he wrote it entirely on his own, with no help from others. In fact, he refused to tell his wife, Michele, and his children what he would say, wanting them to get the full impact from hearing it live on that sweltering day on the grounds of the Hall of Fame. "I wanted to tell them what I had to say while I was up there," he said. "I didn't want them to already know what I was going to tell them. From the very beginning, I never even considered letting them know what I was going to say. I'm glad I did it that way."

After thanking everybody from his Little League coach to Brewers broadcaster Bob Uecker for helping his career, Yount saluted his family for its unwavering support. "I know during the baseball season I usually have blinders on to anything but the game," he said. "I took for granted that family matters would take care of themselves. Often times I was there physically, but mentally my mind was always on the game. I realize now what a great job my wife, Michele, did, not only in raising our children, Melissa, Amy, Justin, and Jenna, but in taking care of me. And I love you all very much."

Those who knew Yount and his penchant for keeping things simple were amazed at his eloquence and poise in front of the tens of thousands of fans. His fellow inductees also were quite impressed. "I was amazed at how good you did it, Robin. It was really great," said Brett, who began blubbering uncontrollably shortly after beginning his speech.

Yount said he practiced his speech many times before that special day but admitted he had trouble getting through it initially. "The first time I did it, I was sitting in my car, waiting for my daughter to get through ice skating, and I had some wet eyes," he said. "And I said to myself, 'Man, I got to try to figure out a way for that not to happen.' Fortunately, I did it over and over again until I got to a point where I could do it clearly."

Later, in a reception for the inductees, Yount admitted he was happy to have the speech behind him despite his outstanding performance that day. "As great an honor as it is, for me personally this has been a pretty stressful weekend," he said. "You know, I've never really liked being the center of attention, although I always wanted to be the guy who drove in the winning run. I wouldn't have minded if I had to go try to get a hit in front of [50,000 people], but go talk in front of them? That was scary."

55 Prince Wins the Derby

Baseball players often worry that participating in home run competitions will mess up their swing. When asked about that possibility, Prince Fielder just shrugged it off. "That's kind of my swing anyway," he said.

Indeed, the Brewers slugging first baseman was born to hit home runs. With massive power from his tree trunk-like arms and a natural uppercut swing, Fielder can launch balls to places other hitters can only dream of reaching. Thus it was with great anticipation and eagerness that Fielder entered the 2009 All-Star Home Run Derby in St. Louis. Asked beforehand what his strategy would be, Fielder smiled and said, "Just hit the ball hard."

And that's exactly what Fielder did—swing after swing after swing. When the smoke had cleared, Fielder was crowned the new Derby champion, topping Texas Rangers outfielder Nelson Cruz, a former Brewer, in the championship round. One of four National League first basemen in the competition, including hometown favorite Albert Pujols of the Cardinals, Fielder needed only six homers in the final round to win. Cruz went first and hit five out of Busch Stadium before making 10 "outs" (anything that didn't go over the fence).

Fielder was greeted by Brewers teammate and fellow All-Star Ryan Braun, and they engaged in their typical post-home-run boxing celebration, featuring one swinging and the other bobbing and weaving. Fielder also followed the team's tradition at the time by untucking his red All-Star jersey, a habit that had drawn criticism in St. Louis when the Brewers did it during NL Central play. "I was just happy to be able to put on a show and I'm glad I won," said Fielder, who had his sons, Jadyn and Haven, nearby as he put on his power show sans baseball cap.

In the initial round, Cruz went first and set the bar high with 11 homers. Fielder followed and matched that total, but the next contestants could not keep up. Detroit Tiger Brandon Inge had the dreaded whitewash, failing to hit even one out of the park. San Diego Padre Adrian Gonzalez did little better with two homers. Philadelphia Phillie Ryan Howard picked up the pace with seven homers, and Minnesota Twin Joe Mauer, Tampa Bay Ray Carlos

Going, Going, Way Gone

During his six-plus years in Milwaukee, Prince Fielder hit many tape-measure home runs at Miller Park. But no one hit a ball farther at the Brewers' first home, County Stadium, than his father, Cecil Fielder.

Leading off the fourth inning of a game between the Brewers and Detroit Tigers on September 14, 1991, Detroit's powerful first baseman sent a drive off lefty Dan Plesac that carried over the left-field bleachers and landed in the back parking lot, the only ball to completely clear the bleachers at County Stadium—as they were configured at the time—during a game.

The monstrous homer led to a funny telephone exchange the following morning between Plesac and his mother, who was in the kitchen doing dishes when she thought she heard—via the living room TV—that Fielder had homered off her son.

"Danny, did Cecil Fielder hit a home run off you last night?" she asked.

"Yeah, Mom, it just barely went out," Plesac said.

"I didn't tell her it just barely went out of the *entire* park," Plesac later told reporters, laughing out loud.

A couple of days later, the Brewers brought a surveyor out to measure the distance of the blast. (A worker saw where it landed.) They ruled the home run to be precisely 502 feet.

The morning after the blast, Plesac returned to his locker to find a flattened baseball sitting on the shelf. It had a forged postmark from neighboring Waukesha county on one side, and on the other side an inscription saying, "Dan Plesac, meet Cecil Fielder. Gone!"

Prince Fielder launches another blast in 2009, becoming the first Brewers player to win the Home Run Derby.

Pena, and Pujols tied for the fourth and final spot in the second round with five apiece. In the ensuing swing off, Pujols emerged as the fourth player to advance, much to the delight of the St. Louis crowd.

Pujols didn't last much longer. He hit six homers in Round 2 for a cumulative total of 11, but Howard hit eight to reach 15, and Cruz followed with five to get to a total of 16 and enter the championship round. Fielder then put on another impressive display, socking six homers to total 17, the most through two rounds. The

Brewers slugger did this damage off of Sandy Guerrero, the hitting coach for the Brewers' Triple A Nashville, Tennessee, affiliate, who he had invited to pitch to him during the Derby.

Fielder also became the first '09 contestant to reach the 500-foot mark with a blast of 503 feet, surpassing his previous top distance of 497. In the final round, Fielder and Cruz started from scratch, with their previous totals tossed out. Fielder had the advantage of Cruz going first in the championship round, so Fielder knew know how many homers he needed to take home the trophy. He became the first Brewer to ever do so.

56 The Great Collapse of 2014

When the Brewers began a long trip with a resounding 10–1 victory in San Diego on August 25, 2014, all seemed right with the world. They sported a 73–58 record, had a one-and-a-half-game lead in the National League Central, and, for all intents and purposes, were cruising.

Then, out of nowhere, came The Great Collapse.

There was no reason to expect anything ugly when the Brewers lost quietly to the San Diego Padres 4–1 the next night. But with a chance to win the series in the third game, closer Francisco "K-Rod" Rodriguez surrendered a game-tying, ninth-inning home run to Rene Rivera, who then delivered the knockout blow with a walk-off RBI single in the 10th.

It would be a very long time before the Brewers put another "W" on the board. They went to San Francisco, and the Giants thrashed them for three games, including scores of 13–2 and 15–5. Then it was on to Chicago, and the Cubs handed them three more losses. When the Brewers returned home and dropped a 3–2 squeaker to the St. Louis Cardinals, the losing streak had reached nine games, dropping them four games off the pace in the NL Central in the blink of an eye.

There would be a one-game respite with a 6–2 victory against the Cards, but four more losses followed, and the stunned Brewers were as cooked as your Thanksgiving turkey. They held at least a share of first place every day from April 5 to August 31—all for naught. When the smoke cleared, the Brewers were barely above .500 (82–80), in third place, and eight games out of first. They won only nine of their final 31 games, becoming just the fifth team since divisional play began in 1969 to lead its division for at least 150 days and not make the playoffs.

This was a veteran team, and veteran teams are not supposed to fold like a cheap card table. It was time for hard questions, and owner Mark Attanasio, who seethed over the meltdown, told general manager Doug Melvin he wanted answers. What made it harder to swallow was that no team exerted dominance in the division. The Cardinals finished first with 90 victories, and the wild-card-bound Pittsburgh Pirates closed strong to get to 88. "We're going to look at everything," Attanasio vowed. "We need to give the fans a reason to come back. That means we have to identify what went wrong. We have to have a good explanation for how we're fixing it. And if we're not making any changes, we'd better have a damn good reason for why."

The main issue during the epic slide was a disappearing offense that produced a meager 2.73 runs per game over the final month. With an all-or-nothing lineup that relied heavily on home runs, the Brewers struggled to score when the ball stayed in the park. It's no secret that the ball carries well at Miller Park, but the Brewers were out-homered there 92–77, a big factor in their mediocre 42–39 home record. Of the final 31 games, the Brewers scored 0, 1, or 2 runs on 17 occasions. You're not going to win many games with that scarce run support.

After several weeks of contemplation and analysis, Attanasio and Melvin decided the Great Collapse of '14 was an aberration. Instead, they put faith in the 150 days in first place, which turned out to be a colossal mistake. The Brewers staggered to a 5–17 start in April 2015, and the decision was made to fire manager Ron Roenicke, begin stripping the team of veterans, and engage in a large-scale rebuilding plan. So much for the original blueprint.

57 Sit in the Uecker Seats

You hear people grouse all the time about the rising costs of attending sporting events. But how can you complain about spending $1 to attend a Major League Baseball game?

That's what the Milwaukee Brewers charge on a per-game basis to sit in the "Uecker Seats" at Miller Park. As one might expect for that bargain price, there are a few caveats to purchasing one of those 106 seats.

Many of the seats are obstructed views. The Uecker Seats are in the top deck (terrace level) of the ballpark behind home plate and under the pivot mechanism that provides the fulcrum for the panels of Miller Park's unique fan-shaped retractable roof. Two massive support columns stand in the middle of that section, blocking the view of various parts of the playing field.

Uecker Seats also can be purchased only on the day of the game in person at the Brewers ticket office. They go on sale when the parking gates open, usually three hours before the game, and are snapped up quickly because of the cheap price. The one exception is Opening Day when the coveted $1 tickets are sold via online auction.

It was marketing genius by the Brewers to tie the seats to Bob Uecker, the team's iconic Hall of Fame radio voice. The seats are an obvious reference to "Mr. Baseball's" popular Miller Lite commercial. In the ad an usher ousts him from his seat near the playing field, and Uecker responds, "I must be in the front rooooow!" Then he is relocated to the far reaches of the upper deck, where he sits alone. To commemorate that well-received advertisement, the Brewers installed a statue of Uecker sitting in the last row of that section in 2014, leaving an adjacent empty seat perfect for photo ops.

Depending on whether you are sitting in section 421 or section 433, you won't be able to see the pitcher or catcher, or both, and you might not be able to see the second baseman, shortstop, or center fielder. (If you're sitting directly behind one of the support pillars, you might want to bring a good book.) But once you pay your dollar and get into the park, there's nothing preventing you from wandering around, seeing the sights, and perhaps—we're only suggesting here—moving to a better seat if the game is not sold out.

It's the closest you can come to seeing a game for free. You can't beat the value. What else does a buck buy these days? You could spend it on a lottery ticket, but the odds are much better of seeing (or partially seeing) the Brewers win a game than becoming a multi-millionaire.

58 Riding the Cycle

When you think of players hitting for the cycle, you think about offensive stars with the talent needed to collect a single, double, triple, and home run in the same game. Over the course of the Brewers history, however, some of the more obscure or—shall we say—less likely players have accomplished that feat.

Yes, two of the Brewers' icons, Robin Yount and Paul Molitor, are on the list of players who hit for the cycle. Others are more surprising, such as Mike Hegan and Charlie Moore. And the last three to do so—Chad Moeller, Jody Gerut, and George Kottaras—were average or below average hitters.

So let's take a look at the seven Brewers to hit for the cycle:

Mike Hegan—September 3, 1976 at Detroit Tigers

Other than the Brewers' first season in 1970 when he was the team's regular first baseman, Hegan spent most of his 12 seasons in the majors on the bench. In '76, his career was winding down, and he mostly served as a part-time designated hitter.

On September 3, the Brewers faced flamboyant Tigers righty Mark Fidrych, who was putting the finishing touches on his exciting Rookie of the Year season. But Fidrych didn't have it that night, allowing nine runs (seven earned) in 3⅔ innings. Hegan got to him for a two-run double in the first inning. A bases-empty homer in the third was only his fifth dinger of the season. Hegan's bases-loaded triple in the fourth gave the Brewers a 9–0 lead and sent Fidrych to the showers.

Facing reliever Bill Laxton in the sixth, Hegan singled, collecting his cycle in a span of four at-bats. He flied out to center and walked in his other two trips to the plate, finishing with a career-high six RBIs.

Charlie Moore—October 1, 1980 at California Angels

There were only five days left in the season when the Brewers won a 10–7 slugfest against the California Angels. Moore, a catcher who later moved to right field after the acquisition of Ted Simmons, singled off Ed Halicki in the second inning and homered off reliever Chris Knapp in the fourth.

In the sixth, Moore ripped an RBI triple off reliever Dave Schuler, leaving him a double shy of the cycle. Facing his fourth pitcher of the game, Mark Clear, in the seventh, Moore smacked a run-scoring double to put his name in the Brewers record books. He batted one more time in the ninth and grounded out, but the cycle already had been completed.

In 356 plate appearances that season, Moore hit only two home runs and two triples. That lack of production made his October feat all the more special and unique.

Robin Yount—June 12, 1988 at Chicago White Sox

The Brewers didn't need a cycle from Yount when they pounded the White Sox 16–2. But he accomplished the feat nevertheless, beginning with a first-inning single off Joel Davis. In the third inning, Yount stroked an opposite-field, two-run homer off Davis to put the Brewers on top for good 3–2.

Yount drew a walk in the fifth against reliever Bill Long and then ripped a shot to left-center off Long in the sixth for a double. That left a triple, the toughest hit to complete the cycle, but Yount easily legged one out when he led off the eighth with a drive to right-center off Steve Rosenberg.

It would be the only cycle of Yount's brilliant 20-year career with the Brewers, an indication of the difficulty of the feat.

Paul Molitor—May 15, 1991 at Minnesota Twins

Unlike Yount three years earlier, Molitor's cycle was a key component of a 4–2 victory against the Twins. He got right to work off Kevin Tapani, leading off the game with a triple to left-center and scoring on a ground-out by Jim Gantner.

Molitor's one out, third-inning single led to a run that gave the Brewers a 2–0 lead, but he was stranded after a one-out double in the fifth. With the Brewers on top 3–1 in the seventh and Tapani still in the game, Molitor led off with a homer to left-center to account for his club's final run. He batted one last time in the ninth off Steve Bedrosian and grounded out.

Molitor led the American League that season with 13 triples and 216 hits, and on this night had the perfect four-hit combination to ride the cycle.

Chad Moeller—April 27, 2004 vs. Cincinnati Reds

It would be 13 years before another Brewer hit for the cycle, but finally the home fans got to see it. A light-hitting back-up catcher for most of his 501-game career, Moeller had the game of his life in a thrilling 9–8 victory against the Reds at Miller Park.

In his first at-bat in the second inning, Moeller homered off Cory Lidle—one of five dingers he hit that season. He doubled in the fourth off Lidle and then drove a bases-loaded triple to center off the Reds starter in the fifth to snap a 3–3 tie.

Moeller singled in the seventh off reliever Ryan Wagner, but his cycle appeared destined to be a footnote to a Brewers loss when Cincy took an 8–6 lead into the bottom of the ninth. But with a runner on third and two out, third baseman Brandon Larson threw away Moeller's grounder to keep the game alive. Bill Hall followed with a walk-off, two-run homer to allow Moeller to savor both his accomplishment and a victory.

Jody Gerut—May 8, 2010 at Arizona Diamondbacks

Gerut qualifies as the most unlikely of the Brewers cyclists. Plagued by injuries in 2010, he played in only 32 games, batting .197 with four doubles, one triple, two homers, and eight RBIs in 71 at-bats. By August 13, the Brewers had seen enough and released Gerut, who retired before playing another game in the majors.

But on this Saturday at Chase Field, Gerut would have his moment. It began with a second-inning homer off Cesar Valdez, who would get roughed up for seven runs in four innings. Gerut singled during a four-run rally off Valdez in the third and then chased Arizona's starter with a run-scoring triple to right in the fifth.

The Brewers were well on their way to a 17–3 rout of the Diamondbacks when Gerut came to the plate with two outs in the ninth, still needing a double for the cycle. He had flied out in the sixth and grounded out in the seventh, but given one last chance for glory, he came through with a two-run double off Chad Qualls.

George Kottaras—September 3, 2011 at Houston Astros

As the backup to starting catcher Jonathan Lucroy, Kottaras usually started only when lefty Randy Wolf was on the hill. But on this Saturday evening at Minute Maid Park, Kottaras got the start with Chris Narveson pitching because manager Ron Roenicke liked the match-up of the left-handed hitter against Astros righty Bud Norris.

There was no reason to expect something special when Kottaras flied out to left in his first at-bat in the second inning. But he homered in the fourth and then tripled in the sixth on a monstrous shot onto Tal's Hill, the steep incline in deep center. A seventh-inning RBI single off reliever Aneury Rodriguez left Kottaras needing a double, but would he get another at-bat?

Sure enough, Kottaras got one more chance with one out in the ninth, facing David Carpenter. He hit another blast onto Tal's

Hill and had no choice but to stop at second when it bounded over the wall 420 feet away for a ground-rule double and a place in the Brewers' record book. Had the ball stayed in play and rattled around, Kottaras said he would have headed for third, cycle be damned.

59 2002: A Year to Forget

Before the 2002 big league season began, a baseball writer included the Brewers' Davey Lopes on a list of managers on the hot seat. That reporter wrote that Lopes "was skating on thin ice." In his first encounter with that reporter during spring training, Lopes said, "I don't skate."

As it turned out, that reporter was wrong. Lopes wasn't on thin ice. He actually was in open water with no life preserver, and his head about to go under. After winning only three of the season's first 15 games, Lopes was dismissed by general manager Dean Taylor and replaced by bench coach Jerry Royster on an interim basis. "Personally, it was a very, very difficult decision," Taylor said. "I know nobody worked harder, and nobody wanted to win more than Davey Lopes. Unfortunately, it didn't work out. I think everybody in the organization that is involved in the baseball side of the house feels some sense of responsibility that we had to make a managerial change."

Lopes began the year on double-secret probation after the Brewers stumbled to a 68–94 season in 2001, the team's first in wonderful new Miller Park. That was no way to open a much-awaited facility, and the franchise-record 2.81 million fans who came through the turnstiles were more than a little disgruntled.

A Very Rude Guest

Since Miller Park opened in 2001, no player—Brewer or visitor—has enjoyed a better day at the plate than Los Angeles Dodgers right fielder Shawn Green on May 23, 2002. In a 16–3 romp over the Brewers, Green went 6-for-6 with four home runs and a major league record of 19 total bases.

Making Green's performance all the more stunning was the fact that he came to Milwaukee mired in a deep slump with just one hit in his previous 19 at-bats. He was batting .231 and was on pace to hit 11 home runs after knocking 49 out of the park the previous season.

Green perked up after the Dodgers hit town, socking two home runs in the series opener, which the Brewers rallied to win 8–6. In the second game, he tripled in the only run of the game as Los Angeles won a pitching duel between Hideo Nomo and Ben Sheets.

Then came the big day in the series finale, which began with an RBI double and homer off lefty Glendon Rusch. "After that, I relaxed," Green said.

No kidding. The hits and home runs just kept coming. Green homered twice off reliever Brian Mallette and then capped his historic day with a 450-foot shot off reliever Jose Cabrera with two out in the ninth. "It hasn't sunk in yet," Green said. "I wish we had a few days off so I could enjoy it."

The Brewers were just glad when Green left town.

Taylor was named Brewers GM at the end of the 1999 season, during which manager Phil Garner was fired and general manager Sal Bando resigned. One of Taylor's first acts was to hire Lopes, the Brewers' first African-American manager. After dismissing Lopes so early in the season, the spotlight was squarely on Taylor. "You feel heat," he said. "That is part of the job. I realized that. I realized that going in when I took the job 2½ years ago. There is heat in a lot of jobs in baseball. There was heat when I was in Atlanta. It is part of the process and certainly one I have to accept."

If the Brewers thought dismissing Lopes would turn around the club, they were badly mistaken. Morale sunk to the point where the team fractured—with more than one clubhouse fight taking place. Pitching coach Dave Stewart, who had been hired by Lopes after the 2001 season, deserted the team at midseason, citing family reasons.

Outfielder Alex Sanchez and pitcher Ruben Quevedo got into a scuffle outside the players' entrance to Miller Park, a confrontation that even included Quevedo's wife. Not long afterward, catcher Paul Bako, angered by being brushed back by Philadelphia Phillies pitcher Jose Mesa, yelled at teammate Valerio de los Santos for prompting the retaliation by hitting Phillies second baseman Marlon Anderson with a pitch the previous inning.

As the losses began to mount, things got uglier. Royster and reliever Mike DeJean had an argument on the mound in Houston when the manager came out to make a pitching change. DeJean refused to give Royster the ball, stomping off the mound in protest. "Tension has been high at times," Royster said. "You expect that. But I really believe we have done a good job of keeping that clubhouse in order under these circumstances. This is tough. It's something a lot of these guys aren't used to. You will never hear somebody say those guys don't care. If they do, they are full of shit. That gets me hot. They care. I am going to make sure they care. When something needs to be said, we say it. We just have to say it more of the time when things get worse."

As the end of the season neared, it became evident that Taylor's job also was in dire jeopardy. The inevitable occurred when the Brewers lost 100 games for the first time in franchise history, finishing with an unfathomable 56–106 record.

As a further sign that it wasn't the Brewers' year, the All-Star Game at Miller Park ended in a 7–7 tie, a controversy that prompted boos from the local fans, ridicule from the national media, and an eventual change in the game's format—with home-field advantage in the World Series going to the winning league.

It was the bottom of the barrel of what had become 10 consecutive years of losing. And, sure enough, Taylor paid with his job. But he was not the only club executive to go. In a sweeping overhaul of the club's leadership, Wendy Selig-Prieb stepped down as president and CEO to become chairman of the board. She was replaced atop the team hierarchy by local attorney and board member Ulice Payne (whose tenure would last just more than one year).

Before stepping down, Selig-Prieb hired former Texas Rangers general manager Doug Melvin to replace Taylor. That turned out to be a great move, and it pushed the Brewers in the right direction, though it would take several years to dig out from beneath the rubble created by that brutal 2002 season.

60 Not a Happy Camper

You could call Gary Sheffield a malcontent. Shortly after the first-round draft pick arrived in the majors in 1988 as a 19-year-old shortstop, he turned into a conspiracy theorist, deciding those who ran the club "disrespected" him.

The rumblings started during his first full season in '89 when Sheffield said he didn't think Milwaukee's pitchers were protecting the hitters when opponents hit them with pitches. He wasn't keen on manager Tom Trebelhorn, whom he felt overworked him.

Sheffield also told club officials that his foot was bothering him and affecting his play, but they could find nothing of note wrong with it. When he finally was sent to the minors, a bone scan revealed a stress fracture. While vindicated, Sheffield developed a level of mistrust for those who ran the ballclub, and it bubbled under the surface.

During the 1990 season, Sheffield became completely disgruntled. The Brewers decided to put another first-round pick, Bill Spiers, at shortstop and move Sheffield to third, which they felt made the club stronger. But Sheffield didn't want to move off shortstop and even suggested there were racial overtones in going with Spiers, a white player, at that position. After that season Sheffield openly criticized general manager Harry Dalton, saying he was "ruining the team."

Team owner Bud Selig did everything he could to try to patch things up with Sheffield. He even invited Sheffield's parents from Florida to be his guests at a series in Milwaukee in 1991. Although that olive branch did little to ease the situation, Sheffield said at the time, "As long as Bud Selig wants me here, I'm here."

Adding to the problems, Sheffield could not stay healthy. In 1991, he played only 50 games, batting .194 while battling a wrist injury and an ailing shoulder that finally required surgery.

When the Brewers turned over their baseball operation after the season, removing Dalton and Trebelhorn and inserting new general manager Sal Bando and manager Phil Garner, there were hopes that Sheffield would be happier with new leadership. But it soon became evident that the moody slugger wanted out.

Sheffield began looking for ways to make the Brewers trade him. In the spring of '92, he suggested that he had been forced to play through injuries the previous season. Selig was none too pleased, and Bando said Sheffield's sense of entitlement was unfounded. "My feeling is that he has got to earn the right to play third base," Bando said. "He doesn't earn it by being a distraction. He doesn't earn it by complaining. He'll earn it by playing good baseball."

Determined to find a way out of the organization, Sheffield began grousing about his contract. He had filed for $700,000 through arbitration over the winter but eventually agreed on a base salary of $450,000 with incentives that could bring his total pay to his desired level. Sheffield finally found a path out of Milwaukee when he told reporters that Selig reneged on a promise to give him a multi-year deal. In essence, he called the team owner a liar, and that was the final straw.

Within days, Sheffield was traded to San Diego in a package for right-hander Ricky Bones, outfielder Matt Mieske, and shortstop Jose Valentin.

Although other players on the club knew it wasn't beneficial to have a troublemaker on the club, they also knew a considerable talent had been traded. "I'm not surprised it happened because there had been so much speculation," veteran Paul Molitor said. "I have mixed feelings. I'm a little disappointed things didn't work out better for him here. He got off to a rough start, and it never improved. There were disruptions along the way. I'm pleased for Gary because I know he wanted a trade. Maybe this will get him on track for the career that everyone expected for him."

And that's exactly what happened. Finally happy and healthy, Sheffield's talent came through and he led the National League in hitting with a .330 average that season for the Padres, socking 33 homers and driving in 100 runs. Sheffield went on to a long and prosperous career, also playing for the Florida Marlins, Los Angeles Dodgers, Atlanta Braves, New York Yankees, Detroit Tigers, and finally the New York Mets. He drove in at least 100 runs eight times.

The Brewers won 92 games in 1992 but then lapsed into years of losing, with few players even close to the talent level of Sheffield. Ironically, despite his initial complaint of being moved from shortstop, he never played that position again, eventually evolving into an accomplished outfielder. "It's no secret he was unhappy here," Garner said after the trade with the Padres was completed. "Without taking sides, Gary felt like things hadn't been right for him in this organization. He was bitter, and it showed. The kid obviously has talent, but it's a situation where it's best for him to be in another organization."

While Mieske didn't do much with Milwaukee, Bones and Valentin had several productive, though unspectacular seasons. Still, Brewers fans were left to wonder what might have happened had Sheffield stayed with the club and produced as he did for those other organizations.

61 A Star-Crossed Star

Faced with the prospect of losing Teddy Higuera, the highly successful left-hander out of Mexico, as a free agent after the 1990 season, owner Bud Selig and general manager Harry Dalton opted to give Higuera a four-year, $13.1 million contract. After announcing the signing, the biggest financial commitment in club history at the time, Dalton admitted, "I didn't know whether to laugh or cry."

Later, Dalton probably felt like crying. During training camp the next spring, Higuera tore his rotator cuff, a devastating injury for a hurler. He pitched in only seven games during the '91 season before undergoing surgery, and Higuera was never the same. To his credit, he tried desperately to rehabilitate the shoulder, but it wasn't meant to be.

After a 1–5 season in 1994, in which he made only 12 starts, Higuera was finished as a big league pitcher. During the three seasons following the lucrative contract, he won a total of five games. Pitchers get injured all of the time, often at the expense of their careers, but with the Brewers struggling at the time, fans looked at the Higuera deal as one of the worst boondoggles in club history.

Those fans forget, though, just how good Higuera was when healthy. Signed out of Juarez, Mexico, in 1983, he rose rapidly to the big leagues, debuting with the Brewers two years later. Pitching for a 1985 team that won only 71 games, Higuera went 15–8, the most victories ever for a Brewers rookie.

The squatty southpaw did not have overpowering stuff but was a master at hitting his spots, carving up hitters who didn't know what pitch was coming next. His out pitch was his version of a screwball, a diving offering that proved effective against right-handed hitters and lefties alike. "He knew how to pitch," catcher Bill Schroeder said. "He had a good fastball, but he didn't blow you away. He had one of those slower-than-slow changeups. And he was a fierce competitor."

In 1986, Higuera became only the third pitcher in club history to win 20 games, joining Mike Caldwell (22 in 1978) and Jim Colborn (20 in 1973). He compiled a 2.79 ERA and struck out 207 hitters, a franchise record for a lefty. Higuera finished second in the American League Cy Young Award balloting to Boston Red Sox hurler Roger Clemens. The Brewers won only 77 games that season, another indication of just how dominant Higuera could be when on his game.

Speaking of dominance, no Brewers pitcher controlled enemy hitters over a three-game stretch better than Higuera did in late August and early September of 1987. It began with a three-hit, 1–0 victory in Cleveland. In his next start, he pitched a masterful one-hitter in a 2–0 triumph in Kansas City. The Brewers then went to Minnesota where Higuera tossed a two-hitter in a 6–0 victory.

Three starts. No runs. Six hits allowed. Higuera never threw a no-hitter, but pitching a three-hitter, one-hitter, and two-hitter in succession ranks as one of the greatest pitching feats in club history.

"Those three games were as good as it gets," Schroeder said. "He worked fast. He wanted the ball and he got rid of it. He knew what he wanted to do." Before coming back down to earth, Higuera stretched his scoreless streak to a club-record 32 innings.

The next year, Higuera fashioned a 16–9 record, making him 69–38 (.645 winning percentage) through his first four seasons with the Brewers. In 1989, back and ankle injuries limited him to 22 starts, and he fell off to a 9–6 mark. More nagging injuries struck in 1990, and Higuera finished with an 11–10 record.

Then came the lucrative extension and the devastating rotator cuff injury. There was no way to see it coming, and the Brewers deserve little blame for paying to retain one of the most skilled pitchers in the league. "When Teddy was on the mound, you expected to win," Schroeder said. "He was the best pitcher I ever caught when he was throwing the ball like that. Before he got hurt, he was the best."

62 Preview of Coming Attractions

When the Brewers departed on June 5, 1997 for a three-city, nine-game trip, a previously unnecessary piece of cargo was loaded on the equipment truck. The case was labeled, "Pitchers' Bats."

Pitchers needed lumber for the first time because the trip would end with three games against the Chicago Cubs at Wrigley Field, the Brewers' first interleague series, as Major League Baseball began a much-debated venture that would become a huge hit with fans. "Some of them got better wood than we get," moaned first baseman/catcher David Nilsson.

In the first year of interleague play, teams in Milwaukee's division, the American League Central, would play opponents in the National League Central. For the first few years of interleague play, corresponding divisions faced off until the format was expanded to include play against the other two divisions.

In preparation for interleague games, the Brewers conducted pitchers' batting practice for a few weeks. "The first two BP sessions were just awful," manager Phil Garner said. "It was terrible. Everything about it was ugly. The one after that was a lot better. They've continued to get better. Problem is, they've been sneaking in the [batting] cage behind my back and hitting. Some of them are getting sore hands. They're being stupid about it. I'm going to have to calm them down a little bit."

The Cubs started the season 0–14 and were still 14 games under .500 (25–39) when the Brewers arrived at Wrigley Field, but Garner didn't want to hear about having a pushover for his first interleague opponent. "You know darn well that doesn't work with us," Garner said. "How many times have we gone out and played much better against a pitcher with a 2.00 ERA than we have against a pitcher with a 7.00 ERA?"

Nevertheless, in the first interleague game in club history on June 13, the Brewers prevailed against the Cubs 4–2 behind a strong pitching performance by Jeff D'Amico. Garner admitted afterward that he forgot to put D'Amico in the No. 9 spot in the batting order in his original lineup card. "[Catcher] Mike Matheny is normally my ninth-place hitter," Garner said. "I forgot I had to put the pitcher in there today."

Fortunately for the Brewers, Garner quickly made the correction, and the 21-year-old D'Amico went out and pitched eight solid innings, allowing only five hits. Shortstop Jose Valentin drove in three runs with a two-run homer and RBI double, and second baseman Mark Loretta added a clutch run-scoring single in the seventh. "It kind of seemed like a spring training game," said

D'Amico, referring to the fact that the Brewers and Cubs often played each other in exhibition games in Phoenix. "It was different, but everybody was really excited."

The first hit allowed by D'Amico came from his counterpart, Cubs lefty Terry Mulholland. "I took a little abuse from the guys for that," he said.

D'Amico struck out in all three of his at-bats, but it was his arm—not his bat—that was essential that day. Though he picked up the victory, D'Amico didn't take home the game ball. That went to veteran closer Doug Jones, who pitched an uneventful ninth to record his 15th save. When Jones recorded the final out, there were noticeable cheers from the stands as many Brewers fans had made the trek south from Milwaukee. "We definitely had a lot of people who were Milwaukee fans today," Garner said.

The Brewers would go on to lose the other two games of that series, but Game No. 1 of interleague play was a rousing success. At the time, the Brewers had no way of knowing that they'd be playing in the National League the following season, making the jump for a necessary realignment of the majors. The Cubs would become the Brewers' primary NL Central rivals, and AL teams would form the opposition in interleague play. What's that they say about turnabout being fair play?

63 Vukie Pitches Through Pain

Pete Vuckovich's teammates knew he was hurting. The Brewers ace had been getting treatment on his right arm for weeks, and he realized there was something going on beyond mere soreness. Vuckovich, however, was not going to let that stop him from taking the mound in Game 7 of the 1982 World Series against St. Louis.

His mind-set was anything for the team, even to the point of risking further injury. It was a commendable approach, and the plan worked for the first five innings, as the teams battled to a 1–1 tie. When the Brewers went on top 3–1 with a pair of runs in the top of the sixth at Busch Stadium, they could smell a championship.

It had been typical "Vukie" on the mound. He pitched in and out of trouble, never giving an inch, stranding runners, and doing whatever it took to keep his team in the game. It was the way he had pitched all season, and why he would later receive the American League Cy Young Award that year.

Things began to unravel, however, in the bottom of the sixth. With one out, Ozzie Smith singled, and Lonnie Smith followed with a double, putting runners on second and third. Knowing Vuckovich was pitching with an ailing shoulder and getting by mostly on guts and savvy, manager Harvey Kuenn summoned lefty Bob McClure from the bullpen.

That move backfired. McClure walked Gene Tenace to load the bases and then surrendered a two-run single by Keith Hernandez to tie the game. George Hendrick delivered a run-scoring single, sending home what proved to be the decisive run. St. Louis would add two more runs in the eighth to take a 6–3 victory, which gave them the World Series title despite having trailed 3–2 in the series.

Afterward, in a solemn visiting clubhouse, Vuckovich was disconsolate. And for a long time after, he lamented letting down his teammates by failing to go deeper into the game and protecting the lead. "You go out there. It's the seventh game. You have the opportunity to go nine, shut them down, and win," he said. "I failed to do that and I've carried that burden ever since 1982. All these years, I've felt guilty for letting my teammates down. It's that simple."

Despite pitching with a torn rotator cuff, Pete Vuckovich guts through the 1982 World Series.

Vuckovich's teammates felt that guilt was misplaced. In reality, he had been running on fumes for weeks, pitching with a shoulder injury that would cut short his career. Tests would later reveal that he had pitched with a torn rotator cuff, a dreaded injury for pitchers. That explained why he had little left in the tank for the postseason, failing to win either of two starts in both the AL Championship Series against the California Angels and in the World Series. "Vukie pitched anyway, but his arm was blown," said Brewers catcher Ted Simmons, who knew exactly what his teammate had to do before each start to try to control the pain in his shoulder. "He wouldn't quit. He kept going out there and trying to help his team win."

It was no secret in the Brewers clubhouse that Vuckovich took pain injections in his shoulder before many of his starts. He didn't see it as a heroic act or worry about consequences down the road. He merely felt it was his responsibility to go out there every five days and do whatever it took to help his club win a game.

Vuckovich gained his teammates' respect with that approach, and they watched in fascination at times as he won games without having much on the ball. He was in constant motion on the mound, constantly twitching and flinching, jerking his head from side to side, basically doing anything to distract the hitter before throwing a pitch.

It was not uncommon for Vuckovich to walk to the back of the mound, bend over, and dry heave. Sometimes it wasn't so dry. He wore a baggy uniform, sported a sinister-looking Fu Manchu mustache, and glared at hitters from beneath a baseball cap pulled down low on his forehead. But it wasn't all smoke and mirrors, Vuckovich also knew how to pitch. "You can't fake it out there," Simmons said. "You have to have the stuff, too. He just tried to get an edge, whatever it might be."

Pitching hurt eventually took its toll, leaving Vuckovich with the misguided notion that he had betrayed his teammates when it counted most. "I know I had their respect," he said. "That's fine. That's nice. I just personally felt I let them down. I had a goal at that point in time to win the seventh game of the World Series. I failed and I've had to live with it. I've always felt shitty about that."

64 The Losing Ends

When the Brewers finished the 2005 season with an 81–81 record, it was notable because it ended a string of 12 consecutive losing seasons, a stretch of futility matched at the time by the equally woeful Pittsburgh Pirates. But it wasn't the same as a winning season. (In fact, a final day loss in Pittsburgh robbed the Brewers of that chance.) So when the Brewers took a step back in 2006, winning only 75 games, their fans became understandably nervous. Was this rebuilding program actually going to work, or was it just a tease?

The 2007 season would be crucial. General manager Doug Melvin and manager Ned Yost had rebuilt the club from the ground up after a disastrous 106-loss season in 2002, and this was no time for the club to spin its wheels. Not messing around, the Brewers bolted to a 24–10 start, electrifying their fans and getting the attention of folks throughout baseball.

Two months into the season, they called up third baseman Ryan Braun, who would go on to claim National League Rookie of the Year honors. Slugging first baseman Prince Fielder would become the youngest player ever to hit 50 home runs in a season. Right fielder Corey Hart and shortstop J.J. Hardy were establishing themselves as productive players. Anchored by reliable closer Francisco Cordero, the pitching staff held its own.

The potent Brewers obliterated the club record of 216 homers set by "Harvey's Wallbangers" in 1982, socking 231. With the team in first place in the NL Central from the very start, the goal of merely having a winning season changed—now the team wanted to end a playoff drought that went back to that same '82 club.

But 90 miles to the south, the division-rival Chicago Cubs had similar plans to please their long-suffering fans. After watching the Brewers lead the Central for 133 days, including a margin of 8½ games at one point, the Cubs finally broke into the lead in late August. There would be much jockeying back and forth between the clubs in the ensuing weeks.

In the end, the Brewers pitching didn't hold up under the strain. Oft-injured ace Ben Sheets broke down again, the bullpen frayed under the strain of a teetering rotation, and the Brewers stumbled through a 3–7 stretch in late September. And the Cubs finally clinched the division crown on the Friday of the final weekend of the season.

As disheartening as that turn of events was, the Brewers still had work to do. They were 81–79 with two games remaining and needed to win one more to achieve their first winning season since 1992. Another win wouldn't come easily either as they faced the visiting San Diego Padres, who were on the cusp of securing a playoff berth.

The Brewers' quest for a winning season seemed destined to go down to the final game when they entered the bottom of the ninth inning on Saturday trailing 3–2. The Padres had vaunted closer—and future Brewer—Trevor Hoffman there to nail down the victory, and he was one strike away against pinch-hitter Tony Gwynn Jr., son of legendary Padre Tony Gwynn. But Gwynn yanked one of Hoffman's trademark change-ups into the right-field corner for a triple, tying the game.

The game would go into the 11th inning when another pinch-hitter, Vinny Rottino, delivered the game-winning single with one out for the Brewers. Rottino, a native of nearby Racine, Wisconsin, and a September call-up, had delivered one of the biggest hits for the team he grew up cheering, ending a 14-year spell in which Milwaukee went without winning seasons.

The next day the Brewers would pummel San Diego 11–6, forcing the Padres into a one-game playoff with the Colorado Rockies for the NL wild-card spot, which the Padres would lose to suffer their own heartbreak. The Brewers couldn't be worried about that, finishing with an 83–79 record that somewhat lessened the disappointment of failing to hold off the Cubs.

At long last Brewer Nation had a winner. The next season, the Brewers would break through with their first playoff berth in 26 years. The corner officially had been turned.

65 From Garbageman to MLB Pitcher

Some unlikely characters have worn a Brewers uniform over the years, but none traveled a more unlikely path to Milwaukee than Joe Winkelsas. You just don't get that many former Buffalo, New York, sanitation workers in the major leagues.

When the Brewers summoned the 32-year-old reliever from Double A Huntsville, Alabama, on May 23, 2006, he could barely believe his ears. He hadn't pitched in the major leagues since 1999 with the Atlanta Braves, for whom he allowed four hits and two runs in one-third of an inning.

That's a long time to sit on a 54.55 ERA.

In the interim Winkelsas spent time in drug rehab, had three stints in independent baseball, and a thankfully short-lived career

The fact that Joe Winkelsas is signing autographs on the major league level is startling, considering he worked in Buffalo, New York's sanitation department shortly before resuming his baseball career. (Getty Images)

in waste management. He was signed by the Brewers in January 2006 at a tryout camp in Phoenix.

How he ended up in that camp was a story in itself. Winkelsas had been released by the Chicago White Sox from their Triple A Charlotte club in April 2005. He briefly hooked on with the Grays, a club in the independent Canadian-American League that played nothing but road games. He quit after one appearance. "It was brutal," Winkelsas said. "The hotel was their home."

Figuring his pitching days were over, Winkelsas returned home to Buffalo and took a job collecting garbage for the city sanitation department. It soon dawned on him that his new job had improved the velocity on his fastball. "I started to gain some strength, lifting

The Unusual Suspects

Joe Winkelsas wasn't the only unlikely player to see action with the Brewers during the 2006 season. The bullpen was in a constant state of flux, with Chris Mabeus and Chris Demaria also getting summoned from the minors.

Mabeus was done after one of the worst one-game performances in major league history on May 29 in Pittsburgh. With the Brewers trailing 10–3 after six innings, manager Ned Yost put Mabeus in to mop up. Mabeus pitched a scoreless seventh but completely melted down in the eighth, allowing four runs on three hits, two walks, and three wild pitches. Yost was forced to remove Mabeus before he could get the third out. (Winkelsas came in to record it.) Mabeus was sent down afterward and never made it back to the majors, retiring with a one-game ERA of 21.60.

Demaria, who made eight relief appearances the previous season with the Kansas City Royals, lasted long enough to make 10 outings out of the pen for the Brewers, compiling a 5.93 ERA. He actually was sent down to make room for Mabeus and would never pitch in the big leagues again.

Other no-names given shots in the Brewers bullpen that season were Allan Simpson (two games) and Chris Spurling (seven). The Brewers didn't confine their list of unlikely big leaguers in '06 to relief pitchers. They also called up 27-year-old second baseman Chris Barnwell, who had played six years and 616 games in the minors without a sniff of the majors. (Winkelsas was sent down in a corresponding move.) Alas, Barnwell fared no better than the aforementioned relievers, batting .067 (two for 30) in 13 games. He, too, would be returned to the minors, never to rise to the top level again.

Hey, at least you can't fault the '06 Brewers for one thing: they looked under every rock for talent.

and dragging things through the snow," he said. "It was like physical therapy that I got paid for."

The Brewers invited Winkelsas to camp, though most hopefuls were a dozen years younger. But Winkelsas threw the ball well and was offered a spot on the Huntsville roster. He was determined not to cheat himself this time as he did during his stint in the Atlanta organization when he developed a drug problem that quickly spiraled out of control. He came forward and admitted his problem and kicked the habit at a rehabilitation clinic.

Winkelsas had overcome obstacles as a youngster, coming from a family background that included drugs in the home. At age 15, he discovered that he had been adopted. With that remarkably difficult personal history, he joined the Brewers in Cincinnati, ready for another chance.

Winkelsas would pitch more than one-third of an inning for the Brewers, but his stay was not destined to be a long one. After posting a 7.71 ERA over seven relief outings, he was sent back to the minors, never to return to the major leagues.

It was a good story while it lasted. And people still chuckle at how legendary Brewers radio broadcaster Bob Uecker pronounced the pitcher's name when he would enter a game. Uecker would intentionally and distinctly say, "Winkels-ass," breaking up anyone within earshot.

Winkelsas similarly left behind a memorable and amusing line when asked if he had received any messages from folks after finally making it back to the big leagues. "Yes," he said. "The only messages I got last year [was] when I forgot to pick up somebody's garbage."

66 Learn the Secret to the Secret Sauce

Whether you're a regular visitor to Miller Park or a first-timer, you'll order a brat at some point during the game. Or a wiener of some kind, be it the traditional hot dog or a zesty Italian sausage. But what do you put on that ballpark delicacy? It has been a long-standing tradition among those in Brewer Nation to slather on a generous helping of Secret Stadium Sauce. Which often raises the question: what exactly is the secret to the Secret Stadium Sauce?

Upon first glance, it appears to be part ketchup, part barbeque sauce. But there has to be more to it than that, right? Before we get to the actual ingredients, let's take a course in Secret Sauce history.

The sauce was developed by Sportservice, the food vendor at Miller Park and its predecessor, County Stadium. It became so popular—in part because of NBC broadcaster Bob Costas' stated fondness for enjoying brats covered in that condiment—that it begun to be sold at the ballpark and local grocery stores in 18-ounce bottles.

Rick Abramson, who worked his way up from a vendor at County Stadium to president of Sportservice, is credited with inventing the sauce during the 1970s. Abramson told the *Milwaukee Journal Sentinel* that he wanted to come up with a new condiment that would include three ballpark standards—ketchup, mustard, and barbecue sauce. "It just sprung up and people walked up and started using it," Abramson said. "Bob Costas became a fan of it and started talking about it. We began to bottle it, package it, and sell it in grocery stores. It has been a cult treat since."

Another version of the story is that Sportservice thought it was receiving a shipment of ketchup to County Stadium, and it turned out to be barbecue sauce. It was doctored in some fashion to give it a turn toward ketchup, and Secret Stadium Sauce was born.

Abramson later indicated a different matter of necessity resulted in the invention. He said the supply of ketchup and mustard had run unexpectedly low at County Stadium, so he combined what he could find with some barbecue sauce and came up with the soon-to-be coveted secret sauce.

Eating brats with the sauce became nationally known when Costas openly stated his love for the ballpark treat during "Game of the Week" broadcasts with Tony Kubek, a Wisconsin native, during the 1980s. He talked about his fondness for brats and Secret

Have a Brat (or Three)

What exactly is a brat, you ask? Well, for starters, it's not a hot dog. Brat is short for bratwurst, a sausage usually made from veal, pork, or beef. The name is German, derived from "brat," which means finely chopped meat, and "wurst" or sausage. Germans now associate the name with the verb "braten," which means to pan fry or roast.

The brat has been a longtime favorite in Wisconsin because of the rich German heritage of that state. And the favorite way to prepare it is over a grill, though preparations prior to the cooking vary according to taste.

Not surprisingly, Wisconsin is known as the origin of the "beer brat," where the sausages are soaked in beer (usually with butter and onions) prior to grilling. The popularity of the brat dates to the 1920s in Sheboygan County, where local butchers would take orders and hand make them to be picked up on a certain day. The fat content was high, making daily pickup necessary to avoid spoiling. Much of that fat burns off during grilling, but no one ever ordered a brat because of its nutritional value.

The brat was first introduced to baseball fans by Bill Sperling at Milwaukee's County Stadium, which opened in 1953. It became an instant hit and a staple of the popular tailgating parties before games.

So if you want the true culinary experience of attending Brewers games, forget the hot dog and savor a brat…or two…or three.

Stadium Sauce in Curt Smith's book, *Storied Stadiums: Baseball's History Through Its Ballparks.* "The secret sauce has a formula, that's in a vault that makes it taste like another planet," Costas said. "Put beer on the grill and steep it in sauerkraut. On camera I'd say it's now an official game because we have the bratwurst." Because of Costas' national promotion, Sportservice sent packages of brats and cases of Secret Stadium Sauce to his home.

In Smith's book, Costas relates a story of being contacted by Ma Pesh of Stevens Point, Wisconsin. Pesh claimed he established the record for eating the most brats, during an August 1972 game between the Brewers and Baltimore Orioles, and challenged Costas to a brat-eating contest. That challenge went unanswered.

So now you're probably wondering what the "secret" ingredients are in the Secret Stadium Sauce. Well, they're listed right on the bottle, as mandated by the Food and Drug Administration: water, tomato paste, corn syrup, vinegar, high fructose corn syrup, salt, modified food starch, spice blend (salt, paprika, onion powder, garlic powder, spices, and spices extractives), BHA and BHT (preservatives, less than 2 percent triacalcium phosphate added to prevent caking), sodium benzoate, and capsicum.

But, shhh! Keep the ingredients a secret. It adds to the allure!

67 Restocking the Pantry

After one year on the job, two things had become quite apparent to general manager Doug Melvin following the 2003 season. First, he didn't have enough experienced major league players on his roster to field a competitive club. Second, it did little good to have slugger Richie Sexson on a club with so many holes.

Sexson was coming off three superb seasons with the Brewers in which he hit a total of 119 home runs and accumulated 351 RBIs. Yet the Brewers' win totals during those three seasons were 68, 56, and 68. So on December 1, Melvin swung a massive nine-player deal with the Arizona Diamondbacks, exchanging Sexson, reliever Shane Nance, and a minor leaguer to be named later for infielder and Milwaukee native Craig Counsell, second baseman Junior Spivey, catcher Chad Moeller, first baseman Lyle Overbay, and lefthanders Chris Capuano and Jorge De La Rosa.

It was a deal that allowed the Brewers to turn the corner toward being a competitive team again, including an 81–81 record in 2005. "We finally have depth that we can use to our advantage," said manager Ned Yost after the swap was announced. "We can do other things. That's important."

Overbay would replace Sexson at first base, Spivey took over at second, and the veteran Counsell became the everyday shortstop (and later returned for a second tour of duty with his hometown team), accounting for three-fourths of the Brewers infield. Capuano settled into the starting rotation and served in that role for four-plus seasons, leading the club with 18 victories in 2005. De La Rosa would eventually make the staff, and Moeller would serve as a reliable backup catcher for two-plus seasons.

The deal made perfect financial sense for a ballclub intent on cutting payroll until it regrouped on and off the field. Sexson was headed for free agency after the 2004 season anyway, and his agent gave Melvin every indication the 6'7" slugger would test the market. "That's part of the business of baseball today," Melvin said. "We didn't feel we could take the chance of having Richie leave as a free agent after next year. My job as general manager is to acquire as many good players as we can. We would have liked to acquire an outfielder, but clubs we talked to did not have outfielders available that were ready for the big leagues.

"It's not something you enjoy as a general manager, to trade your best player. We have to move on, and we feel we filled a lot of holes."

Better yet for the Brewers, the trade became the gift that kept on giving. In June 2005, with Milwaukee ready to make the commitment to second base prospect Rickie Weeks, it traded Spivey to the Washington Nationals for starting pitcher Tomo Ohka. In July 2006 when De La Rosa failed to develop to their liking, the Brewers sent him to the Kansas City Royals for veteran infielder Tony Graffanino. Weeks had gone down with a wrist injury, and the Brewers needed help immediately, prompting them to give up on De La Rosa too soon, they later would admit.

Overbay had two nice seasons as the Brewers' first baseman, setting a club record with 53 doubles in 2004. But with the team ready to commit to young slugger Prince Fielder at first base for the '06 season, Overbay was traded to Toronto for right-hander Dave Bush, outfielder Gabe Gross, and pitching prospect Zach Jackson. Bush would pitch for five seasons in the Brewers' starting rotation before leaving via free agency. Gross would play for two-plus seasons in Milwaukee as a platoon outfielder and valuable left-handed bat off the bench. Jackson was included in the July 2008 trade with the Cleveland Indians that netted ace lefty CC Sabathia.

So the family tree that sprung from the Sexson trade was a fruit-ful one for the Brewers. Making the trade lopsided in Milwaukee's favor, Sexson would injure his shoulder the following season with Arizona, play in only 23 games, and then leave via free agency for the Seattle Mariners.

By restocking their major league roster with experienced players, the Brewers were able to buy time for their developing prospects such as Weeks, Fielder, Corey Hart, and Ryan Braun. It sped up the rebuilding process, culminating with Milwaukee's first playoff berth in 26 years in 2008.

68 The Perfect Mother's Day Present

In 2006 Major League Baseball began asking players to use pink equipment on Mother's Day to bring awareness to the battle against breast cancer. That first year, knowing his mother, Vergie, would be in the stands at Miller Park, Brewers infielder Bill Hall used a pink bat in the game against the New York Mets.

With that pink bat, Hall delivered one of the most memorable home runs in Brewers history, socking a walk-off blast in the bottom of the 10th inning to beat the Mets 6–5. "If it wasn't the biggest moment in my career, it was one of them," Hall said. It wasn't until later, though, that Hall realized the impact his home run had on others. "I knew it was a big home run with my mom in the stands, but little did I know that it would mean a lot more for a whole lot of people," he said. "The notes and letters I received from hitting that home run, I knew I raised a lot of people's spirits."

MLB.com put up the pink bat for auction, with the proceeds designated for the Susan G. Komen Breast Cancer Foundation. Brewers principal owner Mark Attanasio won the auction with a magnanimous bid of $25,000 and presented the bat to Vergie Hall.

It was that bat that came to the rescue during a competitive, back-and-forth game. The Brewers took a 5–4 lead into the ninth against the Mets. But Carlos Delgado pounded a ground-rule double to right-center against Milwaukee closer Derrick Turnbow, and Xavier Nady delivered the tying run with a two-out single.

The Brewers did nothing in the bottom of the ninth, and left-hander Jorge De La Rosa stranded a pair of Mets runners in the top of the 10th to keep the game knotted. New York reliever Chad Bradford, who had come on in the ninth, retired J.J. Hardy on a grounder to third. The side-armed thrower caught a break when

Rickie Weeks tried to stretch a single to right into a double and was thrown out by Jose Valentin, a former Brewers shortstop seeing duty in the outfield.

Up to the plate stepped Hall, who already had a reputation in Milwaukee for walk-off hits. But with three strikeouts in three at-bats, Hall was having a miserable day up to that point. The beauty of baseball, though, is that it only takes one at-bat, one swing, to change the outcome of a game.

Bradford fell behind in the count 2–0 and came back with a fastball that Hall drove over the fence in right-center to win the game and send the Miller Park crowd, including his mom, into a frenzy. The following year featured déjà vu. Hall would hit another Mother's Day home run with a pink bat, and the blast again came versus the Mets. That one would not be nearly as dramatic, however, as it proved to be the only run in a 9–1 loss to New York at Shea Stadium.

Hall matched Attanasio's $25,000 donation to the Komen Foundation, saying he felt it was the right thing to do after getting such a terrific response for his game-winning blast in '06. "I got a lot of letters and I read them all," he said. "It was an inspiration to know that people watching on TV got a lift when they saw that home run."

Eleven years later, catcher Manny Piña would add to that Mother's Day legacy by smacking a three-run homer in the eighth inning to lead the Brewers to an electrifying 11–9 victory against the Mets. The Brewers seemed done when they trailed 7–1 in the fifth but kept fighting back until Piña delivered the deciding blow. Piña's mom, Minda, wasn't in the stands at Miller Park but was watching on television back in Venezuela and texted her son after his dramatic home run. "She said she started screaming. She was so happy," Piña said with a big smile.

69 Eric Thames

During the three years he played professionally in the Korean Baseball Organization, Eric Thames compiled offensive numbers so mind-boggling that he earned the nickname *Hananim*, which translates to "God." That's what you call high praise. Thames also was known as *Sang Namja*, which means "real man," or more colloquially, "bad ass." That's how intimidating he was.

In his version of real-life fantasy baseball during three seasons with the NC Dinos, the left-handed-hitting first baseman batted .348 with 124 home runs, 379 RBIs, and 64 stolen bases in 388 games. He was named MVP of the KBO in 2015 by producing the first 40/40 season (home runs/stolen bases) in league history, batting .381 with 47 homers, 140 RBIs, and 130 runs scored.

Half a world away, the Brewers took notice, though not in person. They had no scouts in South Korea at the time. Relying merely on videos of Thames' at-bats and statistical analysis of his production, the Brewers offered him a three-year deal for $16 million with a club option for 2020 at $7.5 million. That's what you call thinking out of the box. The Brewers' commitment to Thames was a gamble in more ways than one. To open first base for him, they cut loose Chris Carter, who tied for the National League lead with 41 home runs in 2016. No major league club ever had cut loose a reigning home run champ, so it was hardly a no-risk proposition. "We spent a good amount of time with Eric throughout this process," general manager David Stearns said of the club's courtship of Thames. "There is a lot of networking that goes on in this game whenever you're making any acquisition. Regardless of the size of the investment, big or small, you do a lot of work to make sure that you understand the person you're getting, along with the player. That was no different in this case."

Drafted out of Pepperdine University in the seventh round by the Toronto Blue Jays in 2008, Thames made little impact during his initial foray into the major leagues. Playing in 181 games over two seasons as an outfielder with Toronto and the Seattle Mariners, he batted a modest .250 with 21 homers and 62 RBIs. But he figured out some things about his swing in Korea and also learned how to handle breaking balls, which pitchers heavily relied on in that circuit.

Because he could speak only a few words of the native language, Thames also delved deep into Eastern philosophies of meditation and self-awareness. Put simply: he learned a lot about himself, on and off the field, all for the better. He also spent much of his spare time in the weight room, turning an already impressive physique into one that Charles Atlas would have envied. "You always respect and admire someone who has gone through a journey like this and ended up in a place like this and a day like this," manager Craig Counsell said at Thames' introductory press conference. "You respect and understand that his journey is not finished."

Thames was thrilled to return to the states—both for the second chance to prove himself in the majors as well as the simple socialization of interacting with teammates in the clubhouse. In Korea he dressed in his hotel and went straight to the ballpark with no pregame card playing or chat sessions. "Most stadiums didn't even have clubhouses," Thames said. "You just went right on the field and played."

One month into the 2017 season, the Brewers looked like geniuses for signing Thames. He became the talk of the game, slugging a club-record 11 home runs in April while batting .345 with 19 RBIs and a gaudy 1.276 on-base-plus-slugging-percentage (OPS). Along the way, Thames became well acquainted with

MLB's "random" drug testing policy, getting asked many times to submit blood and urine samples. "If people keep thinking I'm on stuff, I'll be here every day," Thames said defiantly. "I have a lot of blood and urine."

Alas, teams adjusted to how they pitched to Thames after that torrid first month, and he had trouble making reciprocal adjustments. The rest of his season was a roller-coaster ride with tremendous ups and downs. He finished with 31 homers and .877 OPS but only a .247 batting average, 63 RBIs, and 163 strikeouts. "This league becomes a league of adjustments," Counsell said. "The league adjusts to you, and you have to adjust back. Part of staying a productive big leaguer is making adjustments. I think there's no question he exceeded expectations."

70 Return to Sender

Giving free baseballs to everyone in attendance at the Brewers' 1997 home opener at County Stadium seemed like a good idea to club officials. Sometimes, however, what is considered marketing genius can become a "what were they thinking?" moment. When some misguided—and perhaps inebriated—fans among the 42,893 in attendance began tossing balls onto the field in the second inning, play was stopped for 14 minutes, and an announcement was made over the public address system to cease and desist.

After Mike Matheny gave the Brewers a 4–1 lead that inning with a grand slam, more baseballs rained down from the stands, prompting Texas Rangers manager Johnny Oates to pull his club off the field. Rather than stopping the flow of baseballs from the stands, it only increased the number.

Another announcement was made, this time warning fans that the Brewers would forfeit the game if the barrage of baseballs didn't stop. And that wasn't just an idle threat. "I was going to give them the three-strikes-and-you're-out policy," umpire crew chief Jim McKean said. "If I had to go off the field one more time, we would have forfeited the game." Manager Phil Garner took the unprecedented step of requesting a field microphone to implore fans to stop throwing the freebies onto the field. "I was scared to death that was going to happen," Garner said of the possible forfeit. "It was damn frightening."

Order finally was restored, and the Brewers went on to a 5–3 victory against the Rangers.

The baseball giveaway took place on Opening Day in every ballpark, but the incident was an embarrassing moment for the Brewers, in particular because team owner Bud Selig also was serving as interim commissioner of Major League Baseball. "As of 2:15 today, we have changed our policy on this promotion," declared Selig, noting that all future baseball giveaways would take place after games were completed.

Texas left fielder Rusty Greer said there was no option but to leave the field after a baseball went buzzing by his head, barely missing him. "I'll just say it was close," Greer said. "It does distract you, but there's nothing you can do about it until a call is made to come off the field."

Oates said it was never his intention to secure a victory by forfeit. "That wasn't the option," he said. "The idea was to get them to stop throwing baseballs. That was what we were all trying to do—Phil, myself, and the umpires. The goal was to get them to stop throwing baseballs so we could play. I'm not worried about looking for a forfeit. All I'm trying to do is put some sense in people. Hey, there's much more at stake out there than one baseball game—much, much more. Do you think I'd want my family sitting out there? After someone throws a baseball down and hits someone in the head and they're blind for the rest of their life, then what? I'm sorry? I didn't mean to? It's unacceptable. It's too late then. Do something about it beforehand, not afterward."

Already chilly due to the zero-degree wind chill, the cold day became even more miserable for fans in Section 17—for reasons that had nothing to do with the ball-throwing incident. A water main burst in that seating section, spraying cold water on the fans and sending them scattering.

First it rained baseballs. Then it rained water from a burst pipe. Other than that, Mrs. Lincoln…

71 One Game, Two Days

Okay, the game between the Brewers and Chicago White Sox—which began on May 8, 1984—didn't really last two days. The actual game time was eight hours, six minutes, as if that wasn't long enough. But the 25-inning game at old Comiskey Park was suspended the first night because of a Major League Baseball rule, stating that no inning could begin after 12:59 AM. Thus the game was stopped with the score tied 3–3 after 17 innings. "You began to wonder if the game would ever end," said Brewers catcher Bill Schroeder, who entered the game in the bottom of the 13th inning for Jim Sundberg.

Chicago finally won 7–6, but not until another eight innings were played the next day. It was the longest game in major league history in terms of time and was one inning short of the longest game in terms of innings. Only a 26-inning affair in 1920 between the Brooklyn Dodgers and Boston Braves, which was called with a 1–1 tie due to darkness, surpassed the Brewers-White Sox game.

Feeling a Bit Foggy

As if losing a game 20–8 isn't bad enough, how about having it delayed for nearly two hours by fog? Sounds like a nightmare, doesn't it?

Unfortunately for the Brewers, that scene was all too real on May 15, 1996 as they took on the Chicago White Sox at County Stadium. After the visitors scored two runs in the top of the first inning off Ricky Bones, a thick fog moved into the ballpark and blanketed the playing field. "It was spooky," said Brewers manager Phil Garner.

When Kevin Seitzer slapped a one-out double to right field, and Chicago's Danny Tartabull never moved, the umpires called the teams off the field to wait for the fog to dissipate.

As it would turn out, the best scenario for the Brewers—considering the carnage that awaited them—would have been for the game to be called right then and there. But after surreal fungo sessions, in which coaches from both teams hit fly balls to outfielders to assure they could see them, play resumed.

White Sox hitters certainly had no trouble seeing the ball. The first six batters in the second inning reached base against Bones, who exited for an early shower after Frank Thomas doubled in three runs. Lefty Mike Potts took over but was unable to stem the tide, surrendering a three-run homer to Thomas in the third that made it 11–0. In hopes that the fog would prompt umpires to call

The 1984 contest featured a chaotic ninth inning with both teams scoring, and a fading Rollie Fingers unable to hold the two-run lead for the Brewers.

When play resumed the next afternoon, the White Sox were in position to win. They had loaded the bases with two outs, but Carlton Fisk struck out. The Brewers finally broke through with three runs in the 21st. Ben Oglivie's massive homer into the upper deck in right off Ron Reed put Milwaukee on top 6–3. "We thought for sure we had won when Benjie hit that homer. That was a blast," Schroder said.

Surely that blast ended the marathon, right?

Wrong!

the game before the requisite five innings made it official, Potts was urged by teammates to take his sweet time between pitches, but play went on.

The Brewers offense finally offered some resistance in the fifth inning. With a run in, two on, and one out, Greg Vaughn hit a towering fly ball into the fog that bounded off the padding high atop the right-field wall. First base umpire Dale Ford hesitated before signaling a home run.

After Vaughn circled the bases and Bernie Brewer went down his slide in celebration, Ford met with other umpires and reversed his decision, sending Vaughn back to second and Jose Valentin to third. An irate Garner charged onto the field and vehemently argued the decision, earning an ejection. "I saw Dale make the home run call and wanted him to stand on his call," said Garner, who had barely ducked down the tunnel when John Jaha sent another drive into the fog. That three-run homer sailed far over the right-field wall and cut Chicago's lead to 11–5.

The White Sox barrage, however, was not over. Chicago poured six more runs across in the sixth inning and three more in the eighth to reach 20 for the game. The Brewers had yielded that many runs in a game just once in their history—on September 6, 1975 against the Boston Red Sox. And they haven't allowed 20 since.

Capped by Tom Paciorek's two-run single, the White Sox came back with three runs in the bottom of the 21st inning, and play continued. Paciorek had taken over for the White Sox's Ron Kittle in left field for the fourth inning and ended up playing 22 innings—not your typical action off the bench.

The 21st inning began with an astounding throwing error by Brewers third baseman Randy Ready on a groundball by Rudy Law. The overthrow was so egregious that the ball carried far into the stands and is still talked about by players who witnessed it.

Chicago would have won in the 23rd inning if not for a base-running gaffe by Dave Stegman. Running from first to third on a single by Paciorek, Stegman stumbled and lost his balance at the bag when the ball was momentarily bobbled in the outfield, bumping into third-base coach Jim Leyland. Stegman was ruled out for making contact with a coach, rendering a single by Vance Law (his only hit in 10 at-bats) meaningless.

Finally, with one out in the bottom of the 25th inning, Chicago's Harold Baines socked a home run to center off Chuck Porter to win the game. Porter was pitching into his eighth inning, having surrendered the three runs in the 21st. Making his first relief appearance in eight years during that last inning, Chicago's Tom Seaver was the winning pitcher. He then started the regularly scheduled game that followed, winning that contest, as well.

"Chuck Porter actually did a good job, pitching all those innings," Schroeder said. "How many relievers could do that today? When we picked up the game the next day, we figured it might go another inning or two. Nobody dreamed that we'd play eight more innings. Nobody was really tired.

"That was a couple of tough days for us. We lose that game. Then we lose the regularly scheduled game afterward, and Seaver picks up both wins. It was crazy. Without the curfew, that first game would have gone on until about 3:30 AM."

72 The Ax Man Cometh

John Axford's path to becoming a big league closer was an unusual one. The Seattle Mariners selected the Ontario, Canada, native in the seventh round of the 2001 draft, but he chose to attend Notre Dame. There he blew out his elbow and missed his junior year, resulting in his scholarship being withdrawn. Axford transferred to Canisius College in Buffalo, New York, where he could be closer to home.

To Sirs, With Love

On May 11, 2012, John Axford blew a ninth inning lead against the Chicago Cubs at Miller Park, ending his club-record streak of 49 consecutive saves, which dated to the early weeks of the previous season. But Axford's adventures had only just begun that evening. Upon leaving the game, he learned that his wife, Nicole, who was at the ballpark, had gone into premature labor and was taken to a nearby hospital.

Axford knew the local media would want to talk to him after the long saves streak ended, but he also had to get to the hospital. Always a media-friendly player, he went above and beyond by leaving behind a hand-written letter at his locker before bolting.

The note showed both Axford's class and sense of humor: "I put my wife into contractions with my performance tonight! So I had to run to the hospital. The streak is over so now you can talk about it. The luck I've had in the past didn't show up tonight! All I can do is begin another streak and keep my head up! Cliche...cliche...another cliche. Gotta go! Love, Ax."

Axford's letter made the rounds nationwide and for good reason. How many players would have taken the time to cleverly write such a note? "I didn't think it was going to be that big of a deal," he said. "I just wanted to make myself smile a little bit, too, because right after I came in I was obviously pretty upset. I needed to cheer myself up a bit, too, so I wrote the note."

And as it turned out, Nicole's labor was stopped, and she didn't deliver the couple's second son, Jameson, until June 28.

From there, the lanky right-hander pitched for the Melville Millionaires of the Western Major Baseball League in Canada, where a Yankees scout watched him strike out 19 hitters in a seven-inning game. New York offered Axford a minor league contract, and he played in 2007 for three different Class A teams in that system.

The Yankees were unimpressed by Axford's work as a pro and cut him loose after the season. Figuring his baseball career was over, he began working odd jobs in the Toronto area, first as a cell phone salesman and later as a bartender. "I really didn't mind that it was a lot of work," Axford said of mixing drinks for others. "I liked the extra hours because you got good money. If it was a good weekend, you'd get good tips."

Desperate to try baseball one more time, Axford invited teams to watch him throw in a gymnasium outside of Toronto during the

Closer John Axford, another in the long line of Brewers with spectacular mustaches, throws during the 2011 National League Division Series.

winter of 2007–2008. There was a blizzard that day, and the only team that could get a scout there was Milwaukee, who dispatched Jay Lapp, their Canadian bird dog. Axford threw the ball well enough to be invited to the Brewers minor league camp where he was given a contract. He scuffled mightily with his control at Single A Brevard County, Florida, walking 73 hitters in 95 innings, and when his control failed to improve the next spring, Axford feared he'd be released again.

Instead, minor league pitching coaches Fred Dabney and Lee Tunnell helped the hard-throwing Axford harness his pitches, and he shot through the system in 2009, earning a call-up by the Brewers in September. "They helped me pick up velocity, lower my direction toward the plate, lower my arm slot, and lower my walk totals, which was a huge difference," Axford said.

He began the 2010 season at Triple A Nashville, Tennessee, but was called up by the Brewers in mid-May when veteran closer Trevor Hoffman was struggling. Even though Axford had scant experience closing, the Brewers turned that duty over to him, and he prospered. With tutelage from the magnanimous Hoffman, Axford converted 24 saves with a 2.48 ERA over 50 appearances, and a new closer was born.

The outgoing and somewhat eccentric Axford became an instant fan favorite, sporting a variety of mustaches, including a handlebar version that channeled legendary Rollie Fingers. He was given the nickname "Ax Man" and had Miller Park rocking every time he entered a game, thanks to the blaring hard rock music that accompanied his arrival.

Fans feared a Hoffman-like meltdown when Axford struggled at the outset of the 2011 season. On Opening Day in Cincinnati, he surrendered a game-winning home run to Ramon Hernandez in the bottom of the ninth and was only 3-for-5 in save opportunities in late April.

Amazingly, there would be no more blown saves for Axford for the remainder of the season. He converted 43 consecutive opportunities, obliterating the franchise record of 25 saves in a row set by Doug Jones in 1997. On September 24 of that season, Axford established a franchise record for most saves in a single season with No. 45 against Florida. "I try to set lofty goals for myself," Axford said that night. "It's not like I started off the season expecting to have this record. But any opportunity I could get, I want to get the save. The more opportunities you get, the more chances you get to get that record. I have to thank my teammates for that."

Axford would finish with 46 saves in 48 chances, tying Atlanta's Craig Kimbrel for the National League lead. He posted a remarkable 1.95 ERA over 74 appearances and logged 86 strikeouts in 73⅔ innings, earning NL Fireman of the Year honors. Axford finally blew a save in Game 5 of the NL Division Series against Arizona, but the Brewers went on to win that game and advance to the NL Championship Series against the St. Louis Cardinals. In that postseason Axford posted three saves with a 1.29 ERA in six appearances.

He would receive a prestigious honor after the season. He was named the 2011 recipient of the Robert Goulet Memorial Mustached American of the Year Award by the American Mustache Institute. Never mind that Axford is a Canadian (so was Goulet).

Axford also shared Canada's Tip O'Neil Award (named after the old-time Canadian baseball player, not the Speaker of the House) with Cincinnati's Joey Votto for individual achievement and team contribution by a native of that country.

73 The Hit Record

There are lopsided baseball games in which the winning club seemingly can do no wrong. But the Brewers took that to an extreme on August 28, 1992, when they walloped the Toronto Blue Jays by a 22–2 score in the SkyDome.

The Brewers fruitlessly chased the Blue Jays all season in the American League East, arriving in Toronto on a five-game losing streak. The Brewers had scored just 18 runs and collected 36 hits during their skid. But on this night they pounded the eventual World Series champs into submission with a 31-hit barrage, matching the post-1900 major league record for most hits in a nine-inning game. "I'm amazed," manager Phil Garner said. "In all my years of playing ball, I've never seen anything like it."

The 31 hits obliterated the team record of 22, as well as topping the AL record for a nine-inning game of 30, which was set by the New York Yankees way back in 1923. The 22 runs also eclipsed the team record previously established in a 20–7 romp against the California Angels at County Stadium on July 8, 1990.

How bad did it get for Toronto's pitchers? The eight and nine hitters in the Brewers lineup, Kevin Seitzer and Scott Fletcher, each collected five hits and combined for eight RBIs and seven runs scored. Leadoff hitter Pat Listach collected four hits as did No. 2 hitter Darryl Hamilton, who drove in four runs.

By the end of the fourth inning, the Brewers led 13–1. Before the night was done, they would score in every inning but the fifth. Five different hitters scored at least three runs. Amazingly, all but five of the hits were singles as the Brewers bled the Blue Jays hurlers to death, drop by drop.

The Blue Jays used six pitchers, and each surrendered at least three runs. The third Toronto pitcher, Doug Linton, managed to surrender six hits, two walks, and six runs while recording only one out. "You don't go out there and expect to get that many hits," Listach said. "We had some hard ones and some soft ones. Everything went our way tonight. Every ball we hit found a hole."

Well, not every ball. Despite scoring 22 runs, the Brewers stranded 16 runners. When Garner was informed of that total after the game, he ducked out of his office and yelled at hitting coach Mike Easler in mock anger. "'Hit Man,' we left 16 runners on base tonight," Garner said. "What the hell was going on out there?"

74 The Unfriendly Confines

When the Brewers agreed to switch from the American League to the National League before the 1998 season, one of the great advantages the team envisioned was the opportunity to develop a rivalry with the Chicago Cubs. And, sure enough, those clubs started going after each other in a fierce way.

The change also afforded Brewers fans the chance to travel 90 miles to the south and attend games at Wrigley Field, one of the game's meccas. When the Cubs fielded contending clubs, tickets weren't always easy to acquire, and Milwaukee fans would always be greatly outnumbered. But you never want to turn down the opportunity to sit in the sunlight at the Friendly Confines and watch the clubs go at it.

In the early years of the rivalry, particularly on days when the wind blew out at Wrigley, there were wild back-and-forth slugfests.

In their first season in the NL, the Brewers didn't play in Chicago until mid-June, taking two of three, including a nail-biting finale in which closer Bob Wickman surrendered two runs before nailing down a 6–5 victory.

The Brewers would return to Wrigley in September of that season to stage one of the most amazing three-day slugfests in the history of either club. Both teams scored in double figures in each of the games, with the Brewers taking a 13–11 victory before losing 15–12 and 11–10. Those Brewers clubs featured Jeromy Burnitz, Geoff Jenkins, Marquis Grissom, Jeff Cirillo, and Dave Nilsson. The Cubs were led by Sammy Sosa, Mark Grace, Gary Gaetti, and Glenallen Hill. In other words, both sides had plenty of firepower, which was aided by stiff outgoing winds during those three days.

In the second game of the series, the Brewers took a 12–10 lead into the bottom of the ninth—only to watch Chicago score five runs off Wickman, a scoring binge capped by pinch-hitter Orlando Merced's three-run homer. The next day, the Brewers scored four times in the eighth to take a 9–8 lead and added another in the ninth, but the Cubs put two on the board in the bottom of the ninth to tie it. Chicago then won in the 10th on Grace's two-out homer off Al Reyes.

In that game Sosa socked his 61st and 62nd homers as he kept pace with St. Louis Cardinal slugger Mark McGwire in the Great Home Run Race of 1998. "That had to be a great game to watch as a fan," Cirillo said. "It was unbelievable."

"That's the best series I've ever played in," said Grace, who launched Reyes' first-pitch change-up into the right-field stands with Sosa standing on deck. "I'll remember this series until my death bed and I feel like that's coming soon. I'm tired."

During the three-game series, the teams combined to score 72 runs on 94 hits, including 21 home runs. While the Cubs stayed in the thick of the wild-card race by pulling out the last two games, the downtrodden Brewers, two losses away from their seventh consecutive losing season, left town even more discouraged. "This is a nightmare," Brewers manager Phil Garner said. "We scored a lot of runs. We battled back. And we just can't close out the frigging game. It's un-frigging-believable."

And so the stage was set for years of wild series between the clubs. The Brewers have held their own, taking a 78–90 record at Wrigley Field into the 2017 season (including interleague play in 1997). But while fans have found the experience enjoyable at the old ballpark, the same cannot be said for the players, who have to put up with antiquated facilities considered adequate 100 years ago.

The visiting clubhouse, awaiting an overhaul as the Cubs updated other areas of Wrigley, has all the roominess of a walk-in closet, with lockers so close together that the players have to take turns dressing. The showers and training room are outdated, and players have no place to eat except tables in the middle of the clubhouse, further cramping the accommodations. Players have to walk down a series of stairs and then a long, narrow, and damp tunnel to the smallish dugouts.

Call it quaint if you will. The players (and media) are more inclined to call it a dump. That won't stop Brewers fans from journeying through Wisconsin and into Illinois to experience baseball, Wrigley-style. But go to the bathroom before the game or be prepared to miss a few innings.

Much to the chagrin of Brewers fans, I-94 goes both ways between the states. When it becomes difficult to find available tickets to watch Cubs-Brewers at Wrigley, Chicago fans have eagerly snapped up tickets in Milwaukee to watch the teams battle. That trend accelerated in recent years as the Cubs improved on the field and eventually won their first World Series in 108 years in 2016.

In fact, Cubs fans often outnumbered Brewers fans by such significant numbers that you couldn't tell who was the home team. A Chicago rally was just as likely to elicit roars as an outburst by the Brewers. Accordingly, some began calling Milwaukee's ballpark "Wrigley Field North," a designation obviously unpopular in Brewer Nation.

Such is life in the Cubs-Brewers rivalry, which quickly took on spice and continues to simmer.

75 A Baker's Dozen

It was the last game before the All-Star break in 1990, and the Brewers were trailing the California Angels 7–0 in the third inning at County Stadium. With flights to be caught for the three-day break, it would have been understandable if the Brewers rolled over, took their beating, and got out of town. After losing hard-fought extra-innings games to the Angels in the first two games of the series, they were already frustrated to the max.

After scoring once in the third inning, the Brewers drew even with a six-run outburst in the fourth inning and then went crazy in the fifth, scoring 13 runs to pull away to a stunning 20–7 victory. "If that was a game to get rid of our frustrations, we probably fell about 50 runs short," said Don Baylor, who was filling in for manager Tom Trebelhorn.

With their amazing comeback, the Brewers set or tied six club records including: most runs in an inning (13), most RBIs in a game (20) and inning (13), most hits in an inning (10), and most runs scored by a player (four by B.J. Surhoff, tying many).

Darryl Hamilton, a seldom-used reserve outfielder who entered the game with no homers and five RBIs in 45 at-bats, was the offensive sparkplug for the Brewers, igniting the 13-run barrage by singling in a run off Mike Fetters earlier in the inning. He smacked a grand slam, added two singles, and finished with a career-high six RBIs. Seven runners had crossed the plate when Hamilton socked his grand slam off reliever Mark Eichhorn. "I just wanted to make contact and get the run in from third," Hamilton said. "I thought it might go foul at first; it was curving. I won't forget this game for a long time. We've been struggling in the first half, and hopefully this will carry over to the second half."

Every hitter batted twice in the fifth inning as the Brewers accumulated 10 hits—four hitters collected two each—and five walks. Eight Brewers batted before the Angels recorded the first out. The baker's dozen of runs obliterated the team record of nine in one inning, last accomplished on June 21, 1985 against the Baltimore Orioles. "I've never seen anything like that, not at this level," said shortstop Bill Spiers, who collected a single and double during the inning. "Maybe in college but not in the major leagues. That's just how the game goes. You won't see that again."

Before the end of the fifth, three California pitchers combined to throw 77 pitches. After running through six pitchers in an effort to stem the tide, the Angels sent out infielder Donnie Hill to pitch the eighth inning. He proved to be their most effective pitcher, allowing only a walk and ending the inning by striking out Rob Deer.

The Brewers began their comeback by scoring six runs off Angels right-hander Bert Blyleven, a long-time nemesis. (Coming into the game, the Hall of Fame pitcher had a 23–16 career record vs. Milwaukee.) After failing to protect the 7–0 lead, Blyleven turned matters over to the bullpen, which was thrashed. Former Brewers catcher Bill Schroeder, behind the plate that day for the Angels, accurately described the offensive carnage by Milwaukee, which finished with 19 hits. "They hit everything," Schroeder said. "They hit good pitches, bad pitches. They hit line drives, ground balls. They hit dorks and dinks. They hit a lot of balls hard.

"I'm tired and I'm going home."

76 A Questionable Soup Recipe

In 2005 the Brewers finished with an 81–81 record, ending a seemingly endless 12-year streak of losing baseball. But they took a step back the following season, finishing 75–87 to stall the progress made since general manager Doug Melvin and manager Ned Yost began a massive rebuilding project in '03. The Brewers were looking for somebody to help them get over the hump and decided that free agent pitcher Jeff Suppan was their man.

The 31-year-old right-hander had just finished an impressive three-year stint with the St. Louis Cardinals, going 44–26 with a 3.95 ERA to boost his career mark to 106–101, including a 12–2 record against the Brewers. Suppan went 12–7 with a 4.12 ERA for the Cardinals in 2006 but stepped up his game in the postseason, earning MVP honors in the National League Championship Series with two outstanding outings during the seven-game triumph against the New York Mets. St. Louis would go on to knock off the Detroit Tigers in the World Series.

Suppan's postseason surge boosted his value on the free agent market. There was also the fact that free agents weren't tripping over themselves to come to Milwaukee, which hadn't made it to the playoffs since 1982. That combination coaxed the Brewers to overpay Suppan with a four-year, $42 million contract, the biggest deal in franchise history at the time.

The deal was announced on Christmas Eve, and as far as the Brewers were concerned, Santa had brought them an experienced starting pitcher they desperately needed. "We have a pitcher who fills a lot in what we look for in players, as far as talent and character," GM Doug Melvin said. "He's a big game pitcher. He showed that last year. He's had success in Miller Park. He is comfortable pitching here. It's a real good fit for us."

The deal was sealed during a dinner at the home of team owner Mark Attanasio in Los Angeles. Suppan also lived in L.A., and he and Attanasio immediately hit it off, though the final piece to the puzzle proved to be the willingness to add a club option to their original four-year offer. "I tried to make sure I made the right decision and I really think this was the right decision for me," Suppan said. "I always enjoyed playing in Milwaukee. This made sense on a lot of levels."

What neither side knew at the time was that Suppan's best pitching was behind him. The Cardinals had him from age 29 to 31, the prime of his career. The Brewers committed to him from age 32 to 35, a span in which many pitchers start to lose their stuff. Suppan held his own in 2007, going 12–12 with a 4.62 ERA in 34 starts. And he was at his best with the Brewers in August 2008, going 5–0 with a 3.00 ERA in six starts. He collapsed in September, however, going 0–3 with an 8.44 ERA in five outings.

As it turned out, that was the beginning of the end for Suppan as an effective pitcher for the Brewers. He assured the Brewers' elimination from the 2008 National League Division Series against the Philadelphia Phillies with a dreadful performance during a 6–2 loss in Game 4. Suppan surrendered a homer to the first hitter of the game, Jimmy Rollins, and allowed two more before departing after three innings, having given up five runs.

Suppan slumped to 7–12 with a 5.29 ERA in 30 games in 2009 and became a lightning rod for disgruntled fans. He pitched his way out of the rotation at the outset of the 2010 season and was finally released after going 0–2 with a 7.84 ERA in 15 appearances, two of them starts.

Suppan lived up to his reputation as an outstanding citizen during his time with the Brewers and teamed with his wife, Dana, to support several charitable endeavors for the club and community. But he just couldn't get it done on the field anymore, forcing Melvin to cut his losses. The club absorbed the final $10 million it owed Suppan, including a $2 million buyout for his 2011 option. "I can't change what happened in Milwaukee," Suppan said. "When I'm 50 years old, it still happened. I was disappointed in how it turned out. I knew what the contract meant and what the Brewers were looking for. There's pressure in this game everywhere. It's how you handle that pressure. It wasn't for lack of effort. I did everything within my power to be ready when I took the mound. I had some different things happen. I'm accountable. I know what they gave me and I know what I was supposed to do. That was frustrating on my end.

"They have every right to cheer or to boo, to express how they feel. I handled it the best I could. We're all human beings; we all have feelings."

77 Milwaukee's Version of the Home Run Derby

On April 22, 2006 in a game against the Cincinnati Reds at Miller Park, the Brewers socked five home runs in the fourth inning. At the end of that barrage, manager Ned Yost and his players quickly tried to do the math. "There was some confusion at the end of the inning whether there were four or five home runs," said Yost after the 11–0 rout of the Reds. "We just knew that we hit a bunch of home runs." You know you've hit a lot of home runs in one inning when you lose count in the dugout.

Indeed, the long-ball outburst tied a major league record. "It was a special day for the team," said catcher Damian Miller, who matched some personal highs by going 4-for-4 with three doubles, a home run, and five RBIs. "It was just meant to be our day."

Only four other teams had socked five homers in one inning and none since the Minnesota Twins in 1966. Oddly enough, the Brewers became the fourth National League club to accomplish the feat, and all four came against Cincinnati.

Bill Hall started it off in the bottom of the fourth with a homer off left-hander Brandon Claussen. After a single by Rickie Weeks, Miller socked his first homer of the season, yanking it out to left. "It was a cutter in. I was just trying to fight it off," Miller said.

Brewers starter Dave Bush, who turned in a brilliant outing with a four-hit, nine-strikeout shutout, helped his cause with a single to left. Brady Clark and J.J. Hardy then hit back-to-back home runs, the first Brewers to do so that season. "I was just happy to get a hit," said Clark, who was batting a mere .213 in the leadoff spot.

Having notched an unwanted niche in the record book, the shell-shocked Claussen finally got the hook from Cincinnati manager Jerry Narron. Claussen tied the major league record for home runs allowed in one inning, becoming the fourth Reds pitcher to do so and first since Mario Soto in 1986.

Lefty Chris Hammond took over and seemingly restored order by striking out Geoff Jenkins and Carlos Lee, the top home run hitters in the lineup. But rookie Prince Fielder stepped up and blasted his third homer of the season, giving the Brewers a place in major league history. Next up was Hall, who began the Home Run Derby as the first batter of the inning. Admittedly thinking about hitting another blast, he flied out to center. "After the third one went out, we got excited in the dugout," Hall said. "And numbers four and five, it was just unbelievable."

For a team that had lost nine of its 12 previous games to fall below .500, the impromptu Home Run Derby was an uplifting experience. "It was kind of a treat," Yost said. "We had a big crowd [35,768], and they got to see something special. You never know when you're going to wake up and come to a ballgame and see some history."

It was the kind of feat that had the Brewers still trying to wrap their minds around what transpired in the fourth inning. The 36-year-old Miller, who had played in the majors for 10 seasons, thought he had seen it all. "I guess it happens about every 40 years, huh?" he said.

Miller had no trouble counting from 1966 to 2006. The big math quiz was how many home runs the Brewers socked in inning No. 4. You could count them on one hand with no digits to spare.

78 Never Say Die

When the Brewers trailed the Cincinnati Reds in the fourth inning 9–0 on April 28, 2004 at Miller Park, it would have been easy to roll over and accept the beating. After all, no Brewers team ever had come from nine runs behind to win a game. In fact, no *major league* team had come from nine runs down to win a game since August 5, 2001, when the Cleveland Indians rallied from a 12-run deficit to beat the Seattle Mariners 15–14. And Cincinnati hadn't blown a nine-run lead to lose a game since September 28, 1930.

History, though, was about to be rewritten.

The Brewers began pecking away inning by inning. One run in the fourth. Three more in the sixth, which was capped by Ben Grieve's two-run homer off Reds starter Paul Wilson. When Geoff

Jenkins doubled in a run in the seventh and scored on a single by Lyle Overbay, the Brewers had pulled within 9–6, and things were getting interesting.

Cincinnati reliever Todd Jones got himself into a bases-loaded mess in the eighth, prompting manager Dave Miley to summon Ryan Wagner. Brewers shortstop Bill Hall greeted him with a bases-clearing double. And just like that, the game was tied at nine.

The score was still knotted when Trent Durrington led off the bottom of the 10th against Reds righty Todd Van Poppel. Durrington scorched a liner to right that caromed off the top of the fence just inches from his first big league homer, and the speedy infielder settled for a double. Scott Podsednik advanced him to third with a well-executed sacrifice bunt.

Up to the plate stepped Hall, who had beaten the Reds with a walk-off homer the previous evening and was fresh off that booming game-tying double in the eighth. Surely, Hall would be swinging away, right?

Nope.

Manager Ned Yost put on the squeeze play, figuring it would be the last thing the Reds would expect. Hall, who had to look twice to make sure he had the sign right, dropped down a perfect bunt on the first pitch as Durrington raced home to give the Brewers an improbable victory.

Hall demonstrated his versatility and clutchness with two consecutive walk-offs—one on the long ball, the other with small ball. "It's unbelievable," he said. "I've never done either. I've never had a walk-off home run or a walk-off squeeze, especially two nights in a row. The adrenaline is pumping pretty good right now.

"I just wanted to get a good pitch to get one down. I was in a defensive mode. Their manager seems to challenge me a lot. Luckily, I've been able to take advantage of it."

Asked about the unusual strategy, Yost said, "Billy has been swinging the bat so well, but we needed to win that game right there. I told him before the inning that, 'if that situation comes up, we're squeezing on the first pitch.'"

The Brewers' previous franchise record for biggest comeback was eight runs, which was accomplished on May 10, 1969 against the Washington Senators when the team was located in Seattle, and again on May 20, 1986 against the Cleveland Indians.

79 The Home Run Race Comes to Milwaukee

As the days of the 1998 season dwindled, the Brewers were hardly a compelling topic of conversation. They were 72–81, putting them one defeat away from their sixth consecutive losing season.

But something was about to happen that would put Milwaukee squarely in the brightest spotlight of the baseball world. The Great Home Run Race of 1998 was coming to County Stadium. St. Louis Cardinals slugger Mark McGwire and Chicago Cub "Slammin'" Sammy Sosa were engaged in a spirited home run duel that already had toppled the record of 61 home runs established by the New York Yankees' Roger Maris in 1961. With St. Louis coming to town for a three-game series, followed by Chicago for two games, that long ball duel would add some spice to another dismal season for the Brewers.

In a three-game slugfest during the previous weekend in Chicago, the Brewers helped Sosa close on McGwire by serving up four gopher balls to him. But they would balance it out this time around. In the first game of the series against the Cardinals, Rafael Roque yielded McGwire's 64th blast of the season. "It was a mistake," manager Phil Garner said of Roque's pitch. "That's been our problem. We've made mistakes, and they get hit out of the ballpark. They don't get hit at somebody or in the gaps. They go out."

And they would continue to go out as a crowd of 48,194 sat captivated. McGwire came very close to adding two more homers that evening, sending drives into the upper deck in left in the sixth and eighth innings off relievers David Weathers and Eric Plunk, respectively, each carrying foul by a few feet.

By that point of the season, Garner was holding a tattered rotation together with spit and bailing wire. He admitted his pitchers, including the rookie Roque, were easy prey for the protagonists in what was becoming a Home Run Derby. "It's not a good match-up for us right now," Garner said. "McGwire and Sosa are on a roll right now. You're talking about 20 or so years of major league experience. Our whole pitching staff barely has 20 years."

That home run was only the third for McGwire that season against the Brewers, compared to 10 by Sosa at that point. But Big Mac insisted he didn't care who emerged as home run champ. "What we've done in the game of baseball, nobody's ever done," he said. "It's like what we're doing right now. People want more. How much more do you want?"

Whether they wanted it or not, Brewers fans would get more. McGwire would strike out in all four of his at-bats in the second game, but that didn't stop the Cards from winning 7–4. It also set the stage for a wild and memorable series finale on Sunday afternoon, much to the delight of a packed house of 52,831.

McGwire got right down to business, socking his 65th homer in the first inning off lefty Scott Karl, a 423-foot rocket that pushed him two ahead of Sosa. But it would be a drive off the bat of McGwire in the fifth inning that would have folks talking for some time.

McGwire sent an offering from Rod Henderson on a line toward the bleachers in left-center where a couple of fans at the railing fought for the ball. Second base umpire Bob Davidson ruled that one of the fans reached over the yellow railing atop the wall and interfered, making it a ground-rule double. "I saw the ball good," Davidson said. "To me, the fan was over."

Not everyone was convinced. After watching a replay twice on TV after the game, McGwire said, "After further review, it looked like it was a homer. The guy never came into play. He never came over the yellow line."

With the home run race and baseball history at stake, the Cardinals said they'd ask league officials to review the videotape and decide whether the call should be reversed. But they knew it was highly unlikely that McGwire would be awarded No. 66 after the fact. "You've got to let the umpire's decision stand," Garner said. "Who knows? They might have missed a call on Babe Ruth."

When the Cardinals left town, the Cubs moved in, and Sosa was champing at the bit to get more swings off the Brewers' beleaguered staff. Chicago's exuberant right fielder would hit no homers in the first game of the brief series, extending his personal drought to 0-for-21, but he wasn't about to leave town without inflicting more damage.

Sosa hit—not one—but two home runs in the series finale to run his total for the season to an amazing 12 against the Brewers, drawing even with McGwire at 65 home runs apiece. It was the highest total for a player against one team since 1961 when Maris socked 13 against the Chicago White Sox, and San Francisco Giant Willie Mays hit a dozen against the Milwaukee Braves.

Oddly enough, No. 64 was surrendered by Roque, making him the first—and still only—pitcher to surrender two 64th home runs in the same season. "I don't know what to say. I wasn't trying to give up a home run," said the shell-shocked Roque.

"This is my lucky team," Sosa said. "Whatever has been happening with the Brewers, I can't say to you. I was struggling, but I came back today and I feel good."

With the Cubs vying for a playoff spot, the game would not be remembered as much for Sosa's home runs as a three-run error committed in the bottom of the ninth by left fielder Brant Brown, who dropped a bases-loaded drive by Geoff Jenkins, to give the Brewers an improbable 8–7 triumph. As for the home run race, Sosa predicted, "I still have that feeling for Mark. I think he's going to finish ahead of me."

That forecast would prove correct. McGwire would finish with an unfathomable 70 homers, a record that would stand for only three years before it was broken by Giants outfielder Barry Bonds. Sosa would hit only one more and finish with 66, which went along with his league-leading 158 RBIs.

Years later, with the revelation of the so-called "Steroid Era," the gloss came off the long ball battle between McGwire and Sosa. But for a few dramatic and exciting days, the Brewers were unwilling accomplices in the Great Home Run Race of 1998.

80 Sheets' Special K Diet

The Atlanta Braves never had a chance.

On May 16, 2004, all of the stars were aligned for Brewers ace Ben Sheets to have a dominant start. The possessor of a live fastball and knee-buckling curve, Sheets showed up with his best stuff. It also was a bright, sunny Sunday afternoon, guaranteeing the infamous Miller Park shadows would be creeping across home plate as the 1 PM game progressed.

The crowd of 20,654 began to expect something special was unfolding when Sheets whiffed Wilson Betemit to end the fifth inning, matching his previous major league high of 10 strikeouts in a game. From the seventh inning on, Sheets faced 11 batters and struck out eight, finishing with 18 strikeouts and obliterating

Moose Haas' franchise record of 14 strikeouts on April 12, 1978 against the New York Yankees.

A two-out home run by Braves center fielder Andruw Jones on an 0–2 pitch in the seventh accounted for Atlanta's only run in the Brewers' 4–1 victory. "The way he was pitching, he could have thrown a no-hitter," Jones said. "When people pitch like that, there is nothing you can do."

Sheets pounded the strike zone with impunity, throwing 91 of 116 pitches for strikes. "It's unbelievable that you strike out that many people, and your pitch count is there," said Brewers pitching coach Mike Maddux. "It's a testament to throwing the ball over the plate and making it happen."

After surrendering a leadoff double to DeWayne Wise in the first inning, he retired 15 batters in a row. Most of his strikeouts came on nasty curveballs that bounced in front of catcher Chad Moeller, but Sheets insisted his four-seam fastball, not his hammer, was the key to his success. "People will look at it and go, 'Oh, he had a good curveball going,'" Sheets said. "But location of the fastball set up the curveball, for the most part."

Never one to beat his chest, Sheets noted he was lucky that Braves slugger Chipper Jones had the day off and second baseman Marcus Giles was out with an injury. He also admitted the shadows "played a part," making it even tougher for hitters to pick up the spin on his breaking ball. "When I was up there hitting, I could see the ball," said Sheets, a notoriously poor hitter. "But the real hitters go up there and try to pick up the spin. I don't think they could do that."

Moeller, who struck out in all four of his at-bats, wasn't going to deny the shadows were a factor in Sheets' historic outing. "I knew what Ben was throwing, so I knew what the ball was going to do," he said. "There is no doubt shadows helped, but he was still great. He would have been tough to hit under any circumstances."

As he approached the team strikeout record that had stood for 26 years, Sheets acknowledged that he had to rein in his feelings and exercise personal control. "I got emotional out there," he said. "I wanted to get it for [the fans] as bad as I wanted to get it for me. I'm not a big strikeout guy. This is kind of all new for me. It's pretty cool, though."

Braves catcher Johnny Estrada, who would have a brief and ill-fated stint with the Brewers a few years later, waved helplessly at Sheets' final pitch to become strikeout victim No. 18. With the crowd standing and roaring its approval, Sheets walked toward the home dugout, stopped, and tipped his cap in recognition. "It was kind of a blur," Sheets said. "But it was a fun blur."

81 Walk the Walk of Fame

No trip to Miller Park is complete without checking out the ballpark's Walk of Fame. It's the club's version of a local hall of fame, commemorating the greatest names in the history of the Milwaukee Braves and Brewers. The Walk of Fame is located on the plaza area outside the ballpark, starting near the statues of Robin Yount and Hank Aaron. Each inductee is honored with a granite-shaped home plate set in the concrete.

The Brewers hold an annual vote for the Walk of Fame, with a committee of approximately 100 state media members and club officials casting ballots. Former players, managers, and coaches are eligible for consideration and must receive 75 percent of the votes cast. To remain eligible for future years, a candidate must receive 5 percent of the vote.

The inaugural class of 2001 consisted of four Hall of Fame players—Hank Aaron, Robin Yount, Paul Molitor, and Rollie Fingers. Aaron played a dual role in Milwaukee baseball history, beginning his career with the Braves and ending it with the Brewers. Fingers made his name with Oakland but was a key figure as the Brewers became a playoff team in the early 1980s. Yount and Molitor were the first players to enter Cooperstown wearing Brewers caps.

The second class in 2002 featured Bud Selig, the team's founder—and later the baseball commissioner—and Cecil Cooper, an All-Star first baseman during the team's glory years in the late 1970s and early 1980s. Selig led the group that bought the club out of bankruptcy in Seattle and later spearheaded the charge to keep the team in Milwaukee by getting Miller Park built.

In 2003 legendary radio voice Bob Uecker and longtime general manager Harry Dalton received their places on the Walk of Fame. Uecker has been Brewers baseball for generations of fans who follow the game on the radio. Dalton was the architect of two playoff teams in the early '80s, including the 1982 club that fell one victory shy of winning the World Series against the St. Louis Cardinals. Two beloved figures in franchise history were elected to the Walk of Fame in 2004—second baseman Jim Gantner and center fielder Gorman Thomas, known as "Gumby" and "Stormin' Gorman," respectively. Both players remain popular among Brewers fans and still can be found at Miller Park on any given day, helping the ballclub in any way asked.

Another beloved figured was added to the walk in 2005 when former manager Harvey Kuenn was elected. Former infielder Don Money, a key figure on the winning Brewers clubs of the late '70s, also was added that year. Kuenn was named manager early in the '82 season and guided that club to the World Series. He would manage the Brewers only one other season but made an indelible mark on the franchise, including his time as hitting coach. Money played 11 of his 16 seasons in the majors with the Brewers and was a four-time All-Star. He also managed for several seasons in the organization's farm system.

After no one was elected in 2006, former members of the Milwaukee Braves became eligible for the Walk of Fame. That change resulted in Eddie Mathews, Warren Spahn, and former general manager John Quinn being elected in '07. Mathews and Spahn are legendary names in major league history, and Quinn was the architect of standout teams that never suffered a losing season. The voters pitched shutouts in 2008 and 2009, overlooking several worthy candidates from both the Brewers and Braves. In 2010 Braves hero Lew Burdette, known for his incredible performance in the '57 World Series against the New York Yankees, was fittingly elected. Pitching on short rest after Spahn became ill, Burdette beat mighty New York in Game 7 to give Milwaukee its lone World Series crown. He went 3–0 with two shutouts in the series.

After voters failed to elect anyone in 2011–12, popular Braves shortstop Johnny Logan was honored in 2013, shortly before he passed away. Left-hander Teddy Higuera, the Brewers' last 20-game winner in 1986, was added in 2015, and Braves slugger Joe Adcock joined the august group a year later. No one gained enough support in 2017 to be elected.

82 The Future Is Now

As the Brewers went into the offseason after a disappointing 2010 season that led to the dismissal of manager Ken Macha and the hiring of Ron Roenicke, the general assumption was that they'd have to trade slugger Prince Fielder for badly needed starting pitching. Fielder would be a free agent after the 2011 season and the

Brewers presumably wouldn't be able to afford him, so why not deal him for pitching now? But general manager Doug Melvin had a different idea. What if the Brewers kept Fielder, added starting pitching some other way, and went for it all in 2011?

That approach would involve sacrificing some of the club's future by dealing prospects, but Melvin and owner Mark Attanasio figured the window with Fielder was only one more year, so why not go all in? After losing CC Sabathia and Ben Sheets to free agency following the 2008 wild-card season, the Brewers struggled for two years to put together a representative rotation, and Macha subsequently never had a chance.

Melvin knew the Toronto Blue Jays coveted infielder Brett Lawrie, a native Canadian and 2008 first-round draft pick who was considered the Brewers' No. 1 prospect. He asked Toronto GM Alex Anthopolous if he'd be willing to deal right-hander Shaun Marcum, who had bounced back in 2010 from Tommy John surgery to go 13–8 with a 3.64 ERA in 31 starts. To Melvin's surprise, Anthopolous agreed to do so on the eve of the winter meetings in Orlando, Florida, and the Brewers had the first piece to their pitching puzzle. "This came as a little bit of a surprise to us to be able to acquire someone of Shaun Marcum's ability," Melvin said upon announcing the deal. "We felt if we could get someone of his caliber, we were willing to do that. We feel he can fit in at the top of our rotation. It's something we really needed."

Melvin called the deal "the first step" in making necessary improvements to the starting rotation to be able to compete for the National League Central crown. And he wasn't kidding. A second step would take place two weeks later, and it was a stunning one.

Stepping into the breech when a deal fell through that would have sent Kansas City Royals ace Zack Greinke to the Washington Nationals, Melvin offered the Royals a package they couldn't refuse: shortstop Alcides Escobar, center field prospect Lorenzo Cain, and pitching prospects Jake Odorizzi and Jeremy Jeffress. In

Zack Greinke hurls a pitch. Finally playing for a winning team, an inspired Greinke helped Milwaukee capture its first National League Central crown.

return, the Brewers would get Greinke, the 2009 American League Cy Young Award winner, and shortstop Yuniesky Betancourt. To put the finishing touches on the blockbuster swap, Melvin even rushed back to Milwaukee from Ontario, Canada, where he was visiting his parents. "This is what I call a 'now' trade," Melvin said. "We needed to make some big changes with our pitching, and I think we've done that with Shaun Marcum and Zack Greinke."

Melvin conceded that he gave up a lot to acquire Greinke. Escobar was considered the Brewers shortstop for years to come. Cain was a budding big league center fielder, and Jeffress and Odorizzi were first-round draft picks with high ceilings. "It was a costly trade," Melvin said. "We gave up a lot of good young players. This is a credit to our scouting and player development people to have the kind of young players it takes to make a trade like this. I'm excited. This is all about getting both of those pitchers. I live for young guys. I love their emotion and energy. But these guys are young, too. I think coming to Milwaukee will energize Zack a bit."

For the deal to be completed, Greinke had to drop a no-trade clause in his contract, something he refused to do with Washington, which is why that trade fell through. "It's an indication he wanted to come to Milwaukee and thinks we have a chance to compete and win the division," Melvin said.

Melvin couldn't have been more intuitive. Finally on a winning team, Greinke thrived, going 16–6 with a 3.83 ERA and was unbeaten (11–0 in 15 starts) before the home fans at Miller Park. Marcum went 13–7 with a 3.54 ERA in 33 starts, a record somewhat tarnished by a late-season slide. With Greinke and Marcum joining holdovers Yovani Gallardo, Randy Wolf, and Chris Narveson, the Brewers had one of the most consistent rotations in the major leagues. Milwaukee rolled to a club-record 96 victories in 2011 and its first NL Central crown.

The Brewers went all in and hit the jackpot.

83 An NL Win Doesn't Come Easily

Nobody said moving from the American League to the National League was going to be easy. It wasn't that it took the Brewers a long time to win their first NL game. They did so in their second try in the season-opening series in Atlanta in 1998.

It was more about the fight in that second game that eventually ended with the Brewers winning 8–6 in 11 innings. "I just hope all National League games aren't this tough," right fielder Jeromy Burnitz said.

The Brewers thought they were in good shape to win in regulation when Jeff Cirillo bopped a two-out, two-run homer in the top of the ninth off reliever Mike Cather to snap a 2–2 tie. They turned matters over to veteran closer Doug Jones, who was nearly infallible during a brilliant 1997 season.

But stunningly, Jones surrendered home runs to the first two batters he faced—Andres Galarraga and Javier Lopez. The previous season, Jones allowed only four homers in 80⅓ innings. "We were shocked," Burnitz said. "Nobody expected that." The Brewers had suffered a bigger heartbreak in the bottom of the ninth in the season opener when a throwing error by catcher Mike Matheny allowed the winning run to score with two outs. After that disheartening 2–1 defeat, the Brewers were in no mood for another late-inning debacle.

After neither team scored in the 10th, Brewers second baseman Fernando Vina collected his fourth hit with one down in the 11th, a single that struck pitcher Adam Butler and caromed toward third base. After Vina swiped second and Cirillo walked, Braves manager Bobby Cox summoned his seventh pitcher of the night, rookie Brian Edmondson. The young pitcher did his job, inducing John Jaha to hit what should have been an inning-ending double-play grounder to veteran shortstop Rafael Belliard, who entered the game in a double-switch in the sixth. Belliard, however, booted the ball to load the bases.

That brought to the plate Burnitz, who launched a majestic drive that carried into the left-field stands for his fourth career grand slam. It was the second home run of the night for Burnitz, who also smacked a bases-empty blast in the fifth inning off lefty Tom Glavine to snap a 1–1 tie. In keeping with the theme of the night, however, the Brewers would not escape the bottom of the 11th without trepidation.

With two outs, Braves outfielder Gerald Williams belted a two-run homer off Al Reyes to make it a two-run game. When Ryan Klesko followed with a single, it brought Andruw Jones, one of the league's top sluggers, to the plate as the potential tying run. Reyes struck him out on three pitches, and the Brewers had NL victory No. 1, a mere three hours, 42 minutes after the first pitch was thrown. "How about that? My first win in the National League took longer than the movie, *Titanic*," manager Phil Garner said. "I think I need a beer."

84 A Neutral Field No-No

Only one Brewers pitcher—Juan Nieves—has thrown a no-hitter. And only one pitcher—Kansas City Royals hurler Steve Busby—has thrown a no-hitter against the Brewers in Milwaukee's County Stadium. But one pitcher has thrown a no-hitter at Miller Park, even though the Brewers weren't there at the time.

In mid-September 2008, Hurricane Ike was bearing down on the city of Houston. Considerable flooding and damage was expected, and it made no sense for the Houston Astros and Chicago Cubs to try to play a three-game series at Minute Maid Park—even with its retractable roof. After much deliberation commissioner Bud Selig and his staff decided the series would be shortened to two games and moved to Miller Park in Milwaukee, which was vacant while the Brewers were playing in Philadelphia.

The Astros did not like the idea at all but couldn't change the ruling. They protested, in part, by declining to dress in the Brewers clubhouse, even though they were the designated "home" team. The Cubs, on the other hand, were quite pleased to change the venue to a ballpark only 90 miles north of Chicago.

Whether the Astros were distracted or not, they had no chance in the series opener against Carlos Zambrano. The big Cubs right-hander threw the first no-hitter of his career as Chicago cruised to a 5–0 victory opener on September 14. It was the first no-hitter by a Cubs pitcher since Milt Pappas twirled one against the San Diego Padres on September 2, 1972. It also was the first no-hitter in Major League Baseball history in a game in which neither team played at home. "I'm a little confused right now," Zambrano said afterward with a big smile. "I still can't believe it. It's a great feeling, a feeling that you can't describe."

There was little reason to expect something special that night from Zambrano. He was making his first start in 12 days, having previously taken himself out against the same Astros squad because of tendinitis in his right shoulder. Yet the mercurial Zambrano was in complete control of both himself and the Astros from start to finish at Miller Park. He struck out 10, including Darin Erstad to end the game, in his first complete game in more than a year. "He had everything going," Cubs manager Lou Piniella said. "From the first few pitches of the ballgame, you knew his arm was live, and the ball was coming out easy. It was just a great game, and we needed that. He had been struggling. To do this, it's special. I'm very happy for him."

The shell-shocked Astros appeared in jeopardy of being no-hit again the next afternoon by Cubs lefty Ted Lilly before finally breaking through for their only hit in the seventh inning. With those two losses, Houston went into a downward spiral and quickly fell out of the NL wild-card race.

Apparently Milwaukee's not for everyone.

Nothing But Goose Eggs

The Brewers have been sitting on their only no-hitter since 1987 when Juan Nieves accomplished the feat on April 15 in Baltimore. On the flip side, they have been no-hit three times by opposing pitchers, and those occasions have been spaced out over a 33-year period.

Kansas City Royal Steve Busby is the only pitcher to no-hit the Brewers in Milwaukee, doing so on June 19, 1974. The previous year, Busby, at age 22, tossed a no-hitter—the first in Royals history—against the Detroit Tigers in only the 10th game of his career.

It would be 20 years before the Brewers got no-hit again. This time it was by Minnesota Twin Scott Erickson on April 27, 1994 at the Metrodome, the first in that facility. Erickson entered that game with a 1–3 record and 7.48 ERA in his first four starts, so a no-hitter was the last thing anyone expected. "That's the beauty of this game," Brewers manager Phil Garner said, "except it wasn't beautiful on our side."

Thirteen years later, Detroit's Justin Verlander no-hit the Brewers in an interleague game at Comerica Park. Verlander struck out 12 in his 112-pitch masterpiece, becoming the first Tigers pitcher to throw a no-hitter at home since Virgil Trucks dominated the Washington Senators on May 15, 1952 at Briggs Stadium. Oddly enough, the Brewers were coming off a 22-hit performance in their previous game in Texas, a 9–6, 12-inning victory against the Rangers. Indeed baseball is an inscrutable sport where a team can have a difference of 22 hits from one game to the next.

After he flied out to right to end the game, Brewers shortstop J.J. Hardy was asked about the pressure of being the last hitter between a pitcher and a no-hitter. "I think the pressure started mounting in the first inning when he was throwing 100 [mph] with that curveball and changeup," Hardy said.

85 Team Losing Streak

When the Brewers took the field on May 11, 1994 at Fenway Park for a game against the Boston Red Sox, they were feeling pretty good about themselves. They were 17–14 and tied for first place with the Chicago White Sox in their first season in the new American League Central Division. A 7–1 thumping that night at the hands of the Red Sox certainly wasn't fun, but there was no way of knowing what heartache awaited the team over the next two weeks. For 14 consecutive games, the Brewers went without a victory, the longest losing streak in club history.

After losing their 14th in a row to the Baltimore Orioles by a 6–3 score, manager Phil Garner admitted that his team was a bit shell-shocked. "We're caught in a crossfire now and we can't seem to get out of it," Garner said. "When we get pitching, we don't get the offense, and when we get the offense, we don't get the pitching."

The losing streak matched the longest in the major leagues to that point in the 1990s. The Seattle Mariners had dropped 14 in a row in September of 1992, but no major league club had lost 15 in a row since Baltimore began the 1988 season with an astonishing 21 consecutive losses. "We're still battling," reliever Mike Fetters said. "It's all up to the players now. Phil and the coaches can't do it for us. We have to do it ourselves and stop talking about it."

After a much-needed day off on Thursday, May 26, the Brewers reconvened at County Stadium for a three-game series against the Mariners. It was the beginning of what was supposed to be a festive weekend, culminating on Sunday with the Brewers retiring the No. 19 of Robin Yount. Perhaps inspired by the mere presence of the franchise icon, the Brewers put an end to the nightmarish 14-game skid with a 5–2 victory against the Mariners, thanks to a three-run homer in the eighth inning by B.J. Surhoff.

After hearing that Yount was talking up players in the clubhouse prior to the game, the future Hall of Famer was asked if he gave a Knute Rockne-style inspirational speech before they took the field. "I just said 'Hello.' That's all," insisted the modest Yount. No. 19 spent much of the evening in the team's TV and radio booths and said it was thrilling to be on hand to watch the Brewers finally come out on top, which also delighted the crowd of 35,495. "That was great," he said. "I've been there before. We lost 12 in a row [in 1987], remember. They played hard tonight, and I'm sure they've been playing hard. When you're in a down streak, all of the little things seem to go against you."

By losing 14 in a row, the Brewers went from a first-place tie with the Chicago White Sox to 10 games out and in last place in the division. That's what two weeks without a win will do. The Brewers would never see .500 for the remainder of the season. When play was stopped on August 12 because of the players' strike that eventually led to the cancellation of the World Series, they were 53–62, in last place, and 15 games out of the lead.

But on this night, everyone was all smiles afterward, particularly Surhoff, who had missed much of the season with an abdominal strain. Since being the No. 1 pick in the 1985 draft, Surhoff had grown close to Yount, and he admitted his decisive blow was more meaningful, because it came on the weekend the team chose to honor "The Kid." "It adds a little bit," said Surhoff, who went 3-for-3. "It's nice to do something like that. It gives me a lift, too. It makes me feel good about myself. The fans have been looking for something to cheer about. We finally gave them something. It'd be nice to have that many people out here all the time. Maybe we can give them a reason to come back out."

The victory did not come without some late drama. Cal Eldred, who bounced back from three awful starts with eight strong innings, departed after walking the leadoff man in the ninth. Fetters took over and struck out ex-Brewer Dale Sveum, who had homered in the fifth inning. Fetters then induced Felix Fermin to hit what appeared to be a sure double-play grounder, but it took a bad hop off second baseman Jody Reed's chest for a single. Undaunted, Fetters got the next hitter, Dan Wilson, to ground into a game-ending double play. "On that first grounder, I said, 'Oh no, here we go again,'" Fetters said. "But then I caught myself and said, 'No way. This is it. I'm not going to let it happen.'"

Afterward, there was laughter and music in the Brewers clubhouse for the first time in more than two weeks. Yount dropped by for a postgame visit, sporting a shiner under his right eye. "He did it doing a two-and-a-half flip off his diving board," said radio broadcaster and close friend Bob Uecker. "I told him to put water in the pool next time."

At long last, the joke was on somebody other than the basement-dwelling Brewers.

86 The Gold Medalist

The player who received the longest and loudest ovation at the last game at County Stadium on September 28, 2000 wouldn't wear a Brewers uniform until the following season. Right-hander Ben Sheets, fresh off his dominating performance against mighty Cuba in the gold medal game of the Olympic baseball tournament, was asked to stand on the sideline in the middle of the fifth inning to allow the overflow crowd of 56,354 to pay tribute. The applause lasted for several minutes as the Brewers 1999 first-round draft pick waved to the adoring crowd. Having barely slept since leading

Team USA to the gold with a three-hitter over favored Cuba, Sheets had arrived around 2 PM that day after a long flight from Sydney, Australia.

He was joined by his parents, brother, and soon-to-be-wife Julie in a group that watched the Brewers' swan song at County Stadium, a dismal 8–1 loss to the Cincinnati Reds, from the private box of club president Wendy Selig-Prieb. "Ben is a tremendous individual, and his family is so nice," Selig-Prieb said. "They thanked us for allowing Ben to participate in the Olympics [rather than come up to the big leagues]. I said, 'Don't be foolish. It was an honor and thrill for all of us in the organization to watch him pitch in the Olympics.' He brought me a T-shirt, which was very nice of him. I also got to hold his gold medal. I had never seen one up close before. He's on a real high. I know he hasn't slept much, but he seems no worse for wear."

The Kings of K

The 264 strikeouts accumulated by Ben Sheets in 2004 remain the most in a single season by a Brewers pitcher. A look at the Top 10 list in that category shows that Mexican natives Teddy Higuera and Yovani Gallardo made their mark more than once in Milwaukee's world of whiffs. Gallardo remains the only Brewers pitcher to log at least 200 strikeouts in three different seasons.

Rank	Player	Strikeouts	Year
1.	Ben Sheets	264	2004
2.	Teddy Higuera	240	1987
3.	Doug Davis	208	2005
4-*t.*	Yovani Gallardo	207	2011
	Teddy Higuera	207	1986
6-*t.*	Yovani Gallardo	204	2009
	Yovani Gallardo	204	2012
8.	Zack Greinke	201	2011
9.	Yovani Gallardo	200	2010
10.	Jimmy Nelson	199	2017

The 22-year-old Sheets was a genuine pitching prospect, one of the few the Brewers managed to cultivate in recent years. He was absolutely brilliant during the Olympic tournament, allowing just one earned run in 22 innings. Former Los Angeles Dodgers

Before beginning his successful, though injury-plagued major league career, Ben Sheets recognizes the excited Milwaukee crowd, which cheered on his achievements in the Olympics.

manager Tommy Lasorda, selected to serve as Team USA's skipper, was so grateful for what Sheets did to earn the gold that he attended the wedding of Ben and Julie in Louisiana later that year. "He's got ice water in his veins," Lasorda said after Sheets mowed down the mighty Cubans. "He doesn't scare. He wasn't scared all day, knowing he had to pitch the biggest game of his life."

Cuba had won both gold medals since baseball became an official Olympic sport in 1992 and never had lost an Olympic game until running up against Sheets, who was given a leave of absence by the Brewers from his assignment with Triple A Indianapolis. "He's just a baby, as far as baseball is concerned," Lasorda said. "And look what he went out and did in front of the whole world. He pitched a great, great game and shut out a great Cuban team."

Though Sheets was plagued by injuries and a lack of support in the early stages of his Milwaukee career while playing for mostly bad clubs, he proved to be the real deal at the major league level. The 2004 season provided dramatic proof as to how much a poor club can affect a pitcher's results. Sheets posted a 2.70 ERA in 34 starts and struck out a club-record 264 hitters in 237 innings but finished with a 12–14 record because the offense deserted him so often.

In one of the most dominating performances ever by a Brewers pitcher that season, Sheets struck out a franchise-record 18 hitters in a game against Atlanta on May 16. It was a sunny day with the shadows at Miller Park making it difficult for hitters to see, and the Braves hitters never had a chance against Sheets' blazing fastball and knee-buckling curve.

Sheets was an important cog in the Brewers' 2008 push to the National League wild-card berth, ending the organization's 26-year playoff drought. He posted a 13–9 record and 3.09 ERA over 31 starts with five complete games and three shutouts. Sheets also became the first Brewers pitcher to start an All-Star Game, tossing two scoreless innings against the American League at Yankee Stadium in the final year of that historic ballpark.

But the injury bug felled Sheets again at the end of that season. An elbow injury prevented him from getting his first taste of postseason play, and it was understandable, if not a bit painful, when the club allowed him to leave via free agency.

87 Go Watch Some Prospects

For many years, the Brewers had their low Single A affiliate in the Midwest League in Beloit, Wisconsin, a small town with an antiquated facility and very small fan base. They became disenchanted with that arrangement and switched affiliations in 2005 to the newly renamed West Virginia Power and a brand new ballpark in Charleston.

That South Atlantic League affiliation was not geographically pleasing to the Brewers, who were keeping their eye on the situation less than two hours north of Milwaukee. The Wisconsin Timber Rattlers of the Midwest League had been affiliated with the Seattle Mariners for 16 years and played their games at Fox Cities Stadium, a nice facility that opened in 1995 and attracted a solid fan base and was located in nearby Grand Chute on the outskirts of Appleton.

Finally getting the opening they sought, the Brewers worked out a new player development contract with the Timber Rattlers before the 2009 season. Spurred by the attraction of being connected with Wisconsin's major league team, the Rattlers drew 253,240 fans to Fox Cities Stadium, an all-time attendance record. It made so much sense for the Brewers and Timber Rattlers to be affiliated that it was amazing it took so long to happen. Beyond the mutual Wisconsin ties and cross-pollination of fans, it gave the Brewers a nearby minor league club where they could send injured players on rehabilitation assignments, a benefit they use whenever feasible. Rattlers team president Rob Zerjav called the affiliation a win/win situation for both teams.

The drive from Milwaukee to Appleton/Grand Chute up Highway 41 is less than two hours, giving Brewers fans the opportunity to check on younger prospects just beginning their climb up the organizational ladder. In 2009 the Brewers placed 2008 first-round draft pick Brett Lawrie with the Rattlers, though he would be traded a few years later to Toronto. Wily Peralta, considered one of the top pitching prospects in the system, also was on that club.

In 2010 Scooter Gennett showed he was a player to watch, making the Midwest League All-Star Game at second base. Jake Odorizzi, a top pitching prospect later sent to the Kansas City Royals in the blockbuster trade for Zack Greinke, pitched for that club and tossed the first eight innings of a combined no-hitter with Adrian Rosario.

The 2011 Timber Rattlers featured pitchers Tyler Thornburg, Jimmy Nelson, and Matt Miller, all high-round picks from the 2010 draft. Thornburg would skyrocket through the system and make his Brewers debut during the 2012 season. That same year, Wisconsin defeated the Fort Wayne TinCaps three games to one to win the Midwest League championship. It was the first title for the franchise.

As the Brewers have rebuilt their farm system into one of the best in baseball, highly regarded prospects continue to find their way to Fox Cities Stadium. First-round draft picks such as Victor Roache (2012), Clint Coulter (2012), Kodi Medeiros (2014), Trent Clark (2015), and Keston Hiura (2017) all wore Timber Rattlers uniforms shortly after going pro.

So for the true flavor of minor league baseball and the feel of what it's like for a professional player beginning his career, it's worth the drive up to Appleton/Grand Chute. The Timber Rattlers have enticing promotions throughout the year and offer a great entertainment package in a nice ballpark at minor league prices.

88 Saenz: One and Done

On April 24, 2004, right-hander Chris Saenz was scheduled to start for Double A Huntsville, Alabama, against the Tennessee Smokies, an affiliate of the St. Louis Cardinals, in a Southern League game. A funny thing, however, happened on the way to that minor league assignment. Saenz ended up wearing a Brewers uniform, facing the big league Cardinals at Miller Park. How exactly did that happen?

After lefty Chris Capuano went on the disabled list, the Brewers were short a starting pitcher. With no viable option on the Triple A level, they dipped down to Huntsville to select the 22-year-old Saenz, a 28th-round draft pick in 2001.

Exceeding expectations by just a tad, Saenz blanked the Cardinals on two hits over six innings as the Brewers pulled out a 3–1 victory. "What he did is nothing less than phenomenal," Brewers manager Ned Yost said. "We had a lot of confidence in him. He was coming off a real good start against the Montgomery Biscuits."

It's a bit of a leap to go from eating up Biscuits to blanking Albert Pujols and Co., but that's exactly what Saenz did, showing no nervousness whatsoever. "He's probably not very impressed with us," St. Louis manager Tony La Russa said. "He came with good stuff and showed good composure. We didn't do anything with him." Pujols was less complimentary, telling reporters, "I don't think he had anything. He just got lucky, I guess."

Saenz found out he was getting called up to the Show while eating dinner at Outback Steakhouse. The summons to the majors came so quickly and unexpectedly that Saenz didn't have time to get too worked up. "It's exciting," he said "I was shocked and stunned by the opportunity I was given. I just wanted to do the best job I can."

That sterling performance resulted in an extended stay for Saenz in Milwaukee, right? Guess again.

He was sent back to the minors the very next day to open a roster spot for another fresh arm, Victor Santos. "This kid will be back," Yost vowed. "We have a lot of confidence in his ability or we wouldn't have put him in that situation." In terms of predicting the future, Yost failed miserably. Amazingly and sadly, Saenz would never pitch again in the majors. He blew out his elbow shortly afterward and sat out the entire 2005 and 2006 seasons.

In 2007 Saenz signed with the Los Angeles Angels of Anaheim as a minor league free agent and was assigned to Double A Arkansas. He struggled with his command, walking 31 hitters in 46 innings, and was released. Saenz later signed with the Reno Silver Sox of the independent Golden League but went 0–4 with an 8.10 ERA in five starts. The next year, he signed with the Schaumburg Flyers of the Northern League, compiled an 8.42 ERA in 19 relief outings, and was done.

How unusual was it for a pitcher to have such a sparkling debut and then never pitch again at the top level? Saenz became only the fourth pitcher—and first since 1899—to start a major league game, surrender no runs in at least six innings of work, record a victory, and never get another chance.

Saenz may have been a flash in the pan, but he retired with a major league record of 1–0 and a 0.00 ERA. At least he had the satisfaction of knowing that, for one fleeting moment, he was as good as you can be as a major league pitcher.

89 Off on the Right Foot

When the Brewers opened Miller Park, their new retractable-roof baseball palace, on April, 6, 2001, all of the stops were pulled out. President George W. Bush and commissioner Bud Selig, the former owner of the club, took turns tossing out first pitches.

Beyond the pomp and circumstance of the occasion, it was more than just another game for the players. They had opened the season with four losses on the road (one in Los Angeles and three in Houston), getting outscored 28–11 in the process. The Brewers wanted a win any way they could get one, and first baseman Richie Sexson complied by socking an eighth-inning home run off Cincinnati's Dennys Reyes to snap a 4–4 tie and send the home team to a 5–4 victory against the Reds. Reliever David Weathers recorded the first W in the new ballpark. "This was more than just a Miller Park win," Weathers said. "We were 0–4, and things weren't going our way. We needed this one bad."

With a sellout crowd of 42,024 ready to party, Jeff D'Amico started for the Brewers, completing a circle of sorts from one facility to the next. It was D'Amico who started the final game at County Stadium the previous September when the Reds ruined the proceedings by romping to an 8–1 victory.

During the Miller Park debut, the ceremonial pitches from Selig and Bush came first. The president threw his to Brewers manager Davey Lopes, who coached for the Texas Rangers when Bush was the club's owner. The president fired a one-hopper, low and away, that Lopes deftly snared with a backhand grab. "That was right over the middle of the plate," Lopes said. "That's what he told me to say."

The Night the Lights Went Out

The idea behind putting a retractable roof atop Miller Park was to ensure that weather postponements would be a thing of the past. But during the facility's first year in 2001, an interleague game on June 15 between the Brewers and Kansas City Royals was put on hold.

Weather, however, had nothing to do with it.

A power failure at the ballpark forced play to be stopped after one scoreless inning. That outage also partially silenced the public address system, making it difficult to tell the 40,000 fans on hand exactly what was going on. When it became apparent the power could not be restored, the game was postponed and rescheduled for the next day as part of a doubleheader.

The power loss was traced to a piece of equipment called a "buss duct" on the terrace level of Miller Park. With about a third of the field lights out, it became evident the game could not continue, and the umpires made the decision to postpone it. At a hastily called news conference, vice president of stadium operations Scott Jenkins said, "It's a critical part of the power system. We're not sure what caused the problem."

During the wait to determine if power could be restored, the club attempted to entertain the large crowd with T-shirt tosses into the stands, renditions of "Take Me Out to the Ballgame" and "Roll Out the Barrel," as well as a special edition of the sausage race. But as 8 PM approached, many fans were already heading for their cars. The next challenge became getting the parts needed to fix the "buss duct" before the second game of a makeup doubleheader at 6 PM the next day.

The Brewers were forced to charter a plane to bring the replacement parts from the Square D plant in Oxford, Ohio. Before those parts could be transported, however, they had to be made. While the Brewers and Royals played the make-up game at noon under natural light, a team of six electricians furiously worked to repair the "buss duct."

Work was completed a mere 30 minutes before the scheduled start of the nightcap, and with that game sold out, much was at stake in getting the power restored in time. "This could have happened anywhere, any time," Jenkins said. "It just happened to be at Miller Park. It's just one of those things that happens. It's like having a cord to a lamp cut. It doesn't matter how many outlets you plug it into—the lamp won't work. We take all of this very seriously, but it's great irony, and you have to find some humor in it. Hopefully this is the first and last doubleheader at Miller Park."

To this day, it indeed has been the only twin bill in a ballpark designed to avoid postponements.

Shortstop Jose Hernandez put his name in the Miller Park record book by collecting the Brewers' first hit, a leadoff double in the third. He also contributed the Brewers' first RBIs—delivering three with one swing on a bases-loaded double in the fourth off Reds starter Rob Bell.

The game was a seesaw affair. Cincinnati drew even with two runs in the seventh on Dmitri Young's homer off D'Amico and Aaron Boone's RBI single off reliever Mike DeJean. That set the stage for Sexson, who delivered his one-out blow in the eighth. Weathers, who bailed out Ray King from a two-on, two-out jam in the top of the eighth, pitched a perfect ninth, and the Brewers won their first game in the new park. "This is something I'll carry with me forever," said Sexson, who was 0-for-3 with two strikeouts before the homer. "It's going to be one of the high points of my career."

90 The Carr Mutiny

The Brewers trailed the Anaheim Angels 4–1 in the eighth inning on May 16, 1997. Angels lefty Chuck Finley had fallen behind in the count 2–0. Milwaukee needed base runners, and center fielder Chuckie Carr was batting a mere .130 through 26 games. So Brewers manager Phil Garner flashed the take sign to third-base coach Chris Bando, who relayed it to Carr.

Carr, though, ignored the signal, swinging away and popping out to third base.

After the game a livid Garner summoned Carr to his office to ask why he didn't take the 2–0 pitch. Carr's third-person response earned him a place in Brewers infamy. "That ain't Chuckie's game," he said. "Chuckie hacks on 2–0."

Not anymore, Garner and general manager Sal Bando decided. Carr was assigned to Triple A Tucson, Arizona, the next day.

The flamboyant Carr's approach to the game rendered meaningless his primary asset—speed. He had drawn only two walks in 46 at-bats and had an on-base percentage of .184. Plate discipline was merely a theory to him, not a practice.

And this wasn't Carr's first dust-up with Garner. During a pregame workout in spring training, the fiery skipper accused him of loafing through a defensive drill. The two exchanged heated words on the field before Carr walked off. Carr's continued laissez-faire approach prompted Garner to have a one-hour meeting with him before a May 2 game in Seattle. After their closed-door talk, Garner removed Carr from the lineup.

The "Chuckie hacks on 2–0" proclamation was the last straw, leading to his demotion to the minors. Asked if he could envision a scenario in which Carr returned to the Brewers, Garner said, "That's up to him. He knows what my expectations were and are. It's a question of whether he wants to make the commitment. He needs to go down there and focus on the game."

It became a moot point when Carr refused his assignment to Tucson, forfeiting the remainder of his $325,000 salary. A few days later, he signed with Houston and played the remainder of the 1997 season with the Astros, batting .276 in 63 games. It would be Carr's last season in the major leagues. But his last quote as a Brewer was one that never would be forgotten.

91 Dressed to Kill (or Be Killed)

On Sunday, June 24, 2001, the Brewers completed an impressive sweep of the Chicago Cubs at Wrigley Field. The jubilant players retreated to the cramped quarters of the visiting clubhouse to prepare to move on to Pittsburgh for a four-game series. Per the team's dress code, it was mandatory to wear a coat and tie on the trip, but a handful of players put a new twist on playing "dress up."

Pitcher Jamey Wright emerged wearing a bright red pinstripe suit, black shirt, and rose-colored glasses. Reliever David Weathers sported a shiny silver zoot suit right out of the Roaring '20s. Fellow reliever Chad Fox stepped out wearing a colorful plaid outfit that could have been made from the curtains of a no-tell motel. Another reliever, Allen Levrault, wore an electric aqua-colored suit that appeared to have its own power source. Closer Curtis Leskanic chose a canary yellow suit with matching shirt. And last but not least, right fielder Jeromy Burnitz donned a leopard-print outfit that would have stood out in the San Diego Zoo. "These are our sweep suits," Burnitz proclaimed proudly. "We've been waiting to wear them."

The chance finally arrived when the heretofore sputtering Brewers finished off the three-game sweep of first-place Chicago with a 6–3 victory that featured home runs by Burnitz, Jose Hernandez, and Tyler Houston. The strikeout-prone visitors whiffed 12 times, and rookie starter Ben Sheets didn't make it out of the sixth inning, but the bullpen turned in 3⅔ scoreless innings with Leskanic notching his 11th save. "The bottom line is we won," manager Davey Lopes said. "That negates the strikeouts and everything else. Like I've said all year, this is who we are."

As for the sartorial efforts of the "Sweep Suit" gang, Lopes shook his head and said, "You think these guys will make Mr. Blackwell's list? And I don't mean his good list."

The sweep gave the Brewers a 5–1 record on a 10-game journey that began in Cincinnati and would end with the four games against the Pittsburgh Pirates, who were 25–47 and already 17½ games behind the Cubs. Chicago had won 13 in a row at home before the Brewers hit town and beat red-hot Kerry Wood 2–1 in the opener. "That set the tone for the weekend," Lopes said.

The sweep—the Brewers' first at Wrigley Field—allowed them to jump from 7½ games to 4½ behind the Cubs in the National League Central. It was little wonder that Burnitz and Co. decided afterward to break out their happy gear. "Why not have some fun?" Burnitz said "When we go on the road, we dress up for each other. We go right to the plane, so we're the only ones who see each other. It's just for giggles."

The laugh turned out to be on the Brewers, however. It's not advisable to mock the baseball gods by getting too giddy over a victory. The awful Pirates stepped up to sweep the four-game series, making the Brewers 0–6 at shiny new PNC Park that year. That pratfall turned a promising 5–1 trip into a 5–4 disappointment, and Milwaukee never recovered.

The Brewers would go on to lose 10 of 12 and then rally briefly to win three of four before dropping their next 11 games in a row. That disastrous stretch left them with a 43–56 record, 15 games out of first place. The Brewers would finish with 94 losses, ruining their inaugural season in Miller Park.

For the rest of the season, superstitious fans would point to the "Sweep Suits" as the cause of the team's downfall. During the 11-game losing streak, there would be suggestions that the garish attire be burned as a sacrifice to the baseball gods, begging for their forgiveness. But it was too late. The Brewers thought they were dressed for success. Instead, they were dressed to kill—kill their season, that is.

92 Have a Picnic

Can't decide whether to spend a nice summer day picnicking or going to a baseball game? Well, at Miller Park, you can do both.

In 2006 the Brewers unveiled their Right Field Picnic Area in front of the right-field wall that put the fans even closer to the action of a game. (It was later renamed the Right Field Patio.) A new chain-link outfield fence was constructed around the area, allowing you to look through to the playing field. For groups that reserve the area on gameday, up to 75 fans can be accommodated with all the amenities, including a private bar and food items such as hamburgers, bratwursts, hot dogs, barbeque chicken, corn on the cob, and baked beans at an all-inclusive price. Fans also are given replica Brewers batting helmets to avoid being conked on the head by home runs that land in the picnic area.

Beyond getting up-close-and-personal views of the right fielder—and perhaps a conversation, if you're lucky—fans can peek through a window into the visiting bullpen and watch relief pitchers warming up. You can see a breaking ball from the catcher's viewpoint, as well as hear the distinct smack of a fastball hitting the mitt. "We are always looking to create new fan experiences that go beyond the norm," said Rick Schlesinger, now the Brewers' chief operating officer, when the picnic area opened. "We anticipate that the Right Field Picnic Area will be one of our most popular attractions for 2006 as it offers a perspective that few have experienced anywhere in sports." Schlesinger was certainly right in his assessment. With all-inclusive tickets priced from $59 to $105 per person, the picnic/patio area reservations go fast each season.

Brewers fans aren't the only people to benefit from that picnic area. The addition moved the right-field fence in some 20–25 feet, allowing for easier home runs, particularly for left-handed hitters. Surprisingly, you don't see a ton of balls land in that area each season, so it hasn't turned an already hitter-friendly venue into a pinball arcade.

How popular has the picnic area been with Brewers' fans? Since it opened, that space has been occupied for every Miller Park game. "We put it on sale every February, and they go fast," Brewers vice president of ticket sales Jim Bathey said. "It's all-inclusive, which is very attractive to groups. You have to buy a minimum of 75 tickets, and we'll let you squeeze in a few more if need be.

"Before each season starts, that space is sold for most of the games. Sometimes we'll sell it to smaller groups that go in together, such as three groups of 25. That's not as common as selling the entire space to one group. Probably two-thirds of the sales each year are to corporations who bring their employees and families. It's been tremendously popular.

According to Bathey, some fans in the picnic area are amazed that they see the game primarily from the point of view of the right fielder. But to assure none of the action is missed, there are television screens located throughout the picnic area. Another draw—or worry, depending on your perspective—is the chance to snag a ball. "We're not really sure just how many home runs fall right in that area," Bathey said. "You see a few but not as many as people feared at first. Most of the home runs seem to go over the picnic area and into the stands, but every now and then they get a souvenir out there."

93 The 2012 Reliever Roller Coaster

Francisco Rodriguez and John Axford were nearly invincible out of the Brewers bullpen during the second half of the 2011 season. After picking up "K-Rod" during an All-Star break trade from the New York Mets to serve as Axford's set-up man, the Brewers did not lose a game they led after seven innings.

It was no coincidence that the Brewers took off shortly after acquiring Rodriguez, winning 27 of 32 games over a five-week period to take control of the National League Central race and finish with a franchise-record 96 victories. Axford set two club marks by converting his last 43 save opportunities and racking up a total of 46 saves for the season.

With Rodriguez and Axford back for the 2012 season, there was every reason to believe the Brewers would be locking down games with regularity. It, however, didn't work out that way. Both pitchers were plagued by command issues that led to big rallies and a series of late-inning losses. The Brewers had other issues, such as season-ending injuries suffered early in the season to shortstop Alex Gonzalez, first baseman Mat Gamel, and left-hander Chris Narveson. The offense was also inconsistent. But it was the inability to protect late leads, which eventually cut the heart out of the club and knocked it from contention shortly after the break.

Axford ran his consecutive-save streak to 49 before he finally blew one on May 11 against the Chicago Cubs, a game the Brewers won in 13 innings. But the wheels began to come off completely during a mid-June, three-game interleague series in Kansas City. The Brewers were swept in that series by scores of 2–1, 4–3 (11 innings), and 4–3, with the Royals scoring in their final at-bat each time. Axford blew saves in each of the last two games in KC, and that trend continued into July when manager Ron Roenicke decided it was time to give Rodriguez—who set a major league record with 62 saves for the Angels in 2008—a shot at closing. Though he flirted with danger in each of his first two chances in a home series against the St. Louis Cardinals, Rodriguez pulled Houdini acts to escape with saves.

But Rodriguez's magic ran out during a three-game series in Philadelphia in late July as both the bullpen and the Brewers' season blew sky high. In mind-numbing fashion, relievers surrendered late leads in all three games, resulting in losses by identical 7–6 scores. (The finale took 10 innings.) Rodriguez was responsible for two of those losses, leaving Roenicke in a quandary as to whom to choose to protect leads. "This is hard to watch," said Roenicke, echoing the sentiments of fans throughout Brewer Nation.

The sweep by the Phillies ended an 0–6 trip that began in Cincinnati and dropped the Brewers from 7½ games to 13½ games behind the Reds in the NL Central. Management put up the while flag on the season, trading ace Zack Greinke to the Los Angeles Angels for three prospects rather than lose him to free agency and receive only a draft pick as compensation.

But the bullpen implosion continued, reaching a nadir in a July 29 home game against the Washington Nationals. The Brewers took a 7–3 lead into the eighth when Rodriguez and Axford combined to surrender four runs to tie the score. After Norichika Aoki and Carlos Gomez homered in the bottom of the inning to put the Brewers back up 9–7, Axford allowed a two-run homer in the ninth by Michael Morse to tie it again.

The Brewers eventually lost 11–10 in 11 innings yet another gut-wrenching defeat. It was the final straw as far as the team's brain trust was concerned, and bullpen coach Stan Kyles became the scapegoat and was fired the next day. The Brewers bullpen ranked last or close to it in nearly every category, an unexpected collapse that sucked the life out of the team. Obviously, it wasn't

Kyles' fault that the relievers, and Rodriguez and Axford in particular, didn't do their jobs, but coaches often pay when those under their guidance fail.

Then, almost magically, Axford, Rodriguez, and the rest of the bullpen got their act together a couple of weeks later. Support arrived in the form of 29-year-old rookie Jim Henderson, who battled for 10 years in the minors to finally get a chance that he wasn't going to blow. Axford converted 17 of his last 18 save opportunities to finish 35 for 44. Rodriguez did not allow a run in 21 of his last 24 outings, compiling a 1.93 ERA over that span.

Not coincidentally, the Brewers caught fire, winning 24 of 30 games to roar into the chase for the second wild-card playoff berth in the NL. They eventually climbed within 1½ games of the St. Louis Cardinals before being eliminated with three contests remaining. The Brewers, though, salvaged a winning season (83–79), which no one thought was possible in mid-August. "I'm not happy with the season. Nobody is happy with the season," said Roenicke, emphasizing that the goal is always to make the playoffs. "But when you look at where we were and where we finished up, I think it was successful. We all feel a lot better about this year."

94 Worst Interview Ever

The Brewers knew that tempestuous pitcher Jeff Juden had a history of indiscretions on and off the field, including conflicts with teammates and beanball wars with opponents. But they accepted him as a throw-in to a five-player deal with the Cleveland Indians on December 1997 mostly because they wanted veteran center fielder Marquis Grissom badly.

Juden lived up to his mercurial reputation, particularly on the evening of July 24, 1998 during the first game of a doubleheader against the Montreal Expos at County Stadium. The Brewers played a twin bill two days earlier, and the pitching staff was running on fumes, so manager Phil Garner told Juden he needed him to go as deep in the game as possible.

Unhappy with his interpretation of the strike zone almost from the outset, Juden began woofing at home-plate umpire Jim Quick about balls and strike calls. Garner came out to the mound and told Juden to knock it off because he couldn't afford to go to his weary bullpen too early.

Juden, however, didn't listen. After Montreal's Shane Andrews smacked a home run in the fifth inning to put the Expos ahead 5–3, Juden protested a called ball in that at-bat. That was enough for Quick, who ejected him.

Juden responded to his ejection with a profanity-laced tirade that was audible through much of the stadium. He also threw the baseball into the screen behind home plate and chucked his glove into the dugout as he stomped off. "I really don't know what I did," Juden said. "If I did anything to offend the man, I'll try not to do it again."

Juden was asked by a reporter to relate the beef he had with Quick. "That's not a question. I only answer questions," Juden said.

When the reporter rephrased the inquiry into a question, Juden answered, "Next question."

That was his answer to a question from a different reporter, as well. When Juden was asked why he agreed to talk to reporters, if he wasn't going to answer questions, he growled, "End of interview," and returned to the Brewers clubhouse.

As he walked away, Juden turned to media relations director Jon Greenberg and asked, "How did I do?"

Despite Juden's ejection the Brewers went on to win that game 10–7. But because Garner had to use reliever David Weathers for the final 4⅓ innings, he was in a bad spot for the nightcap, lacking available arms. He was forced to leave starter Paul Wagner in the game for seven innings despite an 11-run barrage by the Expos that resulted in Montreal's 11–2 victory. Garner was furious with Juden and announced that he was suspending him. "That put us in a bad situation," Garner said. "I certainly didn't need to have him kicked out of the game. That's for sure."

A few weeks later, Juden would be gone. Winless in his last seven starts and 7–11 with a 5.53 ERA overall, he was placed on waivers and claimed by the Anaheim Angels, his seventh organization in six years.

Juden lived up to his reputation as being a poor teammate. When a group of players returned from a baseball chapel gathering one Sunday morning, they entered the clubhouse to hear Juden playing "Highway to Hell" on his electric guitar—not exactly the best post-chapel ditty.

There are usually reasons that players bounce around that much. With Juden, it didn't take long to see why his work address changed so often. "I really don't know the reason for this," Juden told his hometown newspaper, the *Salem (Massachusetts) Evening News,* shortly after learning of his release from the Brewers. "Maybe the change will do me good."

Maybe not.

95 Dugout Dustups

Against the New York Mets on August 2, 2007, Brewers manager Ned Yost found himself in the middle of a heated triangle in the Miller Park dugout. Yost criticized shortstop J.J. Hardy—in front of gathered teammates—for making a costly error.

When the Brewers returned to the dugout after a pitching change, catcher Johnny Estrada and utility infielder Tony Graffanino got in Yost's face to tell him he was out of line to rip Hardy in front of teammates. The heated argument, in which Yost and Estrada had to be separated, was captured by television cameras, leaving the parties to explain themselves afterward.

Of course, it didn't help that the Brewers were in the process of getting blistered by the Mets 12–4 for their 10th loss in 14 games. But they were still in the midst of a tight playoff race, and this was no time for the team to splinter.

Yost tried spinning the confrontation as an intentional act to rally the troops. "I did that with every intention of having somebody stand up [for Hardy]," he insisted. "It's part of trying to get a team going. I don't view it as a bad thing at all."

Perhaps, but everyone else involved, including those who stopped things from getting completely out of hand, just wanted to move on. "It's a dead issue as far as we're concerned as a team," said Estrada, a huge disappointment who would be traded after the season. "We have a lot of passion for what we do. We haven't been playing well. We were getting our butts kicked. The weather was hot. Tempers flared. We talked about it and put it behind us." Or as veteran infielder Craig Counsell put it, "It was a disagreement based on frustration among people who compete hard for a living. That stuff happens. If it happens off-camera, nobody ever sees it."

But things that happen in the dugout are usually captured on camera. The Brewers learned that lesson the following season during a game in Cincinnati, almost a year to the day after the Yost-Estrada-Graffanino entanglement.

Another frustrated Brewers squad was in the process of dropping a 6–3 decision to the last-place Reds at Great American Ball Park. Upon returning to the dugout after the bottom of the sixth inning, Prince Fielder lunged at pitcher Manny Parra and shoved him hard twice, forcing a handful of teammates to wrestle the burly slugger to the floor. Yost calmly sat nearby as players broke up the tussle.

Yost had just pulled Parra from the game after a rough couple of innings, and Parra was going to retreat to the clubhouse when Fielder told him to stay in the dugout and watch his teammates try to recover from his poor pitching performance. Words were exchanged. Then it got physical. "It's not a major ordeal," Yost said. "Yes, there's a shock factor to it. But people don't understand that there's a lot of stuff that happens over the course of an eight-month season when you've got guys that live together and play together and trust each other." Afterward, it again was up to the sensible Counsell to try to put things in proper perspective. "We lost a game tonight," he said. "That's the worst thing that happened."

The next day, though, Fielder felt compelled to apologize publicly for his outburst. "We had a little disagreement, obviously," he said. "It's something that happened. I've been playing with Manny since rookie ball. It's not like we hate each other. I apologize for the way it went down. I definitely could have handled it better. That's just something that happened in the moment. I can't take it back. But I don't apologize for the full meaning behind it and the fire."

Boys will be boys.

96 Taking an Intentional Hike

Players get ejected all the time after disputes with umpires. But getting ejected while receiving an intentional walk? That actually happened to the Brewers' Terry Francona during a July 9, 1989 game against the Baltimore Orioles.

The genesis of that bizarre incident actually came six weeks earlier in a game against the California Angels. The Brewers held a 4–1 lead in the bottom of the eighth inning when Francona ripped an opposite-field liner to left off Bobby Witt. Dante Bichette charged in and attempted a sliding catch, obviously trapping the ball. B.J. Surhoff came around from second base to score, and Francona alertly took second on the throw home.

Or so it seemed.

Unbeknownst to Francona, third-base umpire Ken Kaiser had signaled that Bichette caught the ball. Manager Tom Trebelhorn came out to argue the call, asking Kaiser repeatedly why Bichette would make a throw home if he thought he caught the ball. The stubborn Kaiser would have none of it, however, and his call stood, leaving Trebelhorn and Francona furious.

Fast-forward to the game against the Orioles, again at County Stadium. Kaiser was working the plate and took a foul ball right to the throat, a blow that would have tumbled most umpires, but not the burly former wrestler. Kaiser staggered to the Brewers dugout, came down the steps, and was getting a drink from the water fountain when Francona, seated nearby, couldn't help himself. "Hey Kenny, if you weren't such a horseshit umpire, stuff like that wouldn't happen to you!" bellowed the reserve outfielder.

If looks could kill, Kaiser would have murdered Francona on the spot. Kaiser glared at him for several moments and then returned to his post behind the plate. Later in the game, Francona went up to bat. The Orioles opted to intentionally walk him, and when catcher Bob Melvin put up four fingers to signal that move, Kaiser removed his mask and began woofing at Francona. "They must really be desperate to send up a horseshit hitter like you to pinch hit," Kaiser said. "You're fucking lucky they're walking you."

And thus the argument began. Kaiser and Francona began screaming at each other as Orioles pitcher Bob Milacki threw ball one, ball two, and ball three. Francona was so distracted that Milacki could have pumped three batting practice fastballs down the middle and struck him out. Just as ball four arrived, Kaiser pointed at Francona, raised his right arm, and gestured while screaming, "You're out of here!"

Francona couldn't believe it. He actually had been ejected from the game while receiving an intentional walk, perhaps a first in the major leagues. Trebelhorn had no choice but to send in a pinch-runner, Mike Felder, as Francona trudged up the tunnel and back to the Brewers clubhouse.

And the fun and games weren't over. After the game, Kaiser called Trebelhorn, complaining that Francona had just phoned the umpire's room to give him more profanity-laced grief. Trebelhorn told Kaiser he couldn't believe Francona would do such a thing, so he checked into it.

Without Francona's knowledge a clubhouse attendant had called the umpire's room and posed as the player to give Kaiser a piece of his mind. "It really happened," said Francona, who would go on to manage the Boston Red Sox to two World Series crowns. "But when I tell people about it, they don't believe me."

97 Who Let the Dog Out?

During a series against the New York Yankees in mid-June 1993, County Stadium began to resemble a set from Alfred Hitchcock's disconcerting movie, *The Birds*. Gulls had begun to circle and land on the outfield grass, and nobody was quite sure why. Lake Michigan was a few miles away, and why the water-loving birds decided to make the Brewers ballpark their new home was a mystery.

Something, though, had to be done about it. The gulls were disrupting play, forcing outfielders to navigate around them to pursue balls. Players would shoo them away, but the winged intruders would circle back around and land again. Because the gulls seemed to favor left field, the Brewers' Greg Vaughn and the Yankees' Dion James were left to do most of the chasing. It proved to be a futile effort, and the delays in the game were distracting to everyone.

The Brewers decided it was time to enlist help in chasing the gulls away. Enter Gus the Wonder Dog. Actually, the yellow Labrador's name was merely Gus, but he earned the additional moniker due to his prowess for chasing away the unwanted birds. The Brewers grounds crew had contacted the dog's owner, a member of the Wisconsin Waterfowl Association named Ray Kirkpatrick and from Cedarburg, Wisconsin.

Gus made his first appearance in the middle of the first inning of the June 12 game against the Yankees, running back and forth in the outfield, prompting the gulls to take flight. The Brewers fans roared their approval. The loudest ovation, however, came in the sixth inning when Gus left an unscheduled deposit in left field. Dogs will be dogs, and when you've got to go, you've got to go.

"I thought at first when everybody started screaming, he caught a bird," Brewers outfielder Darryl Hamilton said. "Then I saw they brought the shovel out and I thought, 'Oh well, it was a matter of time.'"

With the Brewers safely ahead 8–0 through five innings en route to a 9–1 romp against the Yankees, the chief source of entertainment proved to be Gus, who would force the birds to take flight and exit the field, only to have them land back in the outfield.

Gus cavorted in the County Stadium outfield for a few days, but as it turned out, the Brewers did not need to sign him to a long-term contract. It finally was discovered that the gulls had flocked to the ballpark because of an infestation of moths in the outfield grass. Once the gulls had gorged themselves, and the moths were all eaten, the birds returned to their lake home.

Sadly, with gulls no longer flocking to the stadium, the dog show left town, as well.

98 Put Up Your Dukes

In a wild, fog-filled game on May 15, 1996, the Chicago White Sox romped over the Brewers at County Stadium by a 20–8 score. Adding to the wildness, Chris Hovorka, a 23-year-old fan from nearby Racine, Wisconsin, began taunting White Sox left fielder Tony Phillips from the left-field bleachers. Phillips decided to take matters into his own hands, literally.

When the taunting went too far for Phillips, he challenged Hovorka to a fight, telling him he'd meet him under the stands at the end of the game. It might sound like a crazy idle threat, but then you don't know the sometimes volatile nature of Phillips.

After leaving the game in the seventh inning, Phillips changed out of his uniform and headed down the lower tunnel toward the left-field stands. A scuffle ensued, and the next thing Phillips knew, he was in the police holding station at the ballpark along with Hovorka. Witnesses said Phillips struck the fan twice, knocking him to the ground.

The 37-year-old Phillips, a veteran of 14 seasons in the majors, was ordered to appear the following Monday before the Milwaukee County assistant district attorney to face battery charges recommended by the sheriff's department. The maximum penalty was a fine of up to $10,000 and up to nine months in jail. Hovorka, charged with disorderly conduct, faced lesser penalties of a $1,000 fine and up to 90 days in jail. Both eventually avoided incarceration, but Phillips was disciplined by the league.

Phillips, an African-American, testified that Hovorka directed racial epithets at him, as well as derogatory comments about his family, but he said he didn't consider Milwaukee fans any ruder than those in other cities, despite the scuffle. "We hear heckling all over the American League," he said. "It's something you have to deal with. I've always had a pretty good relationship with fans. All I can say is I have nothing against Milwaukee fans. Everyone has a breaking point. I reached mine [Wednesday] night. Now, my breaking point will be further. It definitely was not a pleasant experience for me. I regret doing it."

Hovorka denied making racial taunts and in an interview later said, "Basically what happened is a bunch of us were heckling him. He picked me out and said he'd meet me back there [behind the bleachers]. I'm standing there, and he comes up and bumps me and says, 'You're talking a lot of shit for a fat white boy.' I pushed him back just to get him off me. He swung and hit me twice. Then he ran away."

It was that kind of series for Phillips. Two nights earlier he was involved in a shouting match with a fan, whom he said threw a peanut at him. He was scratched from the starting lineup in the series finale to avoid further incidents but pinch hit in the ninth inning and drew a walk. When called out by umpire Chuck Meriwether on a pickoff play, Phillips became infuriated and was ejected after a heated argument—the perfect way to cap his very combative series.

Get Off My Back!

Bill Spiers never saw his "interaction" with a fan coming.

Playing right field for the Houston Astros in a game against the Brewers at County Stadium on September 24, 1999, Spiers was accosted by a fan who bolted out of the stands behind him and jumped on his back. The Astros had just taken the field to begin the bottom of the sixth inning when the 23-year-old male jumped on the unsuspecting Spiers, who could not shake him off. "The whole thing caught me by surprise. I had no idea what was happening," said Spiers, who suffered whiplash during the incident and was removed from the game the next inning. "I looked down and saw blue jeans wrapped around my neck. I couldn't move, so I fell down backward, trying to get him off me."

As Spiers and the fan tumbled to the ground, the entire Houston team raced to his rescue, including those in the dugout and bullpen. Starting pitcher Mike Hampton shook the attacker loose by delivering some karate kicks. "The good thing was he didn't have a weapon," Hampton said. "I always check right field before I deliver the first pitch. It's just a habit. I looked out there and saw the guy on Billy's back. It was a scary thing. My instincts just took over."

The spectator finally was pulled away and handcuffed on the field by sheriff's deputies, who took him away on battery charges. An infielder/outfielder with the Brewers from 1989–94, Spiers suffered scrapes on his face and was treated by a trainer before going back to the clubhouse.

After that incident delayed the game for about 10 minutes, the Astros would score seven runs over the last two innings to pull out a 9–4 victory.

99 Take a (Baseball) History Lesson

To get a brief yet informative history of Milwaukee baseball, all you need to do is stroll in and around Miller Park. A marker between the Brewers ballpark and adjacent Helfaer Field is titled "In Honor of the 1901 Milwaukee Brewers" and describes how the American League was born in the Republican House, a Milwaukee hotel, in 1900. The following year, the original big league Brewers were one of eight teams to play in what was termed the "Junior Circuit."

That club played its games at the Lloyd Street Grounds, located on the city's north side. Player/manager Hugh Duffy batted .302 and was later inducted into the Hall of Fame. Five Wisconsin natives played for that team: Ed Bruyette of Manawa, Davy Jones of Cambria, George McBride of Milwaukee, Pink Hawley of Beaver Dam, and Pete Husting of Mayville. Alas, those Brewers lasted only one year in Milwaukee. They moved to St. Louis in 1902 to become the Browns and then to Baltimore to become the Orioles in 1954.

The next major league club in Milwaukee was the Braves, and down the left-field concourse at Helfaer Field, near the picnic pavilion, is a monument to the 1957 club that won the World Series, beating the mighty New York Yankees in seven games. That monument is located where home plate was in County Stadium, which served as the home for the Braves during their 13-year stay in Milwaukee. Concrete tablets on each side of a big bronze plaque denote the Braves' first game at County Stadium on April 14, 1953 against the St. Louis Cardinals and the final game on September 22, 1965 against the Los Angeles Dodgers. Included in that tribute is a roll call of all of the players, managers, and coaches who suited up for the Milwaukee Braves.

On the main concourse on the third-base side inside Miller Park is the Milwaukee Braves Honor Roll, which displays the franchise history, including the '57 World Series champions. There you will find bronze plaques of Henry Aaron, Warren Spahn, Eddie Mathews, Joe Adcock, Johnny Logan, Andy Pafko, Frank Torre, Bobby Thomson, Felix Mantilla, Bob Uecker, Del Crandall, Gene Conley, Joe Torre, Red Schoendienst, Bill Bruton, and Lew Burdette.

On the concourse near the home-plate entrance is a well-detailed tribute to the Negro Leagues, including the Milwaukee Bears who played for only one season in 1923. That club played at Athletic Park (later known as Borchert Field) but had poor attendance and therefore played most of its games on the road, going 12–41 and disbanding afterward. The Brewers have a tribute night for the Negro Leagues each season, and the team wears replica uniforms of the Bears.

On the Home Plate Plaza outside of Miller Park are dedications to the construction of the facility. A statue entitled "Teamwork" depicts the three ironworkers—Jeffrey Wischer, William DeGrave, and Jerome W. Starr—killed in a crane collapse during the building of the retractable roof. Behind that statue is a wall of honor entitled "Miller Park Heroes" with the names of every worker who helped build the ballpark. Honored separately are four people who played significant roles in getting Miller Park built—former Wisconsin governor Tommy Thompson, Southeast Wisconsin Professional Baseball Park District board chairman Robert Trunzo, construction committee chairman Frank Busalacchi, and former Brewers CEO Wendy Selig-Prieb.

100 Visit the Brewers' Mt. Rushmore

No, the Brewers did not relocate the national landmark from South Dakota to Milwaukee. But in essence, the four statues erected outside of Miller Park form the Mt. Rushmore of Brewers baseball history. The four statues are of Robin Yount, the face of the franchise for 20 years; legendary slugger Hank Aaron, who began his career in Milwaukee with the Braves and ended it with the Brewers; Bud Selig, the team's original owner and later ninth Major League Baseball commissioner; and Hall of Fame radio voice Bob Uecker.

The statues of Yount and Aaron were unveiled on April 5, 2001, the day before the first game played at Miller Park, and were donated by the Allan H. (Bud) Selig Foundation. Selig's statue, donated by current owner Mark Attanasio, was dedicated on August 24, 2010. Last but not least, Uecker's statue ceremony was on August 31, 2012 as a result of Attanasio's funding.

If the bronze statues appear larger than life, that's because they are. Each figure stands seven feet tall and rests atop a large pedestal made of brick and concrete. Yount is depicted swinging the bat; Aaron is in his familiar stance at the plate, Selig is wearing a suit and flipping a baseball into the air with his right hand; and Uecker is dressed casually with his hands in his pockets. The statues were designed and rendered by sculptor Brian Maughan.

Highlights of the career of each man are detailed on bronze plaques on the pedestals. Under Yount's name is his still-used moniker, "The Kid." The plaque mentions Yount being the two-time American League MVP, the 17th player to collect 3,000 hits, the first shortstop to hit .300 with 20-plus homers and 100-plus RBIs in the same season (1982), the only player to have a pair of four-hit games in a World Series, and the AL's "Player of the Decade" for the 1980s.

Some of Aaron's accomplishments include being the all-time home run leader with 755 when he retired; the National League MVP in 1957 when the Braves won the World Series; the 24-time All-Star; the ninth player to collect 3,000 hits; and having his No. 44 retired by both the Braves and Brewers.

The highlights of Selig's career include being president of the Brewers from 1970–1998, being the ninth MLB commissioner, founding the club and bringing it to his hometown in 1970, leading the Brewers to seven Organization of the Year Awards, bringing labor peace to baseball after years of strife, getting revenue sharing passed, getting a drug testing program passed, and implementing innovations in the game such as the wild-card, three-division format, and interleague play. He was elected to the Baseball Hall of Fame in 2017.

Listed under his moniker of "Mr. Baseball," Uecker's career highlights note being the voice of the Brewers, a Major League Baseball player, and world-class entertainer. He received the 2003 Ford C. Frick Award in recognition of excellence in baseball broadcasting, ensuring a place in the Hall of Fame in Cooperstown, New York. His entertainment credits include the TV sitcom, *Mr. Belvedere*; countless appearances on *The Tonight Show*; and the memorable role of announcer Harry Doyle in the *Major League* movies. There is also mention of his participation in one of the most popular ad campaigns of all times as one of the Miller Lite All-Stars and his well-read autobiography, *Catcher in the Wry*.

Acknowledgments

It would be infinitely easier to write a book if one wasn't holding down a job as a baseball beat writer for a daily newspaper. But that challenge is what makes such a project worthwhile, and budgeting your time becomes a primary goal.

Soliciting the advice of others also is essential. I wanted to know what others would like in a list of 100 things that all Brewers fans should want to know and do. You come to grips early on that some items must be omitted to include others you just can't do without, but it helped to hear what former *Milwaukee Journal Sentinel* beat partner Drew Olson had to say, as well as input from former media relations assistant Mario Ziino, who is as close to a club historian as you'll find.

I referenced two books extensively to gather information, dates, and pertinent quotes—*Brewers Essential*, an earlier book I wrote for Triumph, and *Where Have You Gone, '82 Brewers* released by KCI Sports Publishing in 2007 on the 25th anniversary of that team's trip to the World Series. I am thankful to both publishers for asking me to write those tomes, which provided easily accessible reference material.

I am grateful to the folks at Triumph Books for giving me a second chance to work for them and now a third after updating 100 Things. Don Gulbrandsen made the initial contact and trusted me to write this book, and editor Jeff Fedotin worked with me twice, giving advice, support, and feedback as I forwarded sample segments to be perused.

I also must thank my bosses at the *Milwaukee Sentinel* and *Milwaukee Journal Sentinel* for their support and backing in an industry that has undergone countless changes in recent years, forcing an old dog like me to learn new tricks. Senior editor Bill Windler, now retired, has had my back for many years, and his love for baseball is easy to detect. Former executive sports editor Garry D. Howard and current boss Mike Davis have been supportive, as well, while providing the freedom to let me do my job as I've seen fit, for the most part. No one who works at a newspaper in this era takes his job for granted, I promise you that.

The Brewers traditionally have been a media-friendly club, making my job easier to do on a daily basis. Since I came on the beat in 1985, media relations directors Tom Skibosh, Jon Greenberg, and Mike Vassallo, as well as their capable staffs, have provided the proper mix of business and enjoyment, and I thank them for that. From top to bottom, the ownership, front office, managers, coaches, and nearly all of the playing personnel have shown an understanding of the job of a beat writer and all that it entails. I do not take that for granted.

Special thanks goes to former Brewers second baseman Jim Gantner, who agreed to write the foreword for this book. As a Wisconsin native who pursued his dream of playing in the major leagues and had the good fortune to land with his home-state team, "Gumby" seemed a natural to throw out the ceremonial first pitch for a book catered to the fans.

Last, but not least, Trish Haudricourt deserves kudos for living the life of the wife of a longtime baseball beat writer. She learned long ago it's a day-to-day proposition because making plans for any social event or occasion is done with the peril of being ruined by an extra-inning game, unexpected trade, or some other baseball-related event. There is a certain beauty of knowing in January where you're going to be on July 24, but that knowledge is tempered by the possibility that a scheduled off day could turn into anything but a day of rest. Unlike her husband, who latched on to baseball and never let go, she has traveled different paths, all challenging and worthwhile.

Sources

It proved remarkably helpful to have written two previous books on the Brewers when gathering material for this book and the follow-up. One was a previous effort for Triumph Books, *Brewers Essential*, which unfortunately for me, the publisher, and Brewers fans, came out just before the team ended a 26-year drought to return to the playoffs in 2008. It would have been nice to have that highlight included in my first book for Triumph, but what can you do?

My other book, *Where Have You Gone, '82 Brewers?* (KCI Sports Publishing, 2007), was a 25th anniversary look at each player who played for that World Series club. I interviewed every player who saw significant action and dedicated a chapter to each, and it was beneficial to go back and read those interviews in putting together some of the material for this book.

Last, but certainly not least, the archives of the *Milwaukee Journal Sentinel* proved to be my most valuable resource in reviewing events, big and small, that were included in this book. Invariably, the byline on the story would be mine, an indication of how long I have covered the Brewers. My first byline for the old *Milwaukee Sentinel* was in August 1985. Lucky me, I jumped in just when the club was doing poorly. But better days eventually arrived.

There were also many helpful Internet sources, including Baseball-Reference.com, MLB.com, Brewers.com, and Wikipedia. Gathering information at the touch of a keystroke provides an advantage that authors years ago never enjoyed, and I don't take it for granted. Here are the books, websites, newspapers, and other references I used:

Brewers Essential

Brewers media guide

Brewers.com

Milwaukee Journal Sentinel

Baseball-Reference.com

OnMilwaukee.com

Where Have You Gone, '82 Brewers?

MLB.com

Wisconsin State Journal

The Dallas Morning News

Wikipedia

Milwaukee Sentinel

Timberrattlers.com

Boston Herald

Friends of HAST.org

Yahoo! Sports